# Thinking Through SCIENCE

**1**

**teacher's book**

# Thinking Through SCIENCE

1

Arthur Cheney
Howard Flavell
Chris Harrison
George Hurst
Carolyn Yates

teacher's book

thinking science through

HODDER MURRAY

© Arthur Cheney, Howard Flavell, Chris Harrison, George Hurst,
Carolyn Yates 2002

First published in 2002
by John Murray (Publishers) Ltd, a division of Hodder Headline Ltd,
338 Euston Road
London NW1 3BH

Reprinted 2005

Layouts by Stephen Rowling/springworks
Artwork by Oxford Designers and Illustrators Ltd

Typeset in 10/13 pt Lucida by Wearset Ltd, Boldon, Tyne and Wear
Printed and bound in Great Britain by Athenaeum Press, Gateshead,
Tyne and Wear

A catalogue entry for this title is available from the British Library

**ISBN 0 7195 7852 3**
Thinking Through Science Pupil's Book 1 0 7195 7851 5
Thinking Through Science CD-ROM 1 0 7195 7853 1

# Contents

| QCA thinking skills | Investigative skills | Chapter coverage |
|---|---|---|
| Enquiry (planning) | a) Devise questions to be investigated | 7, 10 |
| | b) Use of secondary sources | 2, 8 |
| | c) Make predictions/preliminary work | 1, 11, 12 |
| | d) Controlling variables | Introduction, 1, 5, 6, 7, 9, 10, 11, 12 |
| | e) Decide extent and range of data | 1, 2, 8, 10 |
| | f) Choose equipment and materials – accuracy and safety | 9, 10 |
| | h) Choose sample size/repeat measurements | 1, 2, 8, 9, 10, 11, 12 |
| Obtaining evidence | g) Collect evidence to appropriate precision | 1, 2, 8, 10, 11, 12 |
| Information processing | i) Present data – tables and graphs | 1, 2, 8, 9, 10, 11 |
| | j) Interpret data – patterns | 1, 2, 8, 9, 10, 12 |
| Reasoning | k) Draw conclusions | 2, 4, 7, 8, 9, 10, 11, 12 |
| | m) Explain conclusions | 2, 4, 7, 8, 10, 11, 12 |
| Evaluation | l) Conclusions support prediction? | 8, 9, 10, 11, 12 |
| | n) Anomalous results – explanation | Introduction, 8, 9 |
| | o) Evidence support conclusions? – fair test; accurate; reliable; sample size | 1, 2, 3, 7, 8, 9, 10, 11, 12 |
| | p) Improvements to the investigation? | 7, 9, 10, 11, 12 |

| CASE reasoning pattern | Chapter coverage |
|---|---|
| Control of variables | Introduction, 1, 5, 6, 7, 8, 9, 10, 11, 12 |
| Classification | 2, 4, 5, 10 |
| Ratios, scaling, proportionality | 1, 2, 7, 8, 9, 10 |
| Compound variables | 1, 6, 12 |
| Probability and correlation | 2 |
| Formal models | Introduction, 1, 2, 3, 4, 7, 9, 10 |

# General skills audit

| General skills | Chapter coverage |
| --- | --- |
| **Literacy** | |
| Key words – Etymology, usage | 1, 2, 3, 4, 5, 6, 7, 8, 9, 10, 11, 12 |
| Text types – Recount | 8 |
| Information | 2, 7, 8, 10, 12 |
| Instructions | 8, 9 |
| Explanation | 4, 6, 9, 10 |
| Discursive | 2, 10 |
| Persuasion | 6, 12 |
| Analysis | 2, 4, 8, 9 |
| Evaluation | 2, 4, 8, 9, 12 |
| **Numeracy** | |
| Estimating | 1, 2, 7, 8, 10 |
| Units | 3, 6, 8, 9 |
| Application of number | 1, 2, 4, 8, 9, 12 |
| **ICT** | |
| Finding out (e.g. CD-ROM, Internet) | 8, 9, 10, 11, 12 |
| Capturing data (e.g. datalogging) | 1, 5, 6 |
| Visualising (e.g. simulations, animations) | 4, 8, 10 |
| Interpreting (e.g. spreadsheets, graphing, databases) | 2, 8, 10 |
| Modelling (e.g. spreadsheets, 'Croc Clips') | 6, 10, 12 |
| Communicating (e.g. 'Word', 'Powerpoint') | 2, 8, 10 |
| **Graphs** | |
| Interpreting – Pie | Introduction, 1, 8, 10 |
| Bar | Introduction, 1, 2, 6, 8, 11 |
| Scatter | Introduction, 2, 8, 9 |
| Line | Introduction, 1, 2, 3, 5, 6, 7, 8, 9, 10, 11, 12 |
| Plotting – Bar | 2, 8, 12 |
| Scatter | 2, 8, 9 |
| Line | 2, 7, 8, 9, 10, 11, 12 |
| **Ideas and evidence** | 1, 2, 3, 4, 6, 7, 8, 9, 10, 11, 12 |
| **Spiritual, moral, social, cultural** | 2, 8, 9, 11, 12 |
| **Creative thinking** | 1, 2, 3, 4, 5, 9, 12 |
| **Investigations** | |
| Fair testing | 2, 4, 5, 9, 10, 11, 12 |
| Pattern seeking (survey or record) | 1, 2, 9, 10, 11 |
| Identifying/classifying | 4, 9 |
| Exploring (observing over time) | 1, 7 |
| Technology (design to solve a problem) | 9 |
| Test out an explanation | 9, 10 |
| Reference (look up) | 8, 11, 12 |

# Key Stage 3 Programme of Study

During Key Stage 3 pupils build on their scientific knowledge and understanding and make connections between different areas of science. They use scientific ideas and models to explain phenomena and events, and to understand a range of familiar applications of science. They think about the positive and negative effects of scientific and technological developments on the environment and in other contexts. They take account of others' views and understand why opinions may differ. They do more quantitative work, carrying out investigations on their own and with others. They evaluate their work, in particular the strength of the evidence they and others have collected. They select and use a wide range of reference sources. They communicate clearly what they did and its significance. They learn how scientists work together on present-day scientific developments and about the importance of experimental evidence in supporting scientific ideas.

## Knowledge, skills and understanding

Teaching should ensure that scientific enquiry is taught through contexts taken from the sections on life processes and living things, materials and their properties, and physical processes.

| | Chapter coverage |
|---|---|
| **Sc1 Scientific enquiry** | |
| Ideas and evidence in science | |
| **1** Pupils should be taught: | |
| **a)** about the interplay between empirical questions, evidence and scientific explanations using historical and contemporary examples (for example, Lavoisier's work on burning, the possible causes of global warming) | 1, 3, 6, 7, 11 |
| **b)** that it is important to test explanations by using them to make predictions and by seeing if evidence matches the predictions | Introduction, 10, 11, 12 |
| **c)** about the ways in which scientists work today and how they worked in the past, including the roles of experimentation, evidence and creative thought in the development of scientific ideas. | Introduction, 2, 4, 7, 8, 10 |
| Investigative skills | |
| **2** Pupils should be taught to: | |
| *Planning* | |
| **a)** use scientific knowledge and understanding to turn ideas into a form that can be investigated, and to decide on an appropriate approach | 9, 10, 11, 12 |
| **b)** decide whether to use evidence from first-hand experience or secondary sources | 1, 11, 12 |
| **c)** carry out preliminary work and make predictions, where appropriate | 6, 7, 10, 11 |
| **d)** consider key factors that need to be taken into account when collecting evidence, and how evidence may be collected in contexts (for example, fieldwork, surveys) in which the variables cannot readily be controlled | 1, 9, 12 |
| **e)** decide the extent and range of data to be collected and the techniques, equipment and materials to use (for example, appropriate sample size for biological work) | 1, 5, 8, 10, 11, 12 |

**Thinking Through Science** Teacher's Book 1

*Obtaining and presenting evidence*

**f)** use a range of equipment and materials appropriately and take
    action to control risks to themselves and to others                    3, 5, 7, 10, 11, 12

**g)** make observations and measurements, including the use of ICT
    for datalogging (for example, variables changing over time) to an
    appropriate degree of precision                                        1, 9, 10, 11, 12

**h)** make sufficient relevant observations and measurements to reduce
    error and obtain reliable evidence                                     1, 10, 11, 12

**i)** use a wide range of methods, including diagrams, tables, charts, graphs
    and ICT, to represent and communicate qualitative and quantitative data 1, 3, 6, 7, 10, 12

*Considering evidence*

**j)** use diagrams, tables, charts and graphs, including lines of best fit,    1, 2, 6, 7, 8, 9, 10,
    to identify and describe patterns or relationships in data             11, 12

**k)** use observations, measurements and other data to draw conclusions    1, 2, 3, 5, 6, 7, 10,
                                                                           11, 12

**l)** decide to what extent these conclusions support a prediction or
    enable further predictions to be made                                  4, 10, 11

**m)** use their scientific knowledge and understanding to explain and
    interpret observations, measurements or other data, and conclusions    1, 2, 4, 5, 10, 11, 12

*Evaluating*

**n)** consider anomalies in observations or measurements and try to
    explain them                                                           3, 9, 10

**o)** consider whether the evidence is sufficient to support any
    conclusions or interpretations made                                    3, 7

**p)** suggest improvements to the methods used, where appropriate.         5, 7, 9, 11

## Sc2 Life processes and living things                                    **Chapter coverage**

Cells and cell functions

**1** Pupils should be taught:

**a)** that animal and plant cells can form tissues, and tissues can form organs 7

**b)** the functions of chloroplasts and cell walls in plant cells and
    the functions of the cell membrane, cytoplasm and nucleus in
    both plant and animal cells                                            7

**c)** ways in which some cells, including ciliated epithelial cells, sperm,
    ova, and root hair cells, are adapted to their functions               7

**d)** that fertilisation in humans and in flowering plants is the fusion of
    a male and a female cell                                               8

**e)** to relate cells and cell functions to life processes in a variety of
    organisms.                                                             7

Humans as organisms

**2** Pupils should be taught:

*Nutrition*

**a)** about the need for a balanced diet containing carbohydrates,
    proteins, fats, minerals, vitamins, fibre and water, and about
    foods that are sources of these

**b)** the principles of digestion, including the role of enzymes in
    breaking down large molecules into smaller ones

**c)** that the products of digestion are absorbed into the bloodstream and
    transported throughout the body, and that waste material is egested

**d)** that food is used as a fuel during respiration to maintain the body's
    activity and as a raw material for growth and repair                   12

*Movement*

**e)** the role of the skeleton and joints and the principle of antagonistic
    muscle pairs (for example, biceps and triceps) in movement

*Reproduction*

**f)** about the physical and emotional changes that take place during adolescence       8

**g)** about the human reproductive system, including the menstrual cycle and fertilisation       8

**h)** how the foetus develops in the uterus, including the role of the placenta       8

*Breathing*

**i)** the role of lung structure in gas exchange, including the effect of smoking

*Respiration*

**j)** that aerobic respiration involves a reaction in cells between oxygen and food, in which glucose is broken down into carbon dioxide and water    7

**k)** to summarise aerobic respiration in a word equation

**l)** that the reactants and products of respiration are transported throughout the body in the bloodstream

*Health*

**m)** that the abuse of alcohol, solvents and other drugs affects health

**n)** how the growth and reproduction of bacteria and the replication of viruses can affect health, and how the body's natural defences may be enhanced by immunisation and medicines.

Green plants as organisms
**3** Pupils should be taught:

*Nutrition and growth*

**a)** that plants need carbon dioxide, water and light for photosynthesis, and produce biomass and oxygen

**b)** to summarise photosynthesis in a word equation

**c)** that nitrogen and other elements, in addition to carbon, oxygen and hydrogen, are required for plant growth

**d)** the role of root hairs in absorbing water and minerals from the soil

*Respiration*

**e)** that plants carry out aerobic respiration.

Variation, classification and inheritance
**4** Pupils should be taught:

*Variation*

**a)** about environmental and inherited causes of variation within a species   2

*Classification*

**b)** to classify living things into the major taxonomic groups       2

*Inheritance*

**c)** that selective breeding can lead to new varieties.       2

Living things in their environment
**5** Pupils should be taught:

*Adaptation and competition*

**a)** about ways in which living things and the environment can be protected, and the importance of sustainable development

**b)** that habitats support a diversity of plants and animals that are interdependent       1

**c)** how some organisms are adapted to survive daily and seasonal changes in their habitats       1

**d)** how predation and competition for resources affect the size of populations (for example, bacteria, growth of vegetation)    1

*Feeding relationships*
**e)** about food webs composed of several food chains, and how food chains can be quantified using pyramids of numbers    1
**f)** how toxic materials can accumulate in food chains.

## Sc3 Materials and their properties                                    Chapter coverage

Classifying materials
**1** Pupils should be taught:

*Solids, liquids and gases*
**a)** how materials can be characterised by melting point, boiling point and density
**b)** how the particle theory of matter can be used to explain the properties of solids, liquids and gases, including changes of state, gas pressure and diffusion    4, 9

*Elements, compounds and mixtures*
**c)** that the elements are shown in the periodic table and consist of atoms, which can be represented by symbols
**d)** how elements vary widely in their physical properties, including appearance, state at room temperature, magnetic properties, and thermal and electrical conductivity, and how these properties can be used to classify elements as metals or non-metals
**e)** how elements combine through chemical reactions to form compounds (for example, water, carbon dioxide, magnesium oxide, sodium chloride, most minerals) with a definite composition    11
**f)** to represent compounds by formulae and to summarise reactions by word equations    11
**g)** that mixtures (for example, air, sea water and most rocks) are composed of constituents that are not combined
**h)** how to separate mixtures into their constituents using distillation, chromatography and other appropriate methods.    9

Changing materials
**2** Pupils should be taught:

*Physical changes*
**a)** that when physical changes (for example, changes of state, formation of solutions) take place, mass is conserved    9
**b)** about the variation of solubility with temperature, the formation of saturated solutions, and the differences in solubility of solutes in different solvents    9
**c)** to relate changes of state to energy transfers

*Geological changes*
**d)** how forces generated by expansion, contraction and the freezing of water can lead to the physical weathering of rocks
**e)** about the formation of rocks by processes that take place over different timescales, and that the mode of formation determines their texture and the minerals they contain
**f)** how igneous rocks are formed by the cooling of magma, sedimentary rocks by processes including the deposition of rock fragments or organic material, or as a result of evaporation, and metamorphic rocks by the action of heat and pressure on existing rocks

*Chemical reactions*

**g)** how mass is conserved when chemical reactions take place because the same atoms are present, although combined in different ways

**h)** that virtually all materials, including those in living systems, are made through chemical reactions, and to recognise the importance of chemical change in everyday situations (for example, ripening fruit, setting superglue, cooking food) 11

**i)** about possible effects of burning fossil fuels on the environment (for example, production of acid rain, carbon dioxide and solid particles) and how these effects can be minimised. 11

Patterns of behaviour

**3** Pupils should be taught:

*Metals*

**a)** how metals react with oxygen, water, acids and oxides of other metals, and what the products of these reactions are 11

**b)** about the displacement reactions that take place between metals and solutions of salts of other metals

**c)** how a reactivity series of metals can be determined by considering these reactions, and used to make predictions about other reactions

*Acids and bases*

**d)** to use indicators to classify solutions as acidic, neutral or alkaline, and to use the pH scale as a measure of the acidity of a solution 5

**e)** how metals and bases, including carbonates, react with acids, and what the products of these reactions are 11

**f)** about some everyday applications of neutralisation (for example, the treatment of indigestion, the treatment of acid soil, the manufacture of fertiliser) 5

**g)** how acids in the environment can lead to corrosion of some metals and chemical weathering of rock (for example, limestone) 11

**h)** to identify patterns in chemical reactions. 11

**Sc4 Physical processes**                                                    **Chapter coverage**

Electricity and magnetism

**1** Pupils should be taught:

*Circuits*

**a)** how to design and construct series and parallel circuits, and how to measure current and voltage 3

**b)** that the current in a series circuit depends on the number of cells and the number and the nature of other components, and that current is not 'used up' by components 3

**c)** that energy is transferred from batteries and other sources to other components in electrical circuits 3

*Magnetic fields*

**d)** about magnetic fields as regions of space where magnetic materials experience forces, and that like magnetic poles repel and unlike poles attract

*Electromagnets*

**e)** that a current in a coil produces a magnetic field pattern similar to that of a bar magnet

**f)** how electromagnets are constructed and used in devices (for example, relays, lifting magnets).

Forces and motion

**2** Pupils should be taught:

*Force and linear motion*

**a)** how to determine the speed of a moving object and to use the quantitative relationship between speed, distance and time    6

**b)** that the weight of an object on Earth is the result of the gravitational attraction between its mass and that of the Earth    6

**c)** that unbalanced forces change the speed or direction of movement of objects and that balanced forces produce no change in the movement of an object    6

**d)** ways in which frictional forces, including air resistance, affect motion (for example, streamlining cars, friction between tyre and road)    6

*Force and rotation*

**e)** that forces can cause objects to turn about a pivot

**f)** the principle of moments and its application to situations involving one pivot

*Force and pressure*

**g)** the quantitative relationship between force, area and pressure, and its application (for example, the use of skis and snowboards, the effect of sharp blades, hydraulic brakes).

Light and sound

**3** Pupils should be taught:

*The behaviour of light*

**a)** that light travels in a straight line at a finite speed in a uniform medium

**b)** that non-luminous objects are seen because light scattered from them enters the eye

**c)** how light is reflected at plane surfaces

**d)** how light is refracted at the boundary between two different materials

**e)** that white light can be dispersed to give a range of colours

**f)** the effect of colour filters on white light and how coloured objects appear in white light and in other colours of light

*Hearing*

**g)** that sound causes the eardrum to vibrate and that different people have different audible ranges

**h)** some effects of loud sounds on the ear (for example, temporary deafness)

*Vibration and sound*

**i)** that light can travel through a vacuum but sound cannot, and that light travels much faster than sound

**j)** the relationship between the loudness of a sound and the amplitude of the vibration causing it

**k)** the relationship between the pitch of a sound and the frequency of the vibration causing it.

The Earth and beyond

**4** Pupils should be taught:

*The solar system*

**a)** how the movement of the Earth causes the apparent daily and annual movement of the Sun and other stars    10

**b)** the relative positions of the Earth, Sun and planets in the solar system    10

**c)** about the movements of planets around the Sun and to relate these to gravitational forces    10

**d)** that the Sun and other stars are light sources and that the planets
and other bodies are seen by reflected light                    10
**e)** about the use of artificial satellites and probes to observe the Earth
and to explore the solar system.

Energy resources and energy transfer
**5** Pupils should be taught:

*Energy resources*
**a)** about the variety of energy resources, including oil, gas, coal,
biomass, food, wind, waves and batteries, and the distinction
between renewable and non-renewable resources                   12
**b)** about the Sun as the ultimate source of most of the Earth's energy
resources and to relate this to how coal, oil and gas are formed    12
**c)** that electricity is generated by means of a variety of energy resources  12

*Conservation of energy*
**d)** the distinction between temperature and heat, and that differences
in temperature can lead to transfer of energy
**e)** ways in which energy can be usefully transferred and stored
**f)** how energy is transferred by the movement of particles in
conduction, convection and evaporation, and that energy is
transferred directly by radiation
**g)** that although energy is always conserved, it may be dissipated,
reducing its availability as a resource.

**Breadth of study**
**1** During the Key Stage, pupils should be taught the knowledge, skills
and understanding through:
**a)** a range of domestic, industrial and environmental contexts (e.g.
Acids and alkalis, Pupil's Book pages 94 and 100)
**b)** considering ways in which science is applied in technological
developments (e.g. Forces, Pupil's Book page 128; Energy resources,
Pupil's Book page 240)
**c)** considering the benefits and drawbacks of scientific and
technological developments, including those related to the
environment, health and quality of life (e.g. Variation and classification,
Pupil's Book page 51; Reproduction, Pupil's Book page 159)
**d)** using a range of sources of information, including ICT-based sources
(e.g. Environment and feeding relationships, Pupil's Book page 26;
Energy resources, Pupil's Book page 247)
**e)** using first-hand and secondary data to carry out a range of scientific
investigations, including complete investigations (e.g. Simple chemical
reactions, page 237; Energy resources, page 251)
**f)** using quantitative approaches where appropriate, including calculations
based on simple relationships between physical quantities (e.g. Forces,
Pupil's Book page 113; Solutions, Pupil's Book page 177).

**2** During the Key Stage, pupils should be taught to:

*Communication*
**a)** use scientific language, conventions and symbols, including SI units,
word equations and chemical symbols, formulae and equations, where
appropriate, to communicate scientific ideas and to provide scientific
explanations based on evidence

*Health and safety*
**b)** recognise that there are hazards in living things, materials and physical
processes, and assess risks and take action to reduce risks to themselves
and others.

# Preface

*Thinking Through Science* is a set of textbooks and resources produced by experienced science educators and practising teachers for delivery of the Key Stage 3 Science curriculum through innovative activities, reading and study. *Thinking Through Science* activities are designed to promote better thinking in learners so that they become more adept and effective in their studies. While this textbook is intended for average to high ability pupils in Year 7, there is some differentiation within the activities, and the suggested teaching style enables children who are less able to access the work through collaborative group work. The intention of the activities is to encourage children to think and articulate their thinking in an environment that provides both challenge and support.

The textbook activities are built on the strong foundation produced by Michael Shayer, Philip Adey and Carolyn Yates in the Cognitive Acceleration through Science Education (CASE) project developed at King's College London. This project is well known for its effectiveness in raising achievement and developing logical thinking. The curriculum materials for the CASE project, called *Thinking Science*, are available from Nelson Thornes Ltd. While it is not essential for you and your classes to take on CASE in order to use this textbook course, those schools who do CASE intervention lessons will recognise the reasoning patterns and questioning style associated with CASE within many of the activities. *Thinking Through Science* therefore provides useful bridging of the CASE methodology throughout the Key Stage 3 curriculum.

While we have elected to follow the topics suggested in the QCA Scheme of Work for each year, there is some switching round of topics within the year to ensure that the type of reasoning and thinking that pupils are involved in fits with the CASE scheme and provides progression and coherence for all pupils.

## → Thinking

The basis for *Thinking Through Science* lies in a belief that pupils must construct knowledge for themselves. To do this they need to be set challenges that are ahead of where their current learning is, as well as to articulate and consolidate what they think they know and understand already. This idea is based on the work of the psychologist, Lev Vygotsky, whose interest lay in the interaction between people learning together. Vygotsky described the importance of mediation within learning. This refers to the role of one person who encourages others in the group to talk out loud their ideas and thoughts, so that others can hear and comment on these thoughts, enabling the speaker to modify her ideas. Clearly, at the same time, this also sparks off ideas and thoughts in the listeners' heads and, in turn, enables them to challenge or consolidate their understanding. While in many classroom situations the teacher will take on the role of mediator, there are advantages in allowing peers to take on this role for some of the time. It is far more likely that a pupil will question what has been said and comment on ideas in a small group consisting of his/her peers than in the public arena of whole class situations, where the teacher is looked on as the expert. In this way, pupils can build their knowledge base through social interaction. For you, as the teacher, it means honing your classroom management skills to maximise the interactions between pupils. This may need some initial work with groups, to enhance their listening and cooperating skills, so that they make the most use of the times that they interact with one another.

A child's thinking capacity develops, just as their bodies do, throughout childhood and adolescence. Jean Piaget was a psychologist interested in cognitive development. While Piagetian psychology is criticised by some researchers, most accept the terms that Piaget used to describe types of thought processes. For much of the time, pupils in Year 7 will have thought processes that are described by Piaget as 'concrete operational', a cause-and-effect type of thinking. These processes might arise from a practical activity, from what someone has said or from something the pupil has read. The thinking involved in concrete operations is usually limited to a few variables, so that they can explain and predict that 'heavy objects sink while light objects float', but their thinking cannot be extended to an understanding of density. Also, with concrete operational thinking, their language tends to focus on descriptions of situations rather than explanations of processes.

By contrast, 'formal operational' thinking can manage a greater number of variables at one time, so that a pupil might explain situations such as why a grapefruit floats, while a concrete operational thinker might expect it to sink because of its large mass. They might use explanations such as 'the heaviness of the grapefruit is spread through its large size', indicating a real feel for explaining density rather than chanting 'density equals mass over volume', which is how some learners get by with dealing with density without actually understanding it. Much of the science curriculum at Key Stage 4 requires formal operational thinking. If we can develop this type of thinking as pupils work through Key Stage 3, then the thinking that is required for Key Stage 4 is geared up and ready to go. CASE utilises a number of thinking processes to enhance the movement from concrete to formal operational thinking.

- Cognitive conflict – creating a challenge to an idea or previous experience that causes the learner to seek new ways of thinking.
- Construction – allowing learners to pursue ideas and reform thoughts.
- Metacognition – persuading learners to think about their thinking and be aware of their new ideas.
- Bridging – linking newly formed ways of thinking in other contexts both in science and everyday life.

The Scheme of Work for Key Stage 3 Science lists five types of thinking skills:

- information-processing skills
- reasoning skills
- enquiry skills
- creative-thinking skills
- evaluation skills.

## Information-processing skills

Information-processing skills require learners to locate and collect information from a variety of sources and to organise this information into a form that either aids thinking or prepares the information for analysis. This might be making tally-charts, sequencing data or constructing tables for sets of data. It also includes reading points from line graphs and taking information from bar charts and pie charts. In general, most pupils will have acquired these skills to some extent in Key Stage 2. However, it is important that pupils are given the opportunity to use and develop these skills at Key Stage 3. The analysis of graphs, bar charts and pie charts to find relationships and to identify anomalous points in a variety of contexts and progressively more complex situations is gradually introduced.

Transforming data sets into line graphs, bar charts and pie charts can be more difficult than interpreting information from them. Most Key Stage 2 pupils will be able to construct bar charts but their constructing of line graphs will be rudimentary; while some will be able to draw graphs for some sets of data, many will have problems where the axes and data points do not progress in simple sequence or where the graph origin is not zero. *Thinking Through Science 1* has been designed to ensure development of these information-processing skills by gradually helping pupils to select appropriate ways of presenting data sets, decide on the range of scales, know where each variable should go on a graph, draw lines of best fit and plot complex sets of data.

So in chapters 1 and 2 pupils start observing, interpreting information and making inferences and conclusions about data from bar charts, line graphs and tables. They consider how raw data collected by a birdwatcher can be presented in a table to aid clarity. Again, in chapter 3 pupils look at presenting data in a table and interpreting data gathered from an experiment. However, it is not until chapter 6 that pupils start to make decisions about the way data should be presented and begin to plot bar charts and line graphs. Here they are helped in making decisions about which variable goes on the *x* or *y* axis, which scales to use and how to use ICT to help them achieve a better presentation of the data. By chapter 8, pupils are expected to be able to present different types of data in bar charts, and this skill is gradually developed throughout the remaining four chapters, culminating in information processing as part of a whole investigation in chapters 10, 11 and 12. This could provide an opportunity for a practice run of an investigation in chapter 10, that is then developed and more formally assessed in chapter 11. Formative feedback could then be used to prepare for a final summative assessment in chapter 12. Alternatively, all three investigations could be used in a formative manner to help pupils understand better the assessment criteria for investigative work, and to enhance their investigative skills.

## Reasoning skills

Reasoning skills in their simplest form involve pupils in giving reasons for statements, opinions and actions. Teachers might ask, 'Why do you think that?' or 'Why might others think that?' to draw out this skill from pupils. At a more complex level, the skill involves drawing inferences and making deductions, communicating these ideas to others and making informed judgements and decisions. Reasoning skills are closely linked with the type of thinking that the CASE project engenders, and this logical scientific thinking is associated with a problem-solving and investigative approach to science. Through this area of thinking, pupils come to make decisions about the control and manipulation of variables, in that they can select and set up increasingly difficult situations for fair testing. These skills are first met in the Introduction, formalising the terminology for the different types of variables that they will already have met and worked with at Key Stage 2. Throughout all the chapters, pupils are challenged to identify input, outcome and fixed variables, and to comment on or select values for these variables. While the initial work in this area is somewhat atomistic, the chapters increasingly develop investigative skills within the activities. In the final two chapters, these skills are utilised to carry out full investigations. What we believe is important in Year 7, is that the emphasis is placed on helping pupils to develop their reasoning and investigative skills, rather than concentrating on assessing their skills at this early stage of Key Stage 3.

Other reasoning skills that are developed are those of:

- classification, particularly in chapters 2 and 5
- proportionality, particularly in chapters 1, 2, 7, 8, 9 and 10
- correlation, particularly in chapter 2
- using models, particularly chapters 3, 4, 7 and 10.

## Enquiry skills

Enquiry skills enable pupils to ask pertinent questions and to pose and define problems for research purposes. They also involve prediction, making judgements and conclusions. These skills are worked on in all chapters of the book through the gradual development of research and investigative skills.

## Creative-thinking skills

Creative-thinking skills allow the pupils to generate and extend their scientific ideas. Again this is a common feature of the Year 7 textbook where pupils are asked to be imaginative; examples include designing organisms for novel environments (chapter 1), making games to show understanding (chapters 3 and 5) and designing energy leaflets (chapter 12).

## Evaluation skills

Evaluation skills are linked with enquiry skills when they are incorporated into discussing and making decisions about social, moral and ethical issues, such as deciding whether to separate Siamese twins (chapter 8), or which alternative energy resources we should be encouraged to use (chapter 12). They also play an important role in many of the ICT activities that involve research and analysis.

# → *Progression*

Progression and continuity are important aspects of a curriculum and we have built these aspects into the scheme and framework throughout *Thinking Through Science*. This has been made explicit in the Pupil's Book by cross-referencing parts of chapters to support learners in linking ideas between different areas of the curriculum.

Our approach to progression begins at the start of each chapter in the Pupil's Book with one or more activities designed to elicit understanding gained in Key Stage 2 Science and refresh pupils' minds with the terminology and ideas to enable them to make progress in their Key Stage 3 work. It also enables you to pitch the work within the topic at an appropriate level and pace to ensure that knowledge and understanding is enhanced. This method is further developed throughout each topic by including activities that encourage pupils to reflect on their work as well as provide assessment for learning activities. These activities are labelled 'Time to think' and occur part-way through each topic and again towards the end of each topic.

The Key Stage 3 Programme of Study (pages viii–xiv) demonstrates how units and subunits of the curriculum link together and provide progression throughout Year 7 and in future years.

# → *Assessment for learning*

This type of assessment, formerly called formative assessment, is the ongoing feedback that teachers give to pupils during the learning process. Its intention is not to measure, grade or determine level but to inform, support and develop the learning. It also involves helping the learners develop self-assessment strategies, so that they become less reliant on their teacher and become self-regulated learners.

In 1998, Paul Black and Dylan Wiliam carried out an extensive review of the research literature in this area and wrote an article in *Assessment in Education*. They also produced a short synopsis of their findings entitled 'Inside the Black Box'. Their findings showed that introducing formative assessment strategies into classrooms could greatly increase achievement and, while all learners moved forward with this intervention, the achievement of lower-ability learners was particularly enhanced.

From this review, many teachers and researchers put into action its advice and ideas, the best known being the King's, Medway and Oxfordshire Formative Assessment Project (KMOFAP) led by Paul Black, Chris Harrison and Dylan Wiliam. In this project, 24 science and mathematics teachers in six secondary schools interpreted the findings of several of the research studies highlighted in the review into their classroom practice. Several articles have been published in *School Science Review* and other journals, and more are in the pipeline. 'Working Inside the Black Box' which reviews the work of KMOFAP was released in July 2002 and is available from King's College, tel: 020 7848 3189.

Various agencies have taken an interest in the development of assessment for learning, and useful websites to search are QCA, DfES Standards Site and AAIA. Some of the ideas have been taken on board by both the Science Strategy and the TLF strategy.

When teachers work formatively, they need to focus the pupils' learning so that they help the pupils see which aspects of their work are good and which need improvement. They then need to advise the pupils on what they might do to improve, and create the opportunity for them to do so, preferably in a supportive environment where the pupils can check on their work as they move forward. The teacher then needs to assist the pupils in judging the improved quality of their work so that a similar quality can be attempted in a new context. Eventually this should lead to the pupils attempting similar work without the support networks in place.

In essence, it is finding out where pupils are at in their learning, being clear about where they need to go with their next learning step and then supporting pupils as they close the gap. While schemes of work may provide a context, regular opportunities should be created within a teaching programme for pupils to reveal their ideas and conceptual understanding either orally or in written form, followed by a time space for pupils to move these ideas forward. So teachers are seeking and improving the depth of understanding of specific aspects of a topic for their pupils, rather than planning for coverage of a topic.

In the classroom, assessment for learning varies from context to context, but some of the features that it has are listed here.

- A supportive classroom environment where the emphasis is on improvement rather than right or wrong.
- A belief by the teacher and the learners that good performance is incremental and not purely dependent on IQ or some other trait.
- Questioning strategies whereby the teacher tries to find out what is inside learners' heads rather than pupils guessing what is inside the teacher's.
- Teachers asking challenging and sometimes open-ended questions and then giving enough time for learners to think (and sometimes practise what to say) before giving an answer.
- Collaborative group work, where learners support and challenge one another; peer assessment.
- Feedback that provides detail of what the learner needs to do to improve.
- Sometimes giving feedback without a grade or a mark so that learners focus on the comments for improvement, rather than comparing outcomes with their peers.
- Prime time being given to improve and redraft work.
- Opportunity for learners to see other pupils' work that has better or worse features than their own, so that they can begin to judge good performance and recognise the criteria in action.

- Opportunity for learners to feed back to their teacher on how confident they feel about their work and to identify their improvements and learning needs.
- Encouragement for self-assessment and rising to a challenge.
- Support in setting short- and medium-term targets with action plans to achieve these.

Various strategies to help you create a good culture of assessment for learning are included in the Pupil's Book. For example, traffic lighting, where pupils mark their work with a red, amber or green dot depending on their confidence in understanding a section or piece of work, will begin training your pupils in self- and peer-assessment practices and provide you with feedback on their perceptions of their learning. It will enable you to deal with problems as they arise in the learning or fast-forward the work if everyone has grasped a particular idea, so creating a classroom environment that responds to your learners' needs.

## Summative assessment

Each chapter ends with a test, usually of around 20 minutes, to provide an opportunity for checking knowledge in a continuous summative manner throughout the course. These quick tests supplement the wealth of assessment evidence that can be derived from the activities in each chapter. They are not intended as a means of allocating specific levels of attainment.

## Scientific investigation at Key Stage 3

Scientific investigation is the link between the pupils' practical experiences and the key scientific ideas. It involves testing out ideas, developing practical skills, questioning whether evidence supports the scientific interpretation, and evaluating the whole process.

However, investigative work at Key Stage 3 has caused problems for teachers:

> 'Teachers feel under pressure to cover content and see investigative work as time-consuming and less relevant to measurable performance.
>
> 'All too often at Key Stage 3 it [Sc1] is relegated to an assessment activity, bolted on to the rest of the curriculum, mainly in Year 9.'
>
> OFSTED: Progress in Key Stage 3 Science (2000)

and for pupils:

> 'The AKSIS project found that pupils focused on superficial aspects of investigations and failed to understand what they were supposed to be learning from their investigative work. Their interpretation of what they had learnt was different from what their teachers expected.'
>
> AKSIS: Investigations – Targeted Learning (2000)

# Teaching investigative skills

Investigative skills can be successfully taught if:

- the skills are taught separately
- the objectives of an exercise are shared with the pupils
- the teacher has a clear picture of the progression in each particular skill
- the criteria for the progression in each skill are shared with the pupils
- feedback on completion of an exercise points out how the pupils can improve next time
- the development of the skills is written into the Scheme of Work.

## Types of exercise

**1** A very brief exercise within a 'normal' lesson, for example:

'Explain why this practical is a fair test.'
'Are the results of this practical reliable?'
'Can you think of a way of improving the experiment described by the alchemist?'

- It can be done before, during or after practical work depending on the investigative skill to be developed.
- It can also be done within a 'theory' section.

**2** A longer exercise as part/all of a lesson.

The attainment targets for the Sc1 skill areas from the National Curriculum for Science can be converted into 'pupil speak' and separated into ladders of progression.

For example, **Planning** can be separated into:

- making predictions
- controlling variables
- choosing equipment and the data range
- collecting evidence.

Each of these skills can be taught separately, and both teacher and pupil can see the route to improvement through a progression ladder of the learning:

For example, **Making predictions**:

| Level | In my plan, I can . . . |
|-------|-------------------------|
| 3 | make a simple prediction if it is needed |
| 4 | make a prediction if it is needed |
| 5 | make a prediction if needed, **using scientific knowledge and understanding** |
| 6 | make a prediction if needed, **using simple models and theories** |
| 7 | make a prediction if needed, **using models and theories** |

## Objectives

The objectives for investigative activities should be shared with pupils. For example, the Enquiry exercise in chapter 9, Pupil's Book page 179, is mainly about controlling variables for a fair test investigation, whereas the pupils may think that the key objective is about dissolving. It is essential that pupils are aware of the learning intentions of every lesson and helped to understand what and how they are learning. The investigative skills are made explicit in the Pupil's Book and the whole investigations in chapters 10, 11 and 12 provide an opportunity to bring transparency to the processes involved in investigative work and its assessment.

## Ideas and evidence

This aspect of science teaching has re-emerged in the latest National Curriculum for Science. It is important that pupils begin to see how the ideas that we deal with in science today were established. It is also essential that pupils realise that ideas are sometimes challenged and new ways of looking at scientific concepts emerge. Consequently, science is not simply a body of facts, but a collection of ideas that are continually challenged and upgraded.

This book provides a variety of ways of developing an understanding of ideas and evidence by exploring the following:

- the initial ideas used to create stimulus for further research and thought, for example Pupil's Book, page 47
- the development of technology that accompanies or allows the ideas to develop, for example Pupil's Book, page 76
- the historic development of an idea. Pupils are then asked to comment on the different conclusions, giving evidence and reasons for the changing theories, for example Pupil's Book, page 82
- the historical perspective. Pupils consider the work of a particular scientist and a comprehension exercise is used to test understanding, for example Pupil's Book, page 193.

Ideas and evidence is also supported by some of the Research and ICT activities that ask pupils to investigate science from the past as well as current research programmes, such as the Human Genome Project.

➡ # *The key scientific ideas*

There are five key scientific ideas underpinning the Key Stage 3 Programme of Study:

- cells
- interdependence
- particles
- forces
- energy.

These concepts both fall within chapters but are also used in other chapters to encourage coherence. All five key ideas involve abstract concepts and there are many common misconceptions associated with them. The main pupils' misconceptions are given at the beginning of each chapter. The text includes ideas on eliciting misconceptions and how to deal with correcting them.

## Progression

Pupils will have some understanding of some of the key ideas from Key Stages 1 and 2 but the main difference at Key Stage 3 is the progression from the concrete to the abstract. Pupils need to recognise, describe, use and apply these ideas in increasingly complex and unfamiliar contexts from Year 7 through to Year 9. The development of each key idea in Year 7 is set out below.

### Cells

Cells are not part of the National Curriculum at Key Stages 1 and 2. By the end of Year 6, pupils should be aware of micro-organisms and have a limited understanding of their size.

In order to understand life processes and organ systems at Key Stage 3, pupils need to learn about cells as the 'building blocks of life'.

*Chapter 7 Cells*
Pupils should be taught to:

- Describe a simple model for cells which recognises that all plants and animals are made up of cells, but that there are similarities and differences between the cells.
- Explain that in most living things, there are different kinds of cells to do different jobs.
- Explain that similar cells are grouped together to form a tissue with a particular function. Tissues are grouped together to form organs.
- Explain that new cells are made by cell division and that growth occurs when new cells are made and increase in size.
- Explain that the nuclei of all cells contain the information that is transferred from one generation to the next.

*Chapter 8 Reproduction*
Pupils should be taught to:

- Describe fertilisation as the joining of the nucleus of a male sex cell and the nucleus of a female sex cell. These cells contain the information in their nuclei to make a unique individual.

### Interdependence

By the end of Year 6, most pupils have some understanding of a system for the grouping of animals and plants according to their similarities and differences.

In a biological context, they know that feeding relationships can be represented by food chains. In a physical context, the water cycle has been studied as an example of cycling materials.

At Key Stage 3, the idea of interdependence in and between biological and physical systems is fundamental to an understanding of the Earth as a continuous environment, where events in one place can produce marked effects elsewhere.

*Chapter 1 Environment and feeding relationships*
Pupils should be taught to:

- Describe ways in which organisms are adapted to daily or seasonal changes in their habitat and to their food sources.
- Explain how the organisms in a habitat can be linked together by combining food chains into food webs.

*Chapter 2 Variation and classification*
Pupils should be taught to:

- Explain that organisms can be grouped together by their similarities and differences and that a species is a group of very similar organisms.
- Explain the role of habitat in adaptation and variation.
- Identify some of the main taxonomic groups of animals and plants, describing some common features.

**Particles**
By the end of Year 6, pupils know that materials can be grouped into solids, liquids or gases and have been introduced to some reversible changes such as evaporation and condensation.

At Key Stage 3, the particle theory is fundamental to the explanation of a whole range of phenomena in physical, biological and geological settings. It is also essential in explaining the chemical changes in physical and biological systems and the heat transfer mechanisms of conduction and convection.

*Chapter 4 Solids, liquids and gases*
Pupils should be taught to:

- Describe a simple particle model for matter in terms of size, arrangement, proximity and movement of the particles in a solid, a liquid and a gas.
- Use the particle model to explain:
  - why solids have a fixed shape
  - why gases can be compressed
  - why gases and liquids can be poured
  - how diffusion occurs in gases and liquids
  - how air exerts a pressure.

*Chapter 7 Cells*
Pupils should be taught to:

- Recognise that particles are much smaller than cells.

*Chapter 9 Solutions*
Pupils should be taught to:

- Use the particle model to explain:
  - why mass is conserved when a solute dissolves to form a solution
  - dissolving and the formation of a saturated solution
  - distillation in terms of evaporation and condensation
  - separation of solutes by chromatography.

*Chapter 11 Simple chemical reactions*
Pupils should be taught to:

- Begin to use the particle model to explain how chemical reactions take place.

## Forces

By the end of Year 6, pupils have some understanding of different types of forces including friction and weight.

At Key Stage 3, the abstract concepts of forces are developed and used to underpin explanations of the behaviour of moving objects. This includes planetary motion, antagonistic muscle pairs, separating particles in melting and evaporating, and the weathering of rocks by the expansion and contraction of water.

_Chapter 6 Forces and their effects_
Pupils should be taught to:

- Recognise different types of forces and describe some examples of both balanced and unbalanced forces.
- Recognise that a force has magnitude and direction, and represent the direction of a force by an arrow.
- Distinguish between mass and weight, giving examples.
- Recognise situations involving the force of friction and describe some ways of reducing friction and some situations where friction is useful.

## Energy

Energy is not part of the National Curriculum at Key Stages 1 and 2, and pupils are likely to start Key Stage 3 with some of the misconceptions surrounding this key idea.

At Key Stage 3, the abstract concepts of energy transfer and energy conservation are needed to explain a range of physical, biological, chemical and geological processes.

_Chapter 1 Environment and feeding relationships_
Pupils should be taught to:

- Construct food chains in which energy transfer is represented by the arrows.

_Chapter 3 Electricity_
Pupils should be taught to:

- Use a simple model of energy transfer to explain:
  - the purpose of a cell in an electric circuit
  - that the electric current in an electric circuit carries energy to the components where the energy is transferred.

_Chapter 11 Simple chemical reactions_
Pupils should be taught to:

- Explain that fuels are materials that release energy when they burn.

_Chapter 12 Energy resources_
Pupils should be taught to:

- Explain the term 'non-renewable'.
- Name several non-renewable fuels and explain:
  - their use as valuable resources
  - why conservation is important.
- Explain the term 'renewable' and identify a range of renewable energy sources.
- Recognise that all living things need energy for every activity and that food is the energy source of animals.

# Introduction

## → Rationale

This chapter provides an introduction to the Pupil's Book and introduces some of the types of skill and ways of working that pupils will use in later chapters. It is likely to take between 3 and 4 hours to cover the work.

## → Overview

The textbook sections, activities and worksheets have been arranged into 1 hour blocks to aid lesson planning. Clearly several of the activities and worksheets could form part of a homework session. The planning includes reading time for individual sections but some teachers may prefer to organise this as homework preparation for the following lesson. Five types of worksheets – extension (E), support for an activity (S), practical (P), key skills (K) and developmental (D) – allow for differentiation and flexibility to accommodate teachers' preferred practice. The actual timing and emphasis on different sections will depend on the current knowledge base of the pupils, the ability of the teaching group and the preferences of the teacher.

| Lesson | Worksheet |
|---|---|
| 1 Overview<br>Scientists at work<br>Science in schools<br>Working safely | Worksheet 0.1: Drawing apparatus (K) |
| 2 Variables, values and relationships<br>Input and outcome variables | Worksheet 0.2: More ideas about relationships (E) |
| 3 Using graphs and charts | Worksheet 0.3: Sorting out data (D)<br>Worksheet 0.4: Scatter graphs (E) |
| 4 Problem solving<br>Anomalous results<br>Concept maps<br>Models | Worksheet 0.5: Mystery photograph (S) |

## → Scientists at work

→ *Pupil's Book page 1*

Research indicates that many pupils believe scientists are white males dressed in lab coats with spectacles and wild grey hair, and that the work that they do is solitary and in laboratories full of bubbling flasks of liquid. This section tries to provide a more realistic view of what scientists do and that science is inclusive. Discussion of the type of work that the scientists are doing in the photographs provides a useful way of challenging pupils' ideas.

# → Science in schools

→ *Pupil's Book page 1*

This section explains the way that pupils will learn science in school. It emphasises an investigative approach, skills development and the importance of thinking and communicating ideas. It could prove useful to get pupils to reflect on the ways that they learned science in primary school and then to compare that with how this will change in secondary school with specialised laboratories and set lesson lengths.

# → Working safely

→ *Pupil's Book page 2*

This look at safety helps settle the pupils into good working practices in the laboratory.

## Answers

1 Dangers are: apparatus near edge of bench, spillages not wiped up, safety specs missing or worn on top of head, sitting on the bench, drinking in the lab, hair not tied back, bags in gangways, Bunsen without heatproof mat, flasks boiling away unwatched, walking about with a flame.

2 Pupils will probably select six from the following.

- Always wear safety specs when heating things.
- Tie back long hair in science lessons.
- Store bags away sensibly.
- No drinking or eating in the lab.
- Place apparatus away from bench edges.
- Wipe up or report spillages as soon as they happen.
- Take responsibility for your experiment.
- Do not walk across the classroom with a flame to light your Bunsen.
- Always stand to do experiments and push stools under the bench.

3 Pupils compare their six rules with others to see which they have in common and decide which are the more important safety rules.

4 Pupils compare their six rules with the school laboratory rules to show that the rules do make sense.

*Activity* Practical: Laboratory apparatus

→ *Worksheet 0.1 Drawing apparatus (K)*

This worksheet provides an opportunity for pupils to begin recognising and drawing basic glassware and laboratory apparatus. The move from three-dimensional to two-dimensional diagrams is gradually introduced through the Pupil's Book, and so this activity could be completed at this point or later when more experiments are introduced, for example in chapter 5.

*Activity* ## Creative thinking: Safety

➡ *Pupil's Book page 3*

In this activity, pupils are given a choice to convey their ideas about safety through one of a short story, a poem or a poster. The products can be used to get pupils' work on the noticeboards in the laboratory and provide the Year 7 pupils with a sense of belonging in the new environment of secondary school.

➡ # Variables, values and relationships

➡ *Pupil's Book page 3*

Here the terms variables, values and relationships are introduced in much the same way as in the CASE *Thinking Science* curriculum materials, and their value in helping form predictions is emphasised. These terms are used throughout the book as pupils develop the thinking that underpins fair testing alongside the numerous investigative skills that they need to carry out full investigations in chapters 11 and 12.

*Activity* ## Information processing: Variables

➡ *Pupil's Book page 4*

In this activity, pupils practise identifying variables and articulating variables, as well as using relationships to form predictions. Opportunity to articulate the relationship and hear other pupils' ways of describing it, to check whether they are describing the same one, is very important. This activity is best completed in small groups to give pupils the opportunity to discuss and exchange ideas before taking a whole class feedback. It is best to check through the answers to the shape example before moving on to the other two examples.

In Q4 they might say, 'If it's green, then it's a circle and, if it's red, then it's a square,' or 'All squares are red and all circles are green.' Some pupils will only give one side of the relationship, 'Squares are red', and should be encouraged to complete the whole description of the relationship. The emphasis here is on pupils speaking, listening and commenting on each other's ideas and the teacher's role is to facilitate that without correcting anything or signalling that the answers given are correct. This will encourage pupils to rely on one another for building solutions as an alternative to relying on the teacher's expert knowledge.

Answers to Q9 will also provide opportunity for pupils to compare their way of describing the three relationships. This will help them realise that each can be stated correctly in different ways, for example, 'The larger the diamond, the greater the price of the ring' is the same relationship as 'The cheaper the ring, the smaller the diamond', but also that some ways of describing the relationships are better than others, for example, 'The larger the diamond, the greater the price of the ring' is better than 'Big diamond rings are dearer.'

## Answers

1 Variables are shape, size and colour.
2 Shape – circle or square.
  Size – large, medium or small.
  Colour – green or red.
3 Shape and colour are linked.
4 Squares are red and circles are green.
5 Circles are green.
6 Red shapes are squares.
7 The large, green shape would be a circle and the colour helps predict this.
8 Variables are:
  Rings – price of ring and size of diamond
  Vehicles – size of engine and maximum speed
  Cakes – size of cake and number of cakes.
9 The larger the diamond, the greater the price of the ring.
  The larger the engine size, the higher the maximum speed.
  As cake numbers increase, their size decreases.
10 Variables are:
  Batteries – battery power (voltage) and brightness of bulb
  Dissolving – temperature of water and time to dissolve
  Stars – distance from Earth and brightness.
11

|  | Variable | Value |
|---|---|---|
| Batteries | voltage (power) | number of volts |
|  | brightness of bulb | bright, normal, dim |
| Dissolving | temperature of water | number of °C |
|  | time to dissolve | number of seconds |
| Stars | distance from Earth | number of light years |
|  | brightness of star | bright, dim |

12 The higher the voltage of the battery, the brighter the bulb.
  The higher the temperature of the water, the less time to dissolve the solid.
  The farther the star from Earth, the dimmer the star.

# → *Input and outcome variables*

→ *Pupil's Book page 5*

By the end of Key Stage 2, most pupils are familiar with using the term 'fair test' but in fact few can actually control and manipulate variables when presented with a new context to investigate. They may remember that you keep all variables the same, except for the one that you are testing, but a large proportion of most classes will not be able to do this unaided by teacher direction. In most schemes, a table of variables is given to the pupils in each new investigation, which helps create a fair test by dictating what is and what is not to be changed. While this will help pupils test fairly in that particular investigation, it does not help them develop the thinking that underpins fair testing and so they do not acquire skills that they can transfer to new investigations. Indeed, many pupils confuse fair testing with accuracy or reliability issues and a large number see it as giving a variable a 'fair chance'. For example, if you wanted them to find out what affected the speed of a ball down a ramp, they might place a large ball at the top of the ramp and a small ball partway down. This is because they believe that the size of the ball affects the speed that it travels down the ramp and so placing it higher up the ramp makes it fairer on the large ball. You could try putting that problem to pupils to see the sort of responses that you get and so judge how proficient they are at setting up a fair test situation. Those of you following the CASE *Thinking Science* programme will focus on this in the rollerball activity.

The term 'input variable' is used for the dependent variable and 'outcome variable' for the independent variable. The terms input and outcome signal to the pupils much more directly what their role is in manipulating these variables. They need to make decisions about how to vary the input variable, while the outcome variable is the one they measure or observe (their results). Fixed variables are those that they decide to keep the same.

## *Activity* Information processing: Identifying variables

→ *Pupil's Book page 6*
This activity again provides opportunity to articulate ideas and to listen and compare other pupils' ideas with their own and so is best conducted in small groups followed by a whole class feedback session.

## Answers

**1** Outcomes would be 'delicious' or 'horrible'.
**2** Inputs could be amount of chocolate, amount of cereal, type of chocolate, brand of cereal, temperature of cooking, etc.
**3** Krispy cakes made with milk chocolate are more delicious than those made with dark chocolate.
**4** Amount of chocolate, amount of cereal, brand of cereal, temperature of cooking, etc.
**5** Input variable is type of paper towel.
**6** Amount of water remaining in the bucket is the outcome variable.
**7** Values would be ml of water.
**8** Size of towel, starting volume of water.
**9** The thicker the towel, the less water it leaves in the bucket or the more water it soaks up.

## *Activity* Information processing: More variables

→ *Worksheet 0.2: More ideas about relationships (E)*

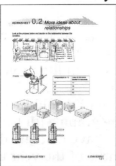

This worksheet provides extra practice at recognising input and outcome variables, and deciding on whether a relationship exists. Pupils will find the presents and mass example difficult as they will expect the relationship to be 'the larger the present, the heavier it will be' and it is not in this case. In fact, there is no relationship between size and mass. This therefore provides cognitive conflict. The final example shows a tulgren funnel. If pupils are not familiar with these, you need to explain that it contains a sample of leaf litter and is used to collect invertebrates, as they move away from the light.

Again one of the benefits gained from this activity is the opportunity to encourage discussion and listening skills in group work and feedback sessions. For some students, it may help to get them to reorder the data for the ice cream sales. All of the relationships given below can be stated in a variety of ways and pupils should be encouraged to decide on which are good ways of expressing the relationships.

- The higher the daily temperature, the higher the ice cream sales.
- The lower the temperature, the slower the treacle flows.
- The brighter the light, the fewer invertebrates were collected.

# → *Using graphs and charts*

→ *Pupil's Book page 6*

During Key Stage 2, pupils become proficient at drawing bar charts and much of the work they do in science at this level requires them to utilise this skill. Many will have also drawn pie charts and line graphs but the awareness of when to present data in one form or another will probably not yet be apparent. This section sets out to emphasise that scientists need to make choices about the way that they present data. This text takes pupils through a problem set in Mr Bertolli's sweet shop, where they have to decide, from a choice of four, on the numbers of particular flavoured sweets that Mr Bertolli needs to top up his 'fruity bon-bon' jar each day. Viewing the numbers in the table does not make it easy to solve the problem but when the table is turned into a pie chart or bar chart, it is easy to see that strawberry and lemon are equally popular and more popular than lime or orange. Spreadsheet 'Sweets.xls' on the CD-ROM can be used here.

*Activity* ## Information processing: Finding information

→ *Pupil's Book page 8*

This activity enables pupils to practise taking readings from bar charts, pie charts and line graphs, and also to interact with different types of data and make decisions about which ways are useful to present the data. Worksheet 0.3: Sorting out data (see below) provides further practice for developing these skills with bar charts, pie charts and line graphs. Scatter graphs are not considered in the textbook but Worksheet 0.4: Scatter graphs (see below) is available as extension work. All pupils will be introduced to scatter graphs in chapter 2.

## Answers

1 In June, the temperature in Ibiza was 20°C and in the UK 12°C.
2 In August, it was 27°C in Ibiza and 17°C in the UK.
3 Water consumption in 1985 was 17 million tonnes.
4 15% of the soya bean is protein.
5 The temperature in Ibiza and the UK could be presented as two separate bar charts or a line graph with two separate slopes. While bar charts usually have discrete data (types rather than a range), when months of the year are the horizontal axis, these can be treated as a range from month 1 to month 12 and so a line graph could be drawn. The way

that it is presented in the book allows holidaymakers to compare the monthly temperatures easily and so is the best way to present it. It could not be presented as a pie chart.

The world water consumption could be presented as a bar chart. Because it has data sometimes at 10 year intervals and sometimes at 5 year intervals, it is better to keep it as a line graph because the horizontal axis does not increase by the same amount each time. If we wanted to present it as a bar chart then it would be better just to select the data at 10 year intervals – but this would reduce the richness of the data. This data could not be presented as a pie chart.

6 The percentage of each food group in soya beans could be presented as a bar chart. In fact it would be easier to take readings from a bar chart than from the pie chart. The pie chart would be useful if comparing lots of foods for their different food groups as we could then pick out foods high in protein or low in fat, for example. This could also be done on bar charts but the comparison would probably not be so easy to see as on pie charts. This data could not be presented as a line graph because there is no range for the horizontal axis.

7 a) Bar chart, but could be a line graph.
b) Pie chart or bar chart.
c) Bar chart or line graph.
d) Pie chart or bar chart.
e) Line graph or bar chart.

## *Activity* Information processing: Presenting data

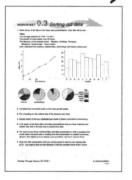

➡ *Worksheet 0.3: Sorting out data (D)*
This worksheet is a 'mix and match' activity where pupils have to select the correct form of data presentation to match the data set. They then have to practise labelling axes or extending scales or taking readings from the presentations. Finally, they devise sensible questions for others to answer by taking readings. They may find that some questions cannot be answered from the data and these should be emphasised as the limitations of that type of presentation.

## Answers

1 The line graph shows the growth of cress, the bar chart shows the average absence of Year 7 and the pie charts show the litter collected. The distance of seaside towns to London cannot be presented as a line graph because the horizontal axis has discrete data. A bar chart would be better. However, it is not the bar chart shown since the labels on the axes are different.

2 Three points need to be added, 30 hours, 40 hours and 50 hours.

3 The axis title should be 'Number of absences in Year 7' or 'Number of children'.

4 The history pie chart is the one with only two categories – paper and other, while the technology has four categories – paper, metal, plastic and other.

5 The average absence of Year 7 in 2001 is a bar chart because it has discrete data for each month and compares two variables – month and absences.

The growth of cress plants over 48 hours also compares two variables but cannot be presented as a bar chart because the horizontal axis is a range with readings not taken at regular intervals.

The types of litter collected from science, mathematics, technology and history classrooms could be presented as a bar chart but it would be complex as a single bar chart as there are four types of classroom. It could be done as four separate bar charts but then the comparison would be more difficult for each type. This data cannot be presented as a line graph.

**6** A variety of questions can be asked such as:

- Which month had the most absences over the year?
- Which school subject produces the most paper rubbish in a month?
- How tall were the cress plants after 30 hours?
- When were the cress plants 2.5 cm tall?
- When did the cress plants grow quickest?

Questions that cannot be asked are:

- What was the total school absence for the year?
- Did all the cress plants grow at the same rate?
- How much did the paper rubbish from mathematics weigh?

**7**

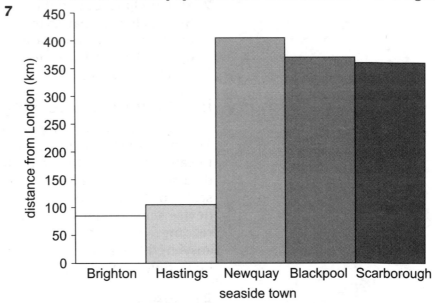

## Activity    Information processing: Scatter graphs

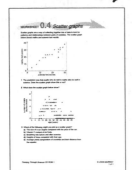

➡ *Worksheet 0.4: Scatter graphs (E)*

This is an extension activity that introduces pupils to scatter graphs as an alternative to bar charts. Point out that you are looking for plots around a line shape to get a positive relationship, whereas, if the plots are scattered then there is no relationship. Sometimes there is a relationship for a subsection of the data and this is shown in Q2.

## Answers

**1** The plots on the scatter graph do indicate that there is a link between doing well in science and doing well in maths. Point out specific points as exemplars. For example, a pupil scored 38 in maths and 30 in science whereas another scored poorly in both maths and science.

**2** Up to around age 30, the scatter graph shows a link between age and number of phones that you have owned but this relationship breaks down above 30.
**3** The following can be plotted as scatter graphs to look for links:
   **a)** the size of a car engine compared with the price of the car
   **d)** heights of trees compared with their age
   **e)** average yearly temperature of countries and their distance from the equator.

# ➡ *Problem solving*

➡ *Pupil's Book page 10*
Presenting science as a problem-solving activity is both motivating and encourages thinking. It also helps improve teamwork, particularly if you ask groups to reflect on the way they solved the problem.

*Activity* ## Reasoning: Mystery photograph

➡ *Pupil's Book page 10*
➡ *Worksheet 0.5: Mystery photograph (S)*
This activity is best done in small groups where the problem can be solved and groups can work out an explanation of how they solved or part-solved the problem. Pupils will solve this problem by following specific variables through, such as the snail trail development or the cat and bird chase. Many will also sequence events either from start to finish or from key events, such as when the ornament is broken. If you are working with a low ability set, it is helpful to use Worksheet 0.5, as this will lower the thinking level to make this task more accessible. Pupils can then either write on the sheet to keep a record of their solution, or cut up the pictures and physically put them into the order of events. Many will miss that the candle is sometimes lit and in some photos is not lit. This is the key clue, along with the broken ornament.

It is a good idea to stop the activity when it is clear that two to three groups have solved it and all other groups have accessed and engaged with the problem. The ones who have not quite solved the problem will be able to complete the solution in their heads as they listen to other groups' explanations.

By using some of the questions and prompts below in the whole class feedback, you can encourage groups to listen to other groups' explanations and compare them with their own:

Your group first ... ?
Which clue helped you decide that?
Why did you think that?
Was your decision the same as X's group or different? How was it the same or different?
How did you decide that this photograph came later than that one?
Does the photograph show everything that is happening in the room at that time?
Which photograph comes next?
How did you decide that?

Why is the broken ornament a good clue to help you
sequence the photographs?
Do snail trails last forever?

Persuade groups to reflect on their solution pathway:

How did you tackle this problem?
Were there any clues that helped?
Were there any clues that did not help?
What was the key piece of information that helped you solve
this problem?
Were there any clues that you thought would help but in the
end did not?
Did you make any notes or use any codes to help you
remember what happened?
Did you check your answer in any way? Could you have
done?
Can you think of other ways of solving the problem?

Learn from one another:

Which groups solved the problem in the way that your group
did?
What is a different way of solving this problem?
Does that way have advantages or disadvantages compared
to your way of solving the problem?
When was it easy to follow someone's explanation? When
was it difficult?
What has this puzzle taught you about problem solving?

There are two possible mystery photographs. The middle one
on the left (3) shows the candle lit and the ornament broken.
The one at the bottom right (6) shows the candle out and the
ornament intact. One of these must be the photograph that
precedes the final photograph, which is top right (2). The other
clue to look at is the picture, which went from askew to
straight. The unknown is what happened between the bottom
left picture (5) and the top right (2). Did the bird fly off, putting
out the candle with its wing beat, straightening the picture and
perhaps knocking off the ornament? Did the cat jump up and
do any of these things? Were all three changes caused by one
event or several?

We have some idea of the right answer but there is
uncertainty. We can use ideas and explanations to explain
changes in variables but sometimes we do not catch events as
they happen. This is how scientists work. Often there are many
variables and scientists have to decide which are the ones to
concentrate on. They collect as much data as they can but
sometimes they simply have to explain what data they have. So
sometimes there are two or more explanations and one might
be favoured over another.

The questions in the Pupil's Book are for groups who finish
early to begin reflecting on their method. They can also be
used for homework questions so that individual pupils can go
through the problem solution again and check that they
understood what their group did and why they chose to do it
that way, and also how this compares with the way other
groups solved the problem.

# → *Anomalous results*

→ *Pupil's Book page 11*

The idea of odd readings or inconsistent findings (as depicted in the previous activity) is picked up in this section. The data table and line graph for stretching a spring with 100 g loads are shown and pupils see that they can use the straight line graph to make predictions. Note that some may use proportional thinking between two results in the data table to do this as well and the fact that you can do both should be emphasised. The 'line of best fit' is explained and this shows that the 400 g reading on the graph gives an anomalous result. The input variable is given as mass in 100 g chunks rather than force in 0.1 N chunks to enable pupils to focus on the interpretative skills here in a simplified way. If newtons are used, it is difficult for pupils to predict readings between the data points because they are not familiar with using decimal points in a range as yet.

## Answers

**5** 12 cm.

**6** Either the graph slope or the fact that each time another 100 g is added the spring stretches a further 3 cm.

**7** Other stretch readings for loads in between, such as 250 g or 375 g.

# → *Concept maps*

→ *Pupil's Book page 12*

Concept maps provide a way of looking at how learners organise their ideas about a topic in their thinking. A concept map can help you see which terminology pupils correctly identify within a topic (selection), how they connect these to other parts of the topic (connectedness), whether the links add to understanding (link quality), whether the map structure can accommodate new ideas (dynamism) or is fixed. In some cases, it is useful to look at concept maps at the start, in the middle and towards the end of a topic to help pupils recognise what learning has taken place and that, often, it is not merely broadening knowledge but sometimes changing the way that you look at a topic. This section encourages pupils to start building concept maps. In the early stages, it is best to provide pupils with words to build their maps from, but as they become more proficient at constructing the maps they can select their own words as part of the task.

## Answers

**8** 'Pollinate' *or* 'identify the colour, shape and scent of'.

**9** 'Carries water from the roots to the' *or* 'holds up the'.

**10** Chlorophyll.

**11** Boxes such as roots, fruits and seeds could be added with appropriate links.

# Models

→ *Pupil's Book page 13*

Models and analogies are used in abundance in science and pupils need to develop the skills of using models to portray their ideas. They also need to develop evaluative skills when using models, to judge how well a model actually fits a situation or not. This section encourages the development of these skills.

## Answers

**12** Balloons represent the lungs.

**13** The glass tube represents the windpipe.

**14** The diaphragm is represented by the rubber sheet.

**15** The ribs or chest wall are/is represented by the bell jar.

**16** There are two lungs and the diaphragm does cover the entire base of the chest region.

**17** The size of the lungs fills the chest cavity which the balloons do not. The ribs and chest wall move as we breathe but the glass bell jar cannot do this.

**18** Answer could be yes or no. Yes, because it has the same parts as the breathing system, and no, because the relative proportions of the parts are different and the movement of some parts is not the same.

# 1 Environment and feeding relationships

## → Rationale

This chapter provides 8 hours of teaching materials. Through Key Stages 1 and 2, children will have been introduced to a variety of animals and plants in their local environment and through television, videos and books. This chapter begins to look at the interrelationships of animals and plants with respect to feeding and develops the ideas of food chains and food webs. It attempts to encourage children to look for evidence and ideas within different habitats to help them bridge concepts developed in a more wide-ranging way. It builds on unit 4B Habitats and unit 6A Interdependence and adaptation in the Key Stage 2 Scheme of Work. The key science ideas developed in this chapter are interdependence and energy.

The chapter moves on to look at adaptation through a structure and function approach again within a number of different types of environment. While it is sometimes difficult to explain adaptation in a Darwinian way when looking at those animals and plants who have been successful in terms of natural selection without considering those that were not, by looking at 'fit' to a range of specific environmental conditions the idea of those organisms who possess particular structures being successful can be emphasised. Creative thinking is included where pupils are asked to create an organism to fit a particular environment, giving reasons for the structures and features that they give their organism. Again here the emphasis needs to be that having particular structures makes an organism successful, rather than it developing some structure to meet the environmental demands.

This chapter links with parts of chapter 2 Variation and classification, and forms a background for work to be developed in Y8 on ecological relationships.

## → Overview

The textbook sections, activities and worksheets have been arranged into 1 hour blocks to aid lesson planning. Clearly several of the activities and worksheets could form part of a homework session. The planning includes reading time for individual sections but some teachers may prefer to organise this as homework preparation for the following lesson. Five types of worksheets – extension (E), support for an activity (S), practical (P), key skills (K) and developmental (D) – allow for differentiation and flexibility to accommodate teachers' preferred practice. The actual timing and emphasis on different sections will depend on the current knowledge base of the pupils, the ability of the teaching group and the preferences of the teacher.

| Lesson | Worksheet |
|---|---|
| **1** Recognising local animals and plants | |
| **2** Samples and estimating | Worksheet 1.1: Sample size (D) Worksheet 1.2: Getting the sample right (E) |
| **3** Changing populations | Worksheet 1.3: How plants cope with the seasons (S) |
| **4** The stream environment | Worksheet 1.4: Looking at stream organisms (P) |
| **5** Who eats who? | |
| **6** What is adaptation? | |
| **7** How much to eat? | |
| **8** Food webs | Worksheet 1.5: Environmental terms (K) |
| Review | Worksheet 1.6: Test on the environment |

➡ # *Chapter plan*

| | Demonstration | Practical | ICT | Activity | Word play | Time to think | Ideas and evidence |
|---|---|---|---|---|---|---|---|
| **Lesson 1** | | | | | | What do you know? | |
| **Lesson 2** | | Using quadrats | | Reasoning: Taking samples  Discussion: Drawing conclusions  Discussion: More samples | | | |
| **Lesson 3** | | | | Information processing: Bird watching  Information processing: changing seasons  Questions: Yearly cycle of an oak tree | | | Population size |
| **Lesson 4** | | Stream organisms | | Information processing: Stream investigation | | | |
| **Lesson 5** | | | | Information processing: Food chains  Information processing: Investigating the compost heap | Food chains | | |
| **Lesson 6** | | | | | | Food chains | |
| **Lesson 7** | | | Using a spreadsheet | Reasoning: Party time | | | |
| **Lesson 8** | | | | Summary: Environmental terms | | | Environment and feeding relationships |

# ➡ _Expectations_

**At the end of this chapter**

**in terms of scientific enquiry**

**most pupils will:** make a series of measurements of environmental variables appropriate to the task; identify a question to investigate the activity of an invertebrate, suggesting a suitable approach and sample size; use their results to relate animal and plant activity to environmental changes; collect evidence to appropriate precision; interpret data evidence and draw conclusions

**some pupils will not have made so much progress and will:** make measurements of environmental variables appropriate to the task and make suggestions about investigating the activity of an invertebrate

**some pupils will have progressed further and will:** describe, in terms of approach and sample size, how strongly any patterns or associations identified are supported by the evidence

**in terms of life processes and living things**

**most pupils will:** identify differences between different habitats and relate these to the organisms found in them; describe ways in which organisms are adapted to daily or seasonal changes in their environment and to their mode of feeding; describe food chains within an environment and combine these into food webs; present data from field notes into tables and into chart form; analyse data and make statements about relationships; make decisions on sample size and begin to build ideas on random sampling techniques; and use 'mark and recapture' methods to make informed estimates of population size

**some pupils will not have made so much progress and will:** identify differences between different habitats and describe how familiar organisms are suited to the habitat in which they are found; describe some simple food chains; present data from field notes in tables and in chart form; and analyse data and, with help, make statements about relationships

**some pupils will have progressed further and will:** explain why a variety of habitats is needed in a community; describe how different organisms contribute to the community in which they are found and relate food chains to energy transfer; evaluate graphs and data in relation to sample size and describe associations and correlations

# ➡ *Links with CASE*

Classification ideas will have been used by children at a descriptive level in primary school within science and other subject areas. The ability to classify in terms of grouping similar things is introduced in this chapter through considering whether animals are herbivores or carnivores, and also in the allocation of organisms to feeding levels within food chains. Clearly observational skills, identification techniques and ability to group organisms will play important roles in developing these basic ideas into conceptual understanding.

Proportionality thinking is also developed through pyramids of numbers where pupils need to scale up the ratios set up in food chains through multiplication methods. The idea is introduced through ingredients lists for recipes that have to be scaled up and down according to the total number requiring feeding.

Sampling involves the use of correlation, allowing pupils to judge whether variability is due to chance or has a causal relationship. Pupils come to realise that sample sizes of one or four might miss some of the variability in plant type and cover within the quadrat. Sample sizes of 12 or 100 are more likely to find the whole variation in the field and diminish the effects of those quadrats that show extreme results.

# ➡ *Pupils' misconceptions*

| Misconception | Scientific understanding |
|---|---|
| Photosynthesis is the way that plants respire. | Photosynthesis is plant nutrition. The plant uses carbon dioxide to make sugar when there is light. Plants also respire all the time and need oxygen for this. |
| The arrows in a food chain show who eats whom. | The arrows in a food chain represent the energy flow. |
| Adaptation is the way that an animal or plant changes to fit an environment. | Animals and plants show variation. Some of these variations help them survive in specific environments. This is natural selection. |
| If environments change, the animals and plants will change to become adapted. It is a gradual process. | Animals and plants show variation. Some of these variations help them survive in specific environments. If environments change dramatically, it is likely that a different variation within that species or a different species will be more likely to survive. Such changes are not gradual. |

## ➡ *Literacy, numeracy and other cross-curricular links*

There is considerable scope within this chapter to develop speaking and writing skills. Wherever possible, discussion and comparison of ideas should be encouraged. Pupils are asked to produce writing for specific audiences including producing information posters for a bird-watching site.

This chapter makes a good start on developing numeracy skills through estimation, percentages and sample sizes. Both continuous and discrete data are collected, collated, presented and analysed. It also gets pupils to use calculators and ICT resources to solve mathematical problems and give results to a degree of accuracy appropriate to context.

### Language for learning

By the end of this chapter pupils will be able to understand, use and spell correctly:

- words and phrases relating to feeding relationships – energy, producer, photosynthesis, consumer, herbivore, carnivore, food chain, food web, pyramid of numbers, predator, prey
- words and phrases relating to organisms and the environment – population, adaptation, nocturnal, hibernate, migrate, habitat
- words relating to scientific enquiry – sample, evidence, data, reliable.

## 1 *Recognising local animals and plants*

### Learning outcomes

Pupils:

- use observation and classification skills to identify and group organisms
- use keys

This activity allows pupils to refresh their skills in observation and classification by identifying and grouping animals and plants typically found in school grounds in rural areas. Most pupils will have used keys for identification in Key Stage 2 but may have called these Yes/No Trees. While urban schools may not have such a rich habitat on their doorstep, it is likely that most of these animals and plants will be found in or near the area of the school. The activity will allow teachers to elicit what preknowledge and classification skills pupils have and this can help in making decisions as to the pace and emphasis of the work in this chapter.

It would be a good idea to take pupils out to the school field, if possible, for them to recognise and identify evidence similar to that in this activity.

# What do you know?
# Answers

→ *Pupil's Book page 16*

1 Nine animals (pair of magpies, thrush, robin, fox, spider, woodlouse, ant, snail, worm) and about eight plants (grass, oak tree, fern, plantain, clover, buttercup, daisy, bramble, moss).

2 Birds (feathers), invertebrates (no backbone), arthropods (jointed legs and exoskeleton).

3 These could vary but here is an example.

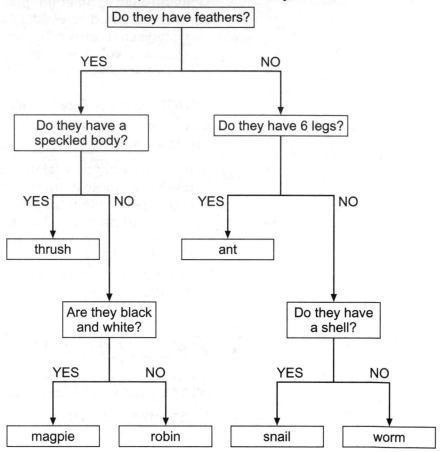

4 These could vary but here is an example.

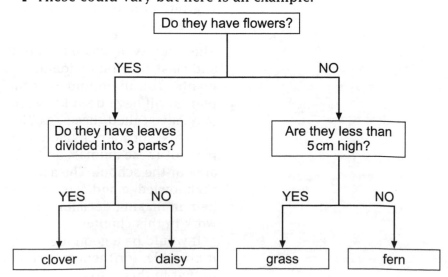

5 Pupils may write about feeding relationships:
Foxes eat birds.
Birds eat worms/insects/invertebrates.
Trees feed by photosynthesis.
Snails eat plants.
Worms eat leaves.
Spiders catch insects in their webs.

They may write about other relationships:
Trees provide a place for birds to build nests.
Worms aerate soil and also make it fertile.
Birds line their nests with moss.
Plants provide good cover from predators for small animals.
Woodlice like to live under piles of damp leaves.

6 Magpies, thrush, fox, spider, woodlice, ant, snail, grass, oak tree, fern, bramble, moss.

7 Squirrels, beetle, ivy, holly, other trees such as ash, different types of fern such as hart's tongue fern.

8 Some animals and plants live in specific habitats where they are successful. Larger numbers of each species live in the wood as there is more food and shelter than on the edge of the school field.

9 Foxes are predators and so only a few can live in an area. Many foxes move to town areas as they have rich pickings in dustbins.

10 More trees to build their homes (dreys) and more food (nuts).

11 Ants scavenge on any small pieces of food and so the school bins and areas where pupils eat lunch are places that they will be found. There are dangers from humans and from predators such as birds and centipedes. Ants have antennae on their heads and sense organs on their legs to detect things in their surroundings.

Early morning and dusk are good times for ants to scavenge as there are no humans in the school and it's more difficult to be seen by predators.

Life for the woodland ant would be similar but the risk of predation would be much greater and food will be mainly plants. Ants are social insects and live with other worker ants and a queen ant in a nest.

# 2 Samples and estimating

## Learning outcomes

Pupils:

- explain why scientists take samples
- consider whether sample size is appropriate for the investigation
- collect results and create results tables
- decide whether the results fit the conclusion given
- decide on appropriateness of sample size used
- collect and interpret experimental results
- explain confidence in results demonstrating a relationship
- explain how scientists carry out population studies

This part of the work concentrates on developing processing skills and enables pupils to gain some understanding of sample size as well as sampling techniques used in fieldwork.

*Activity* Practical: Using quadrats

Using quadrats on the school field or some local grassy area may be a possibility for some schools. The ideas can be worked on in the laboratory by allowing washing up bowls of soil to establish plant growth over the previous summer and using 10 cm quadrats. A cheap way of making your own quadrats is to use four pieces of net curtain wire fastened at the corners. A paper variety of quadrating can be bought from the Field Studies Council, an independent educational charity that works through a network of residential and day centres. To find your nearest centre go to their website, www.field-studies-council.org.

Sample size, confidence in results and reliability are important issues to consider in science. Sometimes other reasoning such as practicability means that we do not always select the most appropriate sample sizes nor carefully interpret results. Pupils need to be made aware of this and be encouraged to give reasons for sample size in an investigation and to realise that chance and other variables may be having some effect on the results.

## Observing and counting
## Answers

➡ *Pupil's Book page 18*

1 Samples are a smaller replica of the real thing and manufacturers produce them so that you can find out what the large-scale product is like before you buy it.

*Activity* Reasoning: Taking samples
## Answers

➡ *Pupil's Book page 20*

1 12 quadrats are taken because this provides a more typical sample of the whole site. If only one or two quadrats were taken these might not be representative.
2 This is partly because plants can grow and overlap one another and partly because we estimate to the nearest 5% when there might only be 3–4% of one type.
3 This is because there might be a large variety and these are not representative of plants in this field because they are so small in number.
4 The data on 12 quadrats is almost the same as that for 100 quadrats and so outlying individual plants do not bias the data as much as in 1 or 6 quadrats' worth of data.

*Activity* Discussion: Drawing conclusions

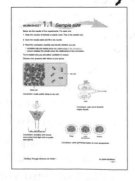

➡ *Worksheet 1.1: Sample size (D)*

This activity encourages pupils to look at sample size, record results systematically and question conclusions that have been suggested. Most pupils will only be able to make judgements about confidence levels at the extremes. They are therefore likely to select the funnel with worms and woodlice as being 'unsure' because of the small sample size and the difference in the results being very small. The darkest place is likely to be in the leaves anyway, rather than furthest from the light and so the conclusion for this experiment is very tentative. They are likely to say that they are confident about the germinating pea and temperature experiment although the fact that only 11 out of the 12 peas germinated at room temperature may cause some pupils concern.

*Activity*

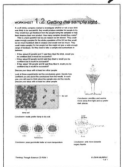

## Discussion: More samples

➡ *Worksheet 1.2: Getting the sample right (E)*

This is an extension worksheet and alternative to Worksheet 1.1 Sample Size. Because it covers the same four experiments, this worksheet could be used for specific groups of pupils within the same classroom as those working on Worksheet 1.1. This worksheet provides the opportunity for pupils to discuss sampling and prepares pupils for making choices in their own investigative work. It moves from an everyday context to considering four experiments in terms of:

**i)** the sample size chosen

**ii)** pupils' confidence in the results showing a relationship.

Pupils should definitely question the conclusion in the ant experiment since one ant changing its mind could give equal choice of variable. There should be some concerns about the conclusion to the woodlice and worms experiment, particularly what is said about the worms. Generally, larger sample sizes are needed for all these experiments since a change in one or two individuals can alter the conclusion.

## Estimating

➡ *Pupil's Book page 21*

This part of the chapter introduces the idea of estimating populations using 'mark and recapture' methods. This concept is introduced at a descriptive level, here focusing more on the ways in which scientists carry this out in the field and collect data rather than on calculating population size as an exercise. This idea is developed in CASE in TS21.

# 3 *Changing populations*

## Learning outcomes

Pupils:

- describe how some animals react to their environment at different times of the day and year
- describe and explain an example of the benefits of population studies
- produce posters to interpret data on seasonal variation
- identify input and outcome variables
- make predictions using patterns emergent from the data
- make decisions about creating results tables
- interpret data from a set of line graphs
- link data from graphs with knowledge of daily and seasonal behaviour of a mammal (squirrel) and an invertebrate (slug)
- identify ways in which habitats vary throughout the year
- describe some strategies that animals and plants adopt to avoid climatic stress
- interpret data from a drawing

## Ideas and evidence: Population size

➡ *Pupil's Book page 22*

This 'Ideas and evidence' activity encourages pupils to see one of the benefits of estimating population size.

### Answers

**1** Population sizes are always changing because animals are born while others die. Also some may migrate.
**2** Scientists were able to work out the areas of bamboo that needed to be put aside in National Parks to support the panda population and prevent extinction.

## Daily and seasonal changes

➡ *Pupil's Book page 23*

This section deals with reasons why population size might change in response to the environment (migration) or seem different depending on when the size is estimated (some animals are nocturnal or may hibernate). Change in population size due to births and deaths is not dealt with here but could be discussed if thought appropriate.

## *Activity* Information processing: Bird watching

➡ *Pupil's Book page 24*

The emphasis with this activity is on helping pupils interpret and present data appropriately to a specific audience (the visitors to a nature reserve) and then to unpick the steps within a bird-watching investigation. Q4 is difficult because pupils will have to interpret the data in the table at the top of the page or look carefully at the information in the four posters produced from Q1 to identify clues about when the bird-watching investigation was done. For some pupils, it might be easier in Q5 to turn the data in the notebook shown into a results table so that they have something concrete to describe.

### Answers

**1** Posters should show that:

- common shelduck and goldeneyes are only around in the autumn and winter
- avocets are only seen in the spring and early summer
- teals and redshanks reduce in number in the late spring/early summer
- the rest of the birds are around in similar numbers throughout the year.

**2** Input variable is the type of bird.
**3** Outcome variable is number.
**4** Spring or early summer because avocets and goldeneye spotted and teal in small numbers. However redshank in large numbers and so perhaps April.
**5** Numbers would be given and not tally marks as in the book and the data would be set out as a two-column table with headings 'Type of bird' and 'Number observed'.

**Attainment targets**

Work in the previous sections should provide evidence that pupils are working towards the following attainment levels.

| | |
|---|---|
| Explain that different organisms are found in different habitats because of different factors | Level 5 |
| Explain that distribution and abundance of organisms in habitats are affected by environmental factors | Level 6 |

*Activity* ## Information processing: Changing seasons

➡ *Pupil's Book page 25*

This is a data analysis activity in which pupils are asked to translate the data into a number of different forms. In Q4, Q6 and Q7, pupils are asked to use their imagination to interpret the data into actual scenes and events. In Q4 it may be possible to use the drawings that pupils produce to focus on changes to plants through the four seasons and discuss how these avoid climatic stress (e.g. leaf fall in deciduous trees, needle-shape leaves in fir trees). This idea is picked up in Worksheet 1.3: How plants cope with the seasons (see below).

### Answers

1 July.

2 January.

3 October – 14 °C, January = 5 °C, April = 15 °C, July = 25 °C

4 Drawings of the four seasons at midday.

5 October = 5 °C, January = 0 °C, April = approx. 5 °C, July = approx. 15 °C

6 In October the squirrel will be eating as much as it can and storing nuts.
In January the squirrel will be hibernating.
In April the squirrel will have come out of hibernation and be searching for nuts and eating young shoots and buds. It may also be looking for a mate or breeding.
In July squirrels are very active feeding on fruits and other plant material.

7 Slugs are 'cold blooded' and therefore their body temperature is only a few degrees above that of the environment. So when the temperature is low they are inactive and when it is high they are active or, if it is too hot, they avoid warm places. In January, they will be hibernating. In April and July they may venture out to feed at night. In October they will be searching for a place to hibernate and feeding on fallen fruits.

*Activity* ## Questions: Yearly cycle of an oak tree

➡ *Worksheet 1.3: How plants cope with the seasons (S)*

This worksheet looks at the yearly cycle of the oak tree, concentrating on the reasons for leaf fall in deciduous trees. It also considers growth rates.

### Answers

1 Sentences should focus on:

spring – buds open, flowers form
summer – leaves fully open (growing period)
autumn – leaves change colour and fall, acorns form
winter – no leaves (dormant period).

**2** If trees kept their leaves in winter, the water would freeze inside the leaf cells and damage them. Losing leaves also streamlines trees to prevent wind damage and snow accumulation breaking branches.

**3** The acorn is the oak's seed and fruit which has grown from its flower. It is an edible fruit and relies on squirrels burying it in the autumn so that it can germinate in the spring.

**4** The terminal bud is found at the tip of the branch. It grows into leaves.

**5** The twig is just over 3 years old because it has three girdle scars. Its best year of growth was the third year because the distance between the girdle scars is greatest.

The research activity should find that tree trunks grow in circumference (as well as upwards) and the rings show a year's growth as two bands. The outer band of each year has larger cells and is the spring growth (when there is usually more water around to swell the cells) and the inner one has smaller celled summer growth. The oldest trees are the giant redwoods found in the USA and Canada and these are over a thousand years old.

# 4 *The stream environment*

## Learning outcomes
Pupils:

- read and interpret datalogging printouts about daily changes
- link data from a table with data from datalogging printouts
- identify and describe how some variables differ in a habitat over an 18 hour period
- identify input and outcome variables
- recognise and articulate relationships
- use observational skills to identify some features of stream organisms
- handle living organisms safely and with respect

The stream provides a different habitat to the woodland and grassy areas considered so far in this chapter. It might be useful here to show pupils a range of stream organisms that include freshwater shrimps. These can be collected from local streams by disturbing the rocks in the stream with kicks and collecting the animals in a net. It is advisable either to wear rubber gloves when handling stream water or to wash hands afterwards. A useful key to stream organisms can be purchased from the Field Studies Council, see page 20 for contact details.

*Activity* ## Practical: Stream organisms

➡ *Worksheet 1.4: Looking at stream organisms (P)*
This worksheet provides information on handling and observing stream organisms and provides a useful opportunity to develop observational skills. Keys to identify stream organisms are available from the Field Studies Council (see page 20 for details).

It is also possible to set up datalogging in a local stream or pond. Temperature and light probes can be used over a 24-hour period to monitor the changing environment for aquatic organisms.

**Safety**
Rubber gloves should be worn when placing hands in stream water. Alternatively, hands should be washed with detergent following the practical.

*Activity* Information processing: Stream investigation
➡ *Pupil's Book page 26*
This activity provides the results table and datalogging printout. Pupils working through the questions are encouraged to read and make sense of the data and decide on the relationship that is shown. Cognitive conflict happens in this activity in that most pupils will think that shrimp numbers would decrease at night. This is because the pupils have little experience of nocturnal animals other than owls and bats. The cognitive conflict also comes from two input variables having effects on the outcome variable of shrimp number. The first is light and this is an inverse relationship. The second input variable that has an effect is increased flow rate, which is also an inverse relationship. In other words, this is a compound variable, but here we treat it as two simple variables. Q10 could be extended to ask for predictions of the effect of the variables.

## Answers

1 13 hours after the start – 3 a.m.
2 4 hours after the start = 6 p.m.
3 Decreased slightly over the first 3 hours and then a lot in the 4th hour. Increased over the next 9 hours and then began to decrease again over the last 5 hours.
4 It affected the flow rate and this reduced the number of shrimps.
5 The light was steady for about 8 hours and then decreased rapidly over the next 1 to 2 hours. It remained low for about 4 hours and then increased for just over 1 hour to its previous high level. Night was from 11 p.m. to around 6 a.m. Daytime was about 6 a.m. to 11 p.m.
6 Temperature was steady for almost 10 hours and then decreased during the night and increased again from around 6 a.m. at daybreak.
7 Sound readings checked that the shrimp samples were being taken on the hour throughout the night and so late measurements or missed measurements could be spotted.
8 Outcome was number of shrimps. Inputs were light, temperature and flow rate.
9 Light. Shrimps are more active at night (nocturnal).
10 Number of predators (measure by trapping at hourly intervals), amount of food (shrimps are scavengers, so collect water samples hourly and then filter out and weigh organic debris), oxygen content (use oxygen meter), pollution (solid can be filtered or allowed to settle, but chemical pollution requires specialist testing.).

# 5 *Who eats who?*

## Learning outcomes

Pupils:

- describe food chains as energy transfer systems
- explain the direction of the arrows in food chains
- construct some food chains
- explain what is meant by and identify carnivore, herbivore, consumer and producer
- describe food chains in terms of feeding relationships

This part of the chapter builds on work begun in Key Stage 2. The emphasis here is on food chains being energy transfer systems with the arrows representing the direction of energy flow. Pupils may draw the arrows in the wrong direction believing that they represent who eats whom and this needs to be pointed out early on in their Key Stage 3 work on this topic.

*Activity* ## Information processing: Food chains
## Answers

➡ *Pupil's Book page 28*

1 Sun → leaves → worms → bird (or fox, or bird → fox)
2 Sun → acorns → squirrel → fox
3 Any two from:

Sun → blackberries → bird
Sun → grass → snail → thrush
Sun → plants → woodlice
Sun → plants → woodlice → bird
Sun → plant → ant
Sun → plant → ant → bird

4 Example would be: 'This food chain shows how energy from the Sun is taken in by plants and then passed on to ants during feeding and finally to birds, when the bird eats the ant.'

## Your place in the chain

➡ *Pupil's Book page 28*

Having established food chains as a means of energy transfer, the terms producer and consumer are introduced. This section also considers food chains from the aspect of feeding relationships and this leads into adaptations for feeding. It would be useful here to let pupils observe carnivore and herbivore skulls and compare the skull shape, teeth types and jaw movement.

## Word play
## Answers

➡ *Pupil's Book page 29*

| ¹G | R | E | E | N | P |
|----|---|---|---|---|---|
| ³S | U | N | ⁴M | E | L |
| R | ⁵C | H | A | A | A |
| O | R | N | I | T | N |
| T | E | T | A | E | T |
| A | D | E | R | ²P | S |

*Activity* Information processing: Investigating the compost heap

→ *Pupil's Book page 29*

This activity encourages pupils to look for patterns in the food chains that they have constructed so that their understanding is more generalisable.

## Answers

1 Nettle, dock, rosebay willow herb, bindweed.
2 Any three from:

Sun → flower → butterfly
Sun → leaves → caterpillar → spider
Sun → plant → ladybird
Sun → rotting plant → fly → spider

3 Producers are green plants which take in sunlight and convert carbon dioxide gas and water into food (energy store).
4 Herbivores always come before carnivores in a food chain, while producers are always first in the chain.
5 Different diets means that the adult and young do not compete for the same food source. Also, more of the energy taken in by the plant can be passed on to the next stage in the food chain.

**Attainment target**

Work in the previous sections should provide evidence that pupils are working towards the following attainment level.

| Recognise that feeding relationships exist between animals and plants in a habitat and describe using food chains | Level 4 |
| --- | --- |

# 6 *What is adaptation?*

## Learning outcomes

Pupils:

- explain adaptation
- identify adaptations for particular habitats
- explain the advantages that adaptation gives an organism
- identify features of predators and prey
- construct a food chain
- explain what is meant by and identify carnivore, herbivore, consumer and producer
- describe food chains as energy transfer systems
- explain the direction of the arrows in food chains
- describe food chains in terms of feeding relationships
- describe some strategies that animals and plants adopt to avoid climatic stress

Explaining adaptation is difficult. Many explanations allow the learner to believe that animals and plants change to match the environment rather than the Darwinian explanation of natural selection. The idea that has to be conveyed is that within any one species there is variety. Some of these types will succeed in the environment that they find themselves in and so live well and breed and pass on their genes. Some types will die off before breeding age and so their genes are not passed on. Over a long period of time, if the environment stays the same, the animals and plants found there will be the ones most suited to that environment because they compete better. Their genes are passed on and so are described as adapted to that environment. Therefore in this chapter, it is important that pupils are encouraged to look carefully at the language and explanations they use.

There are numerous videos showing animal and plant adaptations. These mainly show adaptations in extreme environments, such as cacti in deserts or polar bears on the Arctic ice, but then it is often easier to explain adaptation in such habitats where conditions have high selection pressure.

Pupils use annotated drawings to begin to look at adaptations for feeding in herbivores and carnivores.

## What is adaptation?
## Answers
➡ *Pupil's Book page 30*

2  **a)** Sun → grass → rabbit → fox
   **b)** Eyes at front of the head for keen forward vision. Strong legs to chase the rabbit.
   **c)** Sharp teeth for grasping and killing the rabbit and tearing flesh. Strong back teeth (molars) for eating bones.
   **d)** An animal that is hunted and eaten by another animal.
   **e)** The rabbit has large ears that can move and so any sound the fox makes can be detected and the fox's position found. Eyes on the side of the head mean that the rabbit can see almost all round and so see the fox creeping up.

3  Most are camouflaged. Thrushes have beaks that can pick up snails that they then drop from a height on to a stone to break the snail's shell. Squirrels have large tails for balance and strong legs for jumping from tree to tree. Woodlice 'play dead' when approached and, similar to the worms, prefer dark, damp places where they can hide.

## Time to think
## Answers
➡ *Pupil's Book page 32*

1  **a)**

| Producers | Herbivores | Carnivores |
|---|---|---|
| duckweed | waterflea | water scorpion |
| phytoplankton | watersnail | pond skater |
| | water boatman | tadpole |
| | tadpole | |
| | *Amoeba* | |
| | stickleback | |

**b)** Three from:

Sun → algae → watersnail
Sun → algae → water boatman → water scorpion
Sun → algae → waterflea → pond skater
Sun → algae → waterflea
Sun → duckweed → water boatman
Sun → algae → *Amoeba*

**c)** Water scorpion has large piercing mouthparts for killing and feeding on prey.
Tadpole has strong jaws and rasping teeth to feed on prey. Tadpoles are fast swimmers.

**d)** Water boatman traps air around body and carries it down with it.
Water scorpion has a breathing tube that sticks out of the water.
Watersnail traps air in its shell.

**e)** Fish are streamlined. They have gills with large surface area for getting oxygen from water; a strong muscular tail for swimming; fins for altering direction.

2 Predator needs to have some trapping device or attraction for moths and flies. It might have large feet for moving across mud. It also might have a good sense of hearing, or even radar like bats, as sight is not a useful sense in this environment.

3 If planet has long nights then it is likely that animals are nocturnal and so adaptations for low light such as large eyes or highly developed hearing or radar or smell organs. Predator should have some means of sensing and trapping the prey. It should also have some way of killing and breaking up the prey's body. The prey should have good sense organs for detecting the predator and camouflage or behavioural means of avoiding being detected. Prey is possibly a herbivore and so has means of chewing and digesting plantlife.

# 7 *How much to eat?*

## Learning outcomes
Pupils:

- explain food chains in terms of pyramid of number
- use ideas of proportionality to work out pyramids of number

This section moves forward the idea of food chains quantitatively and begins to look at pyramids of number. The reasoning pattern of ratio and proportionality is developed through an everyday context of scaling up the recipe for a fruit salad. Pupils are then asked to bridge this type of thinking to food chains and make estimates. It is not expected that all pupils will be able to successfully grasp this concept at this stage but the work should be accessible for the majority. The focus is on realising that there are a number of ways of solving the scaling up of the recipe but that 'multiples' (proportionality) can always be used. This activity is not meant as a mental arithmetic session, and calculators or methods without final answers can be used to help make the concept more accessible.

*Activity* ## Reasoning: Party time

Spreadsheet 'Partytime.xls' on the CD-ROM can be used for this activity.

## Answers
➡ *Pupil's Book page 34*

1 20 satsumas, 10 mangos, 10 pawpaws, 10 thick slices of pineapple, 80–100 grapes, 1 litre (1000 ml) of orange juice and 500 ml of lemon or lime juice.
2 15 satsumas, 7.5 mangos, 7.5 pawpaws, 7.5 thick slices of pineapple, 60–75 grapes, 750 ml of orange juice and 375 ml of lemon or lime juice (there could be discussion here about 0.5 of a mango, and so on, and the need to buy in whole numbers).
3 Pupils will probably use 'multiplying by 10' to move from 2 to 20 people but it is important to ask for different ways. For 15, pupils may try a variety of methods such as 'halving recipe for 20 to get recipe for 10 and then halving again to find out quantities for 5, then adding the two numbers together,' or 'working out that 15 is just over 7 times more than 2 so multiplying the recipe by 7 and then adding half the recipe'. For 50, pupils may 'multiply the recipe for 2 by 25' or 'double the recipe for 20 and add half the recipe for 20'.

## Answers
➡ *Pupil's Book page 35*

4 60 lettuce leaves are needed for 5 thrushes.
5 $7\frac{1}{2}$ thrushes numerically, and so 7 thrushes in terms of survival.
6 24 lettuce leaves and 6 snails needed to feed 2 thrushes for 1 hawk in one day.
   168 lettuce leaves and 42 snails for 14 thrushes for a week's food for 1 hawk.
7 Several examples could be given here. It is often difficult to give numbers for plants such as grass or algae, so allow 'lots' or 'many' at producer level.

# 8 *Food webs*

## Learning outcomes
Pupils:

- link food chains to form a food web for a habitat
- identify food chains in food webs
- identify carnivores, herbivores, consumers and producers
- identify features of predators and prey
- identify adaptations for particular habitats
- explain the advantages that adaptation gives an organism
- describe some strategies that animals and plants adopt to avoid climatic stress
- explain how changes in carnivore numbers affect the other organisms in a food chain
- explain how changes in herbivore numbers affect the other organisms in a food chain

This activity brings together several of the ideas developed in this chapter. It provides a new habitat, the seashore, where ideas on food chains, adaptations and feeding relationships can be revisited within a new context. Pupils may need to do research about the organisms shown if they are unfamiliar with rocky shores, or be provided with information cards on these animals and plants. This could form a preparation homework for this section. Ideas of proportionality in a qualitative sense and cause–effect are combined in Q18 and Q19. These are difficult explanations and time should be given for pupils to articulate these through discussion before arriving at an answer that they are satisfied with.

## Answers

→ *Pupil's Book page 37*

**8** Answers such as:

Sun → seaweed → snail → crab
Sun → plankton → fish → seagull
Sun → plankton → mussel → starfish

**9** Seaweeds.

**10** Snails such as limpets and periwinkles, mussels, fish.

**11**

| Producers | Herbivores | Carnivores |
|-----------|------------|------------|
| seaweed | limpets | crab |
| plankton | periwinkles | seagull |
| algae | mussels | fish |
| | fish | starfish |
| | | dogwhelk |
| | | sea anemone |

**12 a)** When the sea comes in, water is cold but brings food animals and plants from the sea.
   **b)** Organisms are likely to warm up and dry out in the sunlight. Less food is available.
   **c)** The tide will come in in waves and this makes conditions difficult as organisms are physically knocked about. Water becomes more aerated by wave action.

**13** Seaweed and some of the snails remain on the rocky shore when the tide goes out. Other organisms may be left in the rock pools.

**14** Seaweed is covered in mucus (slime) to stop it drying out. It is firmly anchored to the rocks. Seaweed and plankton can photosynthesise under water because they have special types of chemical similar to chlorophyll to help them do this.

**15** Many cling on tightly (limpets and mussels) or hide in crevices or on plants (periwinkles). Many feed using a file-like 'tongue' that scrapes algae from rocks. Mussels are filter feeders.

**16** Crabs have claws for breaking open snail shells, move quickly to catch prey, have eyes on stalks so can sense prey quickly. They have a thick exoskeleton to prevent drying out and to resist wave action.

17 Starfish have tube feet that can prise open a mussel shell. They also have stomachs that they can push out and into shells of mussels. The enzymes break the mussel tissue down and then the stomach is pulled back into the starfish with the digested food.

Seagulls have keen eyesight and strong beaks for catching and ripping open fish.

Dogwhelks can drill through snail shells with their radula (a file-like feeding mechanism).

18 The new carnivore competes for food and so the crab population could decrease. Crabs feed on dogwhelks. If the new carnivore predates dogwhelks as well then the dogwhelk population will also decrease.

Seagulls are carnivores but they do not compete with crabs for the same prey and so it is unlikely that there will be any effect on the seagull population.

Any animals that form the feeding level below the crab and the new carnivore will decrease in population size. This means that the producers and any animals in lower food levels in the chain increase in population size as there are fewer animals to eat them.

19 Fewer snails mean that seaweeds are not grazed on so much and so can grow.

Dogwhelks feed on snails and so will decrease in number if fewer snails are around. Any herbivores who also feed on seaweed can increase in number as there is less competition from snails. This could then increase the population size of the carnivores who feed on the herbivores other than snails.

**Attainment target**

Work in the previous sections should provide evidence that pupils are working towards the following attainment level.

| | |
|---|---|
| Construct models to show feeding relationships and explain how these relationships affect population size | Level 7 |

*Activity* ## Summary: Environmental terms

➡ *Worksheet 1.5: Environmental terms (K)*

This is a summary worksheet that checks on some of the key words. It will help some pupils prepare some initial work that can be used in the Time to Think activity. It could be used as an earlier homework activity for those pupils who have already looked at food webs in Key Stage 2 as this is the only term on the worksheet that comes towards the end of this chapter.

The words in the wordsearch are:

- habitat
- producer
- carnivore
- energy
- food chain
- food web
- light
- prey.

## Time to think

➡ *Pupil's Book page 37*

This activity is structured to help pupils summarise each section of the chapter by writing sentences using the key words and then either using these to write a full summary or using the sentences to help them construct a concept map. It will be useful to get pupils to share and compare their summaries and concept maps. One way of doing this is to organise the class into groups of 4 to 5 pupils. Each pupil then presents their summary or concept map to the others. The 'listening pupils' judge how good the information in each presentation was, immediately afterwards using the system:

GREEN = all points covered and clearly explained

AMBER = okay but some points not clear

RED = some points missing or incorrectly explained.

At the end of all the presentations, the 'traffic lights' judgements are given as feedback, with the AMBER and RED judgements explained to the presenter. Pupils who are AMBER or RED then work on their summary/concept map using the feedback given.

Another way is for you to photocopy a very good and a very poor summary/concept map either from this class or another class and ask each pupil to explain how their own summary/concept map is better than or poorer than the ones given. If pupils have not had much practice in self-assessment, then this is best done in groups as a peer-assessment exercise. Time then needs to be given to redraft or tweak their own summary/concept map.

## Review

➡ *Worksheet 1.6: Test on the environment*

This worksheet provides a 20 minute test to check on understanding of this chapter.

## Answers

**1 a)** An area where specific animals and plants live.    (1 mark)

    **b)** A green plant or a plant that photosynthesises.    (1 mark)

    **c)** An animal that captures another animal for food.  (1 mark)

    **d)** An animal that feeds on plants.    (1 mark)

**2 a)** cabbage → snail → thrush → fox (Order correct = 1 mark; Arrows in correct direction = 1 mark)

    **b)** Energy.    (1 mark)

    Sun.    (1 mark)

    Photosynthesis.    (1 mark)

**3 a)** Suited to its environment.    (1 mark)

    Helps it to survive, through evolution.    (1 mark)

    **b)** 1 mark for name; 1 mark for adaptation described; 1 mark for how this helps it survive. (3 marks)

    **c)** 1 mark for name; 1 mark for adaptation described; 1 mark for how this helps it survive. (3 marks)

**4 a)** Pyramid of numbers.    (1 mark)

    **b)** Amount of organisms at each level of food chain. (1 mark)

    **c)** Mice population would increase.

    Wheat population would decrease.    (1 mark)

# 2 Variation and classification

## → Rationale

This chapter provides up to 7½ hours of teaching materials.

Through Key Stages 1 and 2 pupils will have had a wide range of experiences of sorting and classifying animals and materials (Unit 2D Sorting living and non-living things, Unit 3E Sorting magnetic and non-magnetic materials, Unit 4D Sorting solids and liquids, Unit 6D Sorting materials, reversible and irreversible reactions). The key science ideas to be developed in this chapter are linked to interdependence.

When looking at the features of animals and thinking about form and function, pupils will have learnt about internal and external skeletons, and will have examined invertebrates and their habitats (Unit 4A Moving and growing, Unit 4B Habitats). Pupils will have grouped similar organisms together by looking for similarities and differences (as pictures, photographs or real organisms) into plants (trees, flowers) and animals (insects, mammals including humans). They will have also used simple keys to identify plants and animals (Unit 6A Interdependence and adaptation).

In Key Stage 2 pupils will also have explored what is meant by living, non-living and never lived. Now pupils should encounter as wide a range of living things as possible and learn to place them in groups according to their characteristics. They need to know the seven characteristics of living things, that is, they:

- respire
- require a food source for energy
- grow
- reproduce
- move
- respond to stimuli, and
- excrete waste products from the conversions of food into energy to live.

(The differences in the way animals and plants obtain food are not given in this chapter.)

This chapter explains that animals or plants that have many similar characteristics are said to belong to the same species. Within each species there is individual variation. The genes in the cells of an organism are responsible for the characteristics of that organism. These are inherited from the parent organism. There is no need to give details of how the genes are passed on at this stage. Some variation is not genetic but environmental. Although the topic of genetics and inheritance is thoroughly dealt with in Year 9, it is important to deal with some of the terms and concepts that Year 7 pupils will be hearing about through the media, particularly children's current affairs TV programmes and documentaries. Many science fiction films, for example *Jurassic Park* and *AI*, give children all sorts of odd ideas about mutations, cloning and genetic modification. Encourage bridging between their science lessons and the 'world outside' through discussions and creative activities.

# ➡ *Overview*

The textbook sections, activities and worksheets have been arranged into 1 hour blocks to aid lesson planning. Clearly several of the activities and worksheets could form part of a homework session. The planning includes reading time for individual sections but some teachers may prefer to organise this as homework preparation for the following lesson. Five types of worksheets – extension (E), support for an activity (S), practical (P), key skills (K) and developmental (D) – allow for differentiation and flexibility to accommodate teachers' preferred practice. The actual timing and emphasis on different sections will depend on the current knowledge base of the pupils, the ability of the teaching group and the preferences of the teacher.

| Lesson | Worksheet |
|---|---|
| **1** Living things | Worksheet 2.1: Child's play (S)<br>Worksheet 2.3: Examining living things (P) (optional) |
| **2** Sorting | Worksheet 2.2: Classifying vertebrates (S)<br>Worksheet 2.3: Examining living things (P) |
| **3** Scientific classification | |
| **4** Taxonomy and variation | Worksheet 2.4: Fingerprinting (K) |
| **5** Inheritance | Worksheet 2.5: Cystic fibrosis – an inherited disorder (E)<br>Worksheet 2.6: Cloning (S) |
| **6** Measuring variation | Worksheet 2.7: Being average (K) |
| **7** More variation | |
| Review | Worksheet 2.8: Test on variation and classification |

# ➡ *Chapter plan*

| | Demonstration | Practical | ICT | Activity | Word play | Time to think | Ideas and evidence |
|---|---|---|---|---|---|---|---|
| **Lesson 1** | | Looking at living things | | Game: Non-living, never lived and living | | What do you know? | |
| **Lesson 2** | Introducing classifying | Sorting living things | | Reasoning: Can you 'sort it'?<br><br>Discussion: Insects<br><br>Reasoning: Identifying invertebrates | | | |
| **Lesson 3** | | | | Information processing: The otter | | | |
| **Lesson 4** | | | Database search | Discussion: Humans | | Classifying | The Linnean system of taxonomy |
| **Lesson 5** | | | | Discussion: Cystic fibrosis<br><br>Discussion: Cloning | | | |
| **Lesson 6** | | | | Information processing: Average sizes | | | |
| **Lesson 7** | | | | Information processing: Winter holly | Defining new words | Variation and classification | |

# ➡ *Expectations*

**At the end of this chapter**

**in terms of scientific enquiry**

**most pupils will:** use observation to identify questions to investigate about variation between individuals; suggest data to collect to answer the questions; present and analyse the data; identify associations or correlations in their data; use databases and spreadsheets

**some pupils will not have made so much progress and will:** make suggestions about data to be collected to answer questions about variation and, with help, present data using ICT and identify patterns or associations

**some pupils will have progressed further and will:** evaluate graphs and tables of data in relation to sample size and describe how strongly any association or correlation is supported

**in terms of life processes and living things**

**most pupils will:** identify similarities and differences in organisms of the same species and begin to attribute these to environmental or inherited factors; explain the importance of classifying living things; identify some of the main taxonomic groups of animals and describe some features of these

**some pupils will not have made so much progress and will:** identify similarities and differences between organisms of the same species and classify organisms into plants and animals; identify a few taxonomic groups of animals

**some pupils will have progressed further and will:** recognise that inherited and environmental causes of variation cannot be completely separated; name some organisms which are not readily classified as plant or animal

# → Links with CASE

The main thinking skills promoted are those associated with classifying. From about 5 years old children can sort objects into groups based on easily observable characteristics. This is setting and subsetting: dividing things into smaller and smaller groups. There is no one correct method for classifying things. Classification involves first clarifying or identifying the goal for imposing a classification system, by asking 'Why is it helpful to classify or categorise this particular group of items that have similarities and differences?' This in turn determines what characteristics are chosen. If these prove not to be adequate for the purpose, new criteria must be applied and reclassifying takes place through a feedback loop. Characteristics are variables.

Other thinking skills associated with classifying are class inclusion and exclusion, and sequencing (putting items or data into rank order and hierarchies). Class inclusion is easier for children to think about. This is based on grouping objects by their similarities. Class exclusion looks at differences. A formal classification system uses a branching (dichotomous) key to create smaller and smaller groups by setting, for example into animals or plants, then subsetting – animals can be divided into those with backbones and those without. These two groups in turn can be further subdivided.

This chapter is designed to promote problem-solving approaches to classification as well as knowledge of the formal biological classification system.

Probability and correlation reasoning patterns are introduced but not developed beyond the concrete level. A sample represents possible combinations of variables due to chance alone, so we can look for the likelihood of cause and effect. If we suspect there is a cause–effect link then we call this a correlation. Correlation can be negative as well as positive. Biological variables are stochastic. They need to be defined by two parameters, a measure of central tendency and a measure of range. This contrasts with the deterministic variables more typical of physics, which can be defined with one number. This chapter explores this at the descriptive level. Pupils realise that if they take a sample of only one or two they may miss some of the possible effects of natural variation. With larger samples they can be certain of finding all of the variation, but they still cannot be certain that their sample has the same proportion of different characteristics, as does the whole population. These are difficult concepts and will be more fully developed in later years but work in this chapter begins these thought patterns.

## → *Pupils' misconceptions*

| Misconception | Scientific understanding |
|---|---|
| Energy is seen as living, as the fire in 'living flame'. Eating, drinking, moving, walking, breathing and growing characterise living things (and exclude plants). | Seven characteristics of living organisms (COLO) are defined as processes. |
| Plants are not living because they do not move. Photosynthesis is plant respiration. | COLO applies to plants, and plants do move as they grow. Photosynthesis is the way plants feed. Plants do respire (burn food to release energy) and need oxygen, but do not breathe since they have a large surface area to exchange gases. |
| Boys inherit all their characteristics from fathers, girls from mothers. | Some characteristics are sex linked but most are not. Children inherit characteristics from both parents. |
| Genes for eye colour are only in the eyeballs. Genes are bad and are created by radiation or chemical poisons. | Genes are contained in the nuclei of all cells. Mutations are rare and can be caused by 'normal' environmental factors, for example radiation, chemicals. Many mutations are beneficial, for example modern crops are mutants of wild grasses. |

## → *Literacy, numeracy and other cross-curricular links*

There is a lot of scope in this chapter to develop children's speaking and writing skills. Wherever possible pupils should be encouraged to discuss their reasoning about how and why they are classifying organisms in a particular way and how they are analysing data. Examples of two modes of writing (a poem and a piece of scientific writing) show how facts can be communicated in different ways. Asking pupils to find other examples and making a wall display of these could extend this. Newspaper and magazine articles about genetics and inheritance can be read and discussed.

This chapter makes a major contribution to the development of numeracy skills. Thinking about variation demands an understanding of simple statistics. Based on the National Numeracy framework, the following skills are developed:

- having a sense of the size of a number and where it fits into the number system
- calculating both mentally and with pencil and paper, so drawing on a range of calculation strategies
- using calculators and other ICT resources to solve mathematical problems
- selecting the number of figures appropriate to the context of a calculation
- measuring and estimating
- choosing suitable units, reading numbers correctly from a range of scales
- understanding the differences between the mean, median and mode and the purpose for which each is used
- collecting data, discrete and continuous
- drawing, interpreting and predicting from graphs, diagrams, charts and tables
- judging the reasonableness of solutions and checking them when necessary
- giving results to a degree of accuracy appropriate to the context.

If data is entered on a spreadsheet it helps the development of ICT skills as well as science skills.

Children will build on their Key Stage 2 experiences and deepen their understanding of the different kinds of 'average' that we use to handle data. They will calculate and use mean, mode and median. These are particularly important concepts if children are to begin to develop ideas about the representativeness of sampling. Adequate sampling of living material, which has much phenotypic variation, ensures that the sample represents the population as a whole. This is another form of fair testing. It is not always possible to keep all variables the same except the one under investigation (control of variables). Sampling allows us to work with a probability model (see Links with CASE).

This chapter makes some contribution to PSHE. Through data processing and looking at information about human growth and variation, pupils recognise and respect the physical differences between people.

## Language for learning

By the end of this chapter pupils will be able to understand, use and spell correctly:

- words relating to the structure of organisms – segment, abdomen, shell
- words with similar but distinct meanings – for example, limb, leg
- words and phrases related to classification and statistics – vertebrate, invertebrate, mammal, amphibian, reptile, feature, characteristics, taxonomic group, variation, classification, identification, inherited, environmental, association, correlation, confidence, spreadsheet, database.

Pupils will be able to spot the links between how information is presented in different forms and how different modes of writing communicate to different audiences. They will have opportunities for their own creative writing.

# 1 *Living things*

## Learning outcomes

Pupils:

- sort organisms into taxonomic groups
- evaluate and review methods of classifying
- use classification to identify unknown organisms
- classify invertebrates using subgroups
- summarise vertebrate characteristics, using observable features
- know the seven characteristics of living things

## What do you know?

➡ *Pupil's Book page 38*

Some pupils may have categorised mammals in Key Stage 2, others may not. The first question (matching the vertebrates with their characteristics) can be used to assess their knowledge of the main features of mammals, birds, fish, amphibians and reptiles. It could be made into a card matching game which pupils play in groups of three or four.

The next two questions allow concrete preparation for learning more detailed characteristics of the invertebrate groups and identify pupils who are clear about what distinguishes an invertebrate from a vertebrate, and pupils who are not.

For Q2 pupils could work in groups to identify and name eight invertebrates in the picture in the book. At this stage it is not expected that pupils will be able to name the groups. You may have to explain that not all molluscs have shells, for example slug and octopus. You can provide simple keys and books to use for identification as an extension activity. Give the groups 5 minutes to make their lists then summarise the activity as a whole class, asking each group to give one of their answers in turn until all eight are on the board.

The activity to draw a picture called 'under the sea' (Q3) is for individual pupils to do and could be given as homework. Q4 could be used as a short assessment activity.

Q5 asks pupils to spend 5 minutes in their groups discussing how they decide what distinguishes plants from animals. The sea anemone, virus and insectivorous plant will cause cognitive conflict. It is important that pupils argue through the characteristics they are using and debate these rather than that they have the 'correct' scientific knowledge at this stage. After their discussion ask pairs of pupils to make a decision tree (Q6). Making a decision tree is a skill they may have developed in Key Stage 2. If not, show them how to make a series of questions that require yes/no answers and that branch off into smaller and smaller groupings. The sketch on page 43 of the Pupil's Book gives an example. This skill is required for their understanding of which scientific classification systems have been built up. Worksheet 2.2: Classifying vertebrates may be used here or given as homework, or left until the next lesson on sorting (see page 43 for the answers).

The scientific classification of living things (see the Pupil's Book, page 44) could be done as part of this lesson if pupils have shown sufficient understanding. For the answers see page 46.

## Answers

➡ *Pupil's Book page 39*

**1** Birds — Bodies are covered in feathers, have wings, live on land and in the air. Lay hard-shelled eggs.

Amphibians — Bodies are slimy, live on land and in water, lay eggs in water. Swim, walk or hop.

Mammals — Bodies have hair, young develop inside the mother and are fed on milk after birth, live on land, in water or in the air. Walk, swim or fly.

Reptiles — Bodies have dry, waterproof skin with scales, most live on land, some can swim. Some have legs and some slide along the ground. Lay soft-shelled eggs on land.

Fish — Bodies are covered in scales, live in water, swim. Lay eggs in water, have gills to breathe.

**2** The animals are: butterfly, bee, worm, slug, snail, beetle, dragonfly and spider.

**3** The drawing should show the animals listed. The vertebrate could be a fish or a seal, for example.

**4** Worms – earthworm
Insects – butterfly, bee, beetle and dragonfly
Arachnids – spider
Molluscs – slug, snail

**5** and **6** will depend on pupils' explanations. A major difference between plants and animals is in how they move. Plants do not have limbs or other adaptations for locomotion, they usually move by growth towards light or moisture. The fact that not all plants are green and flowering can cause pupils some conflict. You can give pupils a way of helping themselves do this task by reading the section in the Pupil's Book on page 41.

*Activity* ## Game: Non-living, never lived and living

➡ *Worksheet 2.1: Child's play (S)*
Some pupils may still have difficulty distinguishing characteristics for non-living, never lived and living organisms. Worksheet 2.1 could be used to help them develop their understanding (by making a set of playing cards for primary children to use to sort out living things). This worksheet supports pupils who are making slow progress in developing their understanding of the characteristics of living organisms.

*Activity* Practical: Looking at living things

➡ *Worksheet 2.3: Examining living things (P)*

You may decide to give pupils a range of living organisms to observe and sort at this stage rather than in the next lesson. Use Worksheet 2.3, or create your own activity using animals that you have easier access to.

**Equipment**

Each group will need:

- simple keys and books (the Field Studies Council provide a good range of these, see page 20 for their details.)
- range of invertebrates. Label specimens A to F. You can use any organisms available, preserved or fresh. One or two could be pictures or photographs but some indication of size (using a scale) should be given. Make sure that most of the organisms can be easily examined using a hand lens and forceps. Suggested organisms, any six from:

  - a leaf from a tree
  - grass clippings
  - live woodlice or ants
  - live earthworm
  - maggots live or preserved – if live they must be in a suitable see-through aerated container, which should not be opened
  - plant in a pot, for example geranium
  - a fungus (picture can be used if it's the wrong time of year)
  - a fish, such as a trout from a fishmonger or supermarket, or use a picture if you have no live specimens
  - live mammal (hamster, gerbil, rabbit – your local primary school may keep a pet) or use a picture.

Write 'YOU' on another lettered label so that pupils can make scientific observations of each other.

**Safety**
- Treat living organisms with care.
- Wash hands after handling animals.
- Wipe surfaces with disinfectant.
- Some pupils may have allergies to furry mammals or suffer from asthma so discourage handling of animals.

## The seven characteristics of living things

➡ *Pupil's Book page 41*

This section contains knowledge pupils must learn. Q1 is an easy exercise, best done by pairs of pupils helping each other. Each pupil needs to copy the paragraph into his/her notebook and fill in the missing words (or you can provide this on a printed sheet to complete). Make sure any pupils with reading difficulties are paired up with better readers or given extra support. After 5 to 10 minutes, read out the paragraph and ask different pupils to provide the missing words. Pupils correct each other's work.

## Answer

**1** In order the missing words are: excretion, energy, food, respiration, grow, sensitive, reproduction.

# 2 *Sorting*

## Learning outcomes

Pupils:

- handle living organisms correctly
- create and justify their own classification systems
- sort and record living organisms into groups using observations
- describe similarities and differences between two living things
- classify insects into subgroups, using correct terms for body parts (segment, thorax, leg, abdomen, antennae)

*Activity*

## Demonstration: Introducing classifying

➡ *Worksheet 2.2: Classifying vertebrates (S)*

Begin this lesson with a quick 5 minute video clip about classification showing a range of plants and animals, or use a photographic or slide collection. There need be no discussion, before moving into the sorting activity (see below). Alternatively, if pupils are poor at identifying vertebrate groups, use Worksheet 2.2: Classifying vertebrates to support this activity.

## Equipment

Video on classification or a collection of photographs or slides of different plants and animals.

## Answers

➡ *Worksheet 2.2: Classifying vertebrates*

Each group should give their answers to another group for comparison.

**1** Bozargs would be called *birds.*
   Vizargs would be called *reptiles.*
   Nazargs would be called *amphibians.*
   Zigzargs would be called *fish.*
   Wazargs would be called *mammals.*
**2** Animal A is the whale.
   Animal B is the chimp.
   Animal C is the sparrow.
   Animal D is the horse.
**3** Solving the riddle tells you that the animal is an amphibian.

*Activity*

## Practical: Sorting living things

➡ *Worksheet 2.3: Examining living things (P)*

Provide a range of living animals to look at and Worksheet 2.3 Examining living things. This will take about 30 to 40 minutes. The sorting activity can be started at the end of the lesson and continued for homework. It is important that pupils appreciate there is a variety of ways of classifying, through discussing each other's systems and their relative advantages or disadvantages.

### Equipment

- range of living things (see previous notes in lesson 1, page 42)
- access to a binocular mircroscope

### Safety

See notes on page 42.

*Activity*

## Reasoning: Can you 'sort it'?

➡ *Pupil's Book page 42*

The cartoon bedroom picture is an open-ended activity that can be given as homework. It helps pupils develop their reasoning skills by examining their own processes for developing the 'rules' of classifying, viz. that function and usefulness determines the sorting. There will usually be a variety of ways for sorting any collection.

## Answers

The questions are to stimulate group discussion. Give pupils 5 minutes to answer Q1 in groups, then ask each group to tell the whole class what criteria they are using. Lead a brief discussion on the range of criteria, based on Q2. Give the groups 2 minutes to talk to each other about what they have heard and to come up with an answer for Q3, with justification. Get each group to feed their response back to the whole class and encourage evaluation.

## What is an insect?

➡ *Pupil's Book page 42*

*Activity*

## Discussion: Insects

If pupils have not yet had the opportunity to examine living organisms, then you can adapt Worksheet 2.3 to look at a variety of insects. Alternatively, start the lesson by asking pupils to call out named examples of insects. Collect together some pictures and photographs of invertebrates. Show these, one after the other, and ask pupils to call out if the picture shows an insect. Write the names of the invertebrates on the board in two columns headed 'Insect' and 'Not insect'. At this stage offer no explanation as to why some pupils' responses are wrong. It is impossible to give a simple definition of insects beyond the fact that most have six legs at some time in their lives. The best that can be done is to list all those features that distinguish them from other animals.

Insects belong in the phylum Arthropods. This means they have jointed limbs and bodies. All arthropods have hard external skeletons with soft jointed areas. If you have the time you can provide pupils with some insects such as grasshoppers or beetles and hand lenses so they can examine the features for themselves. This activity may be done instead when pupils are studying habitats.

All pupils need to record a simplified drawing of a typical insect in their notes, showing head, thorax, abdomen, leg, and antennae, eyes and body segments.

### Equipment
- examples of live insects *or*
- photographs/OHTs of invertebrates

### Safety
If pupils examine insects, full hygiene precautions should be taken, with pupils washing their hands after handling them or wearing latex gloves (check for allergies) or looking at insects through sealed clear plastic boxes (with breathing holes in the lids).

## Answers
➡ *Pupil's Book page 42*

**2** Insects are invertebrates: they have external skeletons (Key Stage 2).

**3** Insects have six legs.

## *Activity* Reasoning: Identifying invertebrates
➡ *Pupil's Book page 43*

The key activity helps pupils to reinforce knowledge of the characteristics of an insect and practise classification skills. The pupils also develop class inclusion/exclusion reasoning skills. The main arthropod groups are insects, crustaceans, spiders and myriapods (centipedes and millipedes).

## Answers
**1** A = woodlouse, B = crab, C = spider, D = millipede, E = springtail, F = housefly, G = ladybird.

**2** There are three insects, ladybird, springtail and housefly. The crab and the woodlouse are crustaceans (have a hard outer skeleton), the spider is an arachnid (eight legs), the millipede is a myriapod (many legs).

**3** Seven. They are all invertebrates.

**4** Two have wings, the ladybird and the housefly. They are both insects (but not all insects have wings!).

If pupils have not yet examined living animals, you can make a practical activity of this by collecting together living examples of each animal in the key. Remember the usual precautions for handling living material.

# 3 *Scientific classification*

## Learning outcomes

Pupils:

- analyse different styles of writing used to describe living things for purpose and audience
- know about the scientific way of classification and naming of organisms
- define a species
- understand that individual organisms vary within species and describe some of these variations
- describe the inherited and environmental differences in a group of individuals
- know that some characteristics are inherited and give examples
- know that the environment influences some characteristics

## The scientific classification of living things

## Answers

➡ *Pupil's Book page 44*

**4** A frog lives on land some of the time and has legs to swim, walk and hop. Birds have beaks, feathers and lay hard-shelled eggs.

**5** Bats develop their young inside the mother and feed them milk.

**6** Make sure that pupils name reptiles not amphibians. They could include snakes, lizards, turtles, tortoises or crocodiles.

**7** This will depend on how the pupils present the information.

## *Activity* Information processing: The otter

➡ *Pupil's Book page 45*

There are two pieces of writing: one is a poem about an otter, the other a scientific description of an otter from a reference book. The questions ask pupils to develop their language skills by reading with understanding, locating and using information, and evaluating how well these pieces of writing are communicating information for different purposes and different audiences.

## Answers

**1** The otter is an animal, vertebrate and mammal.

**2** This is a matter of opinion but the second piece of writing gives a more factual description. The first piece does give a little more information about appearance and behaviour than a first reading might indicate.

**3** Again, this is a matter for discussion. The poem indicates more about how the otter is adapted to feed on fish and swim:

> '. . . water gifted, to outwit fish;
> With webbed feet and long ruddering tail
> And a round head like an old tomcat.'

The scientific piece just tells you what otters eat.

4 This is an opportunity to develop the pupils' literacy skills and encourage some creative thinking. It makes a good homework activity and the results can be displayed.

**Attainment targets**

Work in the previous sections should provide evidence that pupils are working towards the following attainment levels.

| Identify and group living things systematically | Level 4 |
|---|---|
| Recognise that there is a great variety of living things and understand the importance of classification | Level 5 |

# 4 *Taxonomy and variation*

## Learning outcomes:

Pupils:

- know that species differ
- enter information on a spreadsheet or database to use for classifying

## Ideas and evidence: The Linnean system of taxonomy

➡ *Pupil's Book page 47*

You need to provide dictionaries for this activity. Pupils should have their own, but have a few on hand. Borrow them from the English department if necessary. The short paragraph about Carl Linnaeus requires quite advanced comprehension skills. Ask a good reader to read the passage aloud at the start of the lesson (or read it yourself) then ask pupils to take 2 minutes to check with a partner that they understand every word in the paragraph. Ask the whole class for any words they had to work out the meaning of and then give pupils 10 minutes to answer the questions in their notebooks, working in pairs. The questions are not answered by simple copying from the paragraph but require creative thinking and analysing for meaning.

## Answers

1 A dictionary definition for taxonomy is 'the principles of classification'. Answers that talk about 'rules for classifying' or 'the way we group living things' are acceptable.
2 Everyone used different names so could not easily communicate with each other. Some people thought they were finding new, undiscovered species when these had already been discovered but the names given to them by the discoverer were not recognised by other scientists.
3 Scientists who speak different languages can use the same Latin names without translating them.
4 The Romans.
5 Accept any answer that applies similar logic to that shown in the example of the rhino. Should be: Chordate; Mammalia; Primate or 'human type' (you could encourage pupils to make

up something suitably Latin-sounding); Anthropod (man and ape-like); *Homo*; *Homo sapiens*. There is no need for pupils to know this classification but most find it interesting.

ICT link: www.natureserve.org – allows database searches by plant and animal name, using common or scientific names.

## Time to think

➡ *Pupil's Book page 47*

This could be a homework activity, but give 5 minutes at the start of the next lesson for pupils to compare their work. It is helpful to give pupils a list of the expected learning outcomes for the first three lessons in this chapter, to help them assess their own levels of attainment. How you do this depends on the reading level and self-sufficiency of your pupils. You could make it a tick list or simply put a large poster up. Pupils can use the 'traffic light' technique for self-assessment (see the Introduction). Here is an example of a 'self-evaluation list'.

**Things you know**
- the difference between vertebrates and invertebrates
- the five vertebrate groups
- why it is important to have a scientific way of classifying living things
- some examples of how animal groups differ from each other, for example, insects and crustaceans, or humans and birds
- how some species differ from each other, for example, dogs and humans, ladybirds and butterflies

**Things you can do**
- correctly sort and classify animals into their taxonomic groups
- justify why they are in those groups
- evaluate different ways of classifying things and say why some are better than others
- evaluate different styles of writing descriptions about organisms for different purposes
- handle living organisms safely
- observe and record characteristics of animals, and describe some features of animals and plants using scientific words
- describe similarities and differences between two living things
- use scientific terms to describe an insect's body

## Variation and inheritance

➡ *Pupil's Book page 48*

This section starts the second part of this chapter, where the emphasis shifts to the development of data-handling skills and the use of ICT. Check you can have access to computers and suitable software for the rest of this chapter.

Definitions of the key words are important and pupils should record and learn them:

> variation – differences between individuals of the same species
> characteristics – these are features, or variables between individual organisms, for example eye colour, height
> unique – only one of its kind
> offspring – the young produced by parents
> inherited – (characteristics) passed from the parents to their offspring.

Once pupils have written down their definition of the words in the list there are several activities which ensure they develop their understanding of the concepts.

The 'cat and dog' activity reinforces the idea that within a species some features are the same and some are unique to an individual. Make sure pupils have a definition of 'species' – the smallest group commonly used in scientific classification systems. Each animal or plant in this group is very similar to each other, sharing many characteristics but still showing some individual variation. Animals and plants belonging to the same species can breed with each other.

## Answers

**8** Cats – round head, small pointed ears, eyes to front of head, meow sound.

Dogs – pointed noses, large ears often floppy, eyes on side of head, bark sound.

**9** The cats vary in colour, length and pattern of fur, and size.

## *Activity* Discussion: Humans

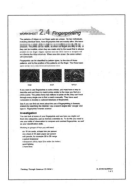

➡ *Pupil's Book page 49*

➡ *Worksheet 2.4: Fingerprinting (K)*

The practical activity on the worksheet develops the pupils' ability to classify and observe as well as developing the concept of variation. Key skills developed here include: use of ICT, enquiry and obtaining evidence. It will take about 40 minutes but if you extend this into a database design activity you need to allow another lesson. You can reduce the time taken for ICT if you design the database and pupils only enter data. Each year you teach this you can add to the database and extend the activity by getting pupils to find 'matches'. It helps to make an overhead projector transparency of 'basic fingerprint patterns'.

Either give each group a Sellotape dispenser and have them tear off their own pieces or put a 'starter set' of three or so pieces on the edge of each desk before pupils start the class. Then circulate and add more pieces as they do the activity. Make sure pupils use the pad of their finger (the area just above the top joint) for their fingerprint, not the tip. Pupils can clean their fingers with a tissue.

It is easiest and cheapest to use the pencil method given here but you can purchase Identiprint materials. Identiprint is a commercial system to put customers' thumbprints on the backs of their cheques without making an inky mess. Special 'ink' pads and self-stick labels take a dark, clear print without leaving any visible residue on the thumb. You can find suppliers on the Internet. There are also several sites designed for children showing how forensic scientists work, including:

www.home.earthlink.net/~thekeither/Forensic/page6.htm
www.cyberbee.com/whodunnit/classify.html

If you have time or are looking for a science project, there are many ways to further investigate both fingerprints and classification. You can create a mock 'crime scene' with a single print from one of your class and time the participants to see who can find a match for the mystery print most quickly using their invented classification system and/or the database. How do their systems vary and why would some be more efficient than others? Investigate other differences: does age, gender or ethnicity seem to predict a type of pattern? Children can compare their prints to those of siblings and parents for evidence of hereditary influence.

The questions in the Pupil's Book about human variation and inheritance are for group discussion. People look a bit like their parents because they inherit their characteristics. By the end of the discussion pupils should be able to identify common variations between individuals, including some features (for example eye colour) that are inherited and others (for example height) that can also be affected by environmental factors (Level 7), and describe some of the causes of variation between living things (Level 6).

The tree drawing shows environmental influences on tree height.

## Answers
→ *Pupil's Book page 49*

**10**, **11**, **12**, **13** will have a variety of answers. Help pupils make the information given relevant to their own experience.

**14** Environmental factors, as well as genetic inheritance, can affect height. For example, under-nourished children usually will not grow as tall as well fed children.

**15** The trees towards the top of the mountain are smaller than the ones below.

**16** If one assumes the trees are all of the same species then it is reasonable to assume they have inherited similar potential for growth, and variations in height would only be small. The large difference in height of trees growing low down, compared with those higher up, indicates strong environmental influence. Give pupils a clue by focusing their attention on what they think the weather will be like higher up the mountain, and if it will be more windy than lower down. If they look carefully, they will see snow on the ground in the picture.

**17** Variations that are inherited in humans include eye colour, hair colour and skin colour. Variations influenced by the environment include weight, school achievement and strength (muscle development). Other characteristics for other organisms can be given. The point is that both inheritance and environment influence variation.

**Attainment targets**

Work in the previous sections should provide evidence that pupils are working towards the following attainment levels.

| Describe some factors that cause variation between living things | Level 6 |
| --- | --- |
| Identify characteristic variations between individuals that are inherited and others that can also be affected by environmental factors | Level 7 |

# 5 *Inheritance*

## Learning outcomes

Pupils

- understand using analogy as a simple model for genetic inheritance, using concepts of genes, chromosomes and organisms
- know what mutations are
- understand some of the issues that concern society about genetics

## What is responsible for inheritance?

➡ *Pupil's Book page 50*

In Year 7 there is no need to go into much detail about genetics. This will be dealt with more thoroughly in Year 9. However pupils hear the word 'gene' almost daily so do need some idea of what the mechanism for inheritance is. This section gives a model using, as an analogy, the idea that genes are like the letters in words. Like all models it is not ideal but does give a concrete representation of inheritance.

## Mutations

➡ *Pupil's Book page 51*

A brief section gives pupils the information that genetic changes (mutations) can be caused by a variety of environmental factors including radiation, temperature and chemicals. Read the paragraph to pupils (or choose good readers to read it to the class) and ask the questions. Allow pupils 5 minutes to write down the answers in their own words, having heard a few responses.

## Answers

**18** A mutation is a change in a gene or chromosome.

**19** Camouflage helps a moth to survive (and so it is more likely to breed and pass on its genes to the next generation) because predators that would eat it, such as birds, find it hard to spot.

## Activity   Discussion: Cystic fibrosis

➡ *Worksheet 2.5: Cystic fibrosis – an inherited disorder (E)*

The worksheet can be used to raise the issue of the effects on health of a mutation and how this can be inherited. It could be used in a group activity to give additional evidence for the discussion, particularly if issues associated with this are currently in the news. This activity links to the development of literacy skills. It can be used to extend pupils who are working towards Level 7.

## Genetic modification

➡ *Pupil's Book page 51*

A new word 'modify' is introduced so this will need some explanation. This section contributes to personal, health and social education by encouraging pupils to debate current social issues and reach their own conclusions. It must be done as either whole class debates, with formal structures to ensure all voices are heard or, more easily, in small groups of five or six with a group reporter feeding back to the whole class at the end of the discussion. You could ask pupils to read and discuss the newspaper clipping at home in preparation for the debate.

## Answers

Answers to **Q20** and **Q22** will depend on the views of the pupils.

*Activity* ## Discussion: Cloning

➡ *Worksheet 2.6: Cloning (S)*

This worksheet is another literacy-based activity. It could also be used as the basis for group activities to collect additional evidence to discuss, particularly if issues associated with these are in the current news. It supports pupils understanding of 'ideas and evidence' as well as offering opportunities to look at ethical issues in science.

This activity need not be done at this stage but could be used as homework in the future or left until the end of the chapter.

## Answers

1 Cloning is a process of producing an animal with a predetermined genetic makeup, by taking a cell from an adult and putting its genes into an egg.
The dangers of cloning are that a genetic defect may result, some cloned animals prove to be more vulnerable to some diseases, it may cause premature aging, and no-one understands what the effects will be on the animals.
Scientists want to continue to experiment with cloning because it may provide new treatments for degenerative diseases, and it could alleviate shortages in human tissues.
Dolly's age is in dispute because she was created using genetic material from a 6-year-old ewe, so it could be argued that she is 11 years old, not 5 years old.
Her arthritis may be a result of a genetic defect caused by cloning, or it could be due to premature aging or just 'an unfortunate accident'.

### Attainment targets

Work in the previous sections should provide evidence that pupils are working towards the following attainment levels.

| Recognise that scientific ideas are based on evidence | Level 4 |
| --- | --- |
| Describe some of the causes of variation between living things | Level 6 |

# 6 *Measuring variation*

## Learning outcomes

Pupils:

- interpret graphs and tables of data
- know what average, mean, mode, median and range mean
- understand that the larger a sample, the more representative it is of species characteristics
- understand that small samples show individual variation, making it difficult to look for patterns

## Measuring variation

➡ *Pupil's Book page 53*

In Key Stage 2 pupils will have had opportunities to learn to classify and rank data and will have calculated mean, mode, median, maximum/minimum value and range. They will be familiar with the terms statistics, average and distribution. They should be familiar with both line and bar graphs but may need reminding. They can keep tally charts and make pictograms.

*Activity*

## Information processing: Average sizes

➡ *Pupil's Book page 53*

➡ *Worksheet 2.7: Being average (K)*

## Answers

➡ *Pupil's Book page 53*

1  'Average' is a slippery concept so this is re-examined in the next section 'Different kinds of averages'. Pupils can respond with something like 'an average is what most things are', or 'it describes what is normal' or give the mathematical answer 'add up all the numbers and divide them by how many numbers you have added up'.

2  A sample is a smaller bit of the whole population that should contain within it a 'mirror' of the whole population (it is 'representative').

3  Twenty-five of each gender in the sample would give the best reliability. Three and five are far too few to look for the 'average' and not be influenced by individual variations. The 'How did you decide?' question encourages thinking about thinking (metacognition).

4  The graphs show differences in both height and weight between the genders related to age.

5  Girls are taller than boys between 11 and 13 but boys are taller from birth to 10 and again from 14 onwards.

6  It is not possible to say for height or weight, as they are still increasing up to 18 when the data stops.

7  Each pupil practises reading the graph axis to fit their height and weight on to the graphs.

8  Both inheritance and environment (particularly diet) influence both height and weight.

Worksheet 2.7: Being average gives a wide selection of variations to investigate and develops numeracy skills.

## Different kinds of averages

➡ *Pupil's Book page 54*

This gives some working definitions, based on reading the graphs from the previous section that will be needed throughout the Year 7 Science course. You may want to extend this with some simple calculations to find means, modes and medians. Activities designed for the Year 6 Numeracy programme are easily available on-line. Your Maths department will also have examples of suitable problem-solving activities.

Pupils must be given experience of framing suitable questions, which can be answered by looking at spreadsheets and databases. The median for the example given is 140 cm.

## Attainment targets
Work in the previous sections should provide evidence that pupils are working towards the following attainment levels.

| Read and interpret graphical data | Level 4 |
|---|---|
| Describe some causes of variation | Level 6 |
| Identify common variations between individuals including some features that are inherited, and recognise that some of these can also be affected by the environment | Level 6 |

# 7 *More variation*

## Learning outcomes
Pupils:

- interpret graphs
- identify strengths of correlation
- understand the importance of sample size

## Correlation
➡ *Pupil's Book page 54*
At this age pupils need only know that a correlation indicates there is a relationship between cause and effect. ICT should play a major part in teaching about correlation.

## Answer
**23** There does appear to be a link between shoe size and height – the taller you are the more likely it is that you wear big shoes. The correlation is not strong and there are exceptions to this 'rule' – you could draw pupils' attention to the 130 cm tall person wearing size 10 shoes. You can ask additional questions to help pupils understand how to analyse a sample of data from a population. For example:

What is the biggest shoe size? What is the smallest?
What is the height of the tallest/shortest person? Are they wearing the biggest/smallest shoes?
What is the average shoe size for this population?
Calculate the mean and the mode – what do they show?

If you have not already used Worksheet 2.7 Being average, it can be used in this lesson.

*Activity* ## Information processing: Winter holly
➡ *Pupil's Book page 56*
Many pupils in Year 7 still do not know when it is most appropriate to use a bar chart or a line graph. The holly data is given in two forms and, with a bit of assistance at reading graphs, pupils can assess that one form makes the data harder to interpret. You can ask them to comment on the sample size. Is it large enough to be a good 'sample', and what do we mean by 'good'?

## Answers

1 The input variable is the temperature, the outcome is the number of berries. The scatter graph has these on the correct axes (input, independent on the *x*-axis; outcome, dependent on the *y*-axis). Note that neither graph shows the years because the relationship being investigated is between the temperature and number of berries, so the data is ranked by temperature. Temperature is a continuous variable here.

2 There is no clear straight-line relationship, but it looks as if the number of berries tends to be lower in colder winters, a very weak correlation. Pupils are expected to make statements such as 'the colder it is the fewer berries' or 'as it gets warmer there tend to be more berries'. Encourage them to use the word 'probably'.

3 The graph does not go down below 0 °C so the only deduction is that it is likely that fewer than 100 berries will be produced.

5 The data does not show individual holly bushes but it would be reasonable to assume there is some inherited (genetic) variation between the bushes, but there is also a weak correlation between temperature and number of berries. The points are scattered along a diagonal. If inheritance alone were responsible for holly berry number we would expect a random pattern of points across the whole graph, that is, no correlation.

## Word play/Time to think

These last two activities make suitable revision homework before an end-of-chapter test. They provide an opportunity for both teachers and pupils to assess pupils' understanding.

### Attainment targets

Work in the previous sections should provide evidence that pupils are working towards the following attainment levels.

| Draw simple graphs | Level 4 |
| --- | --- |
| Select information from a survey provided | Level 4 |
| Select from a range of sources | Level 5 |
| Draw conclusions consistent with the evidence | Level 5 |
| Identify measurements that do not fit the main pattern shown | Level 6 |

## Review

➡ *Worksheet 2.8: Test on variation and classification*
This worksheet provides a test requiring about 20–30 minutes of lesson time to check on understanding.

## Answers

| | | |
| --- | --- | --- |
| 1 | Insect. | (1 mark) |
| 2 | Mammal. | (1 mark) |
| 3 | Fish. | (1 mark) |
| 4 | Mammal. | (1 mark) |
| 5 | Bird. | (1 mark) |
| 6 | Reptile. | (1 mark) |

**7** Drawing quality.                                    (1 mark)
Thorax, abdomen, head.
Wings.
Compound eyes.
Antennae.                                       (Any 3 for 3 marks)

**8 a)** One of: hard outer layer/exoskeleton;
jointed legs; segmented bodies.             (1 mark)

**b)** One of: six legs instead of eight legs; three
body parts instead of two; wings and no wings. (1 mark)

**9** At least three of the following:
Genes are the units of inheritance.
Genes are made from DNA.
Genes code for certain features.
Genes are like the letters that make up words while
chromosomes are like the story.
Chromosomes are a string of genes.
Chromosomes can be seen at cell division.        (3 marks)

**10** Genes/chromosomes; chromosome; radiation; change.
                                                 (4 marks)

**11 a)** 26 + 30 + 28 = 84
84 ÷ 3 = 28 g                                    (2 marks)

**b)** 24 28 29 <u>29</u> 30 30 32
Median = 29 g                                    (2 marks)

**c)** 210 g                                        (1 mark)

**d)** No relationship.                             (1 mark)
Award additional marks for correct statements
such as 'female kittens can be grey or white',
and for proof of statements, for example 'most
of the males are grey but Bubbles is white.'    (3 marks)

**e)** Data does support the statement.            (1 mark)
Award up to 2 additional marks for statements
about individual kittens comparing data at birth
and 8 weeks, or for whole data sets compared.
For example
Kittens are around 30 g at birth and 210 g
at 8 weeks.                                       (1 mark)
This is a increase in weight by seven times.     (1 mark)
This fits with pet care book information.         (1 mark)
Alternatively:
Shadow was the smallest kitten weighing
24 g at birth but by 8 weeks was 195 g.          (1 mark)
This is an increase in weight by eight times.    (1 mark)
This fits with the pet care book information.    (1 mark)

# 3 Electricity

→ ## Rationale

This chapter provides 8 hours of teaching materials. It will consolidate the work covered by the children at Key Stage 2 on electric circuits and the representation of circuits using conventional symbols. Children cover a lot of work on electricity in Years 2, 4 and 6. They will already have done practical work using batteries, bulbs and buzzers; constructed simple circuits to test whether materials are conductors or insulators; and explained how to change the brightness of a lamp.

The work they have done on series circuits at Key Stage 2 will be extended in this chapter and the use of parallel circuits will be introduced. The approach taken encourages pupils to reflect on the circuits that they have seen and made, and asks them to give explanations and consider novel situations, in order to challenge and build their knowledge framework in this area. They will be introduced to the use of ammeters to measure electric current. The key science idea developed in this chapter relates to energy.

The emphasis throughout this chapter is to identify pupils' misconceptions and give them opportunities to reconstruct their own understanding by reference to a range of analogies or models. Pupils are encouraged to interpret graphs, to identify input and outcome variables and to develop their understanding of lines of best fit. Towards the end of the chapter the concept of voltage is introduced and the purpose of fuses in circuits is discussed. Finally the modern medical developments in electro-physiology are related to the early discoveries of Galvani and Volta, providing the opportunity for pupils to understand that science is a developing area where results and conclusions are revisited and sometimes re-interpreted.

Electricity in circuits is not developed further within Key Stage 3 and so the work in this chapter builds, expands and explains work done in Key Stage 2, such that this provides the foundation for considering quantitative relationships between current, voltage, resistance, energy and power at Key Stage 4. The topic also provides input of ideas about magnets and electromagnets (Y8), and energy and electricity (Y9).

→ ## Overview

The textbook sections, activities and worksheets have been arranged into 1 hour blocks to aid lesson planning. Clearly several of the activities and worksheets could form part of a homework session. The planning includes reading time for individual sections but some teachers may prefer to organise this as homework preparation for the following lesson. Five types of worksheets – extension (E), support for an activity (S), practical (P), key skills (K) and developmental (D) – allow for differentiation and offer flexibility to accommodate teachers' preferred practice. The actual timing and emphasis on different sections will depend on the current knowledge base of the pupils, the ability of the teaching group and the preferences of the teacher.

| Lesson | Worksheet |
|---|---|
| **1** What do you know about electrical circuits? | Worksheet 3.1: What do you know? (S) |
| **2** Circuits and symbols | Worksheet 3.2: Electrical dominoes (S) |
| **3** Series and parallel circuits and switches | Worksheet 3.3: Predictions about circuits (S) |
| **4** Measuring current using ammeters | Worksheet 3.4: Measuring electric current (P) <br> Worksheet 3.5: True/false? (S) |
| **5** Varying current in a circuit | Worksheet 3.6: Changing resistance (P) |
| **6** Resistance, fuses and voltage | Worksheet 3.7: To investigate the action of a rheostat (P) <br> Worksheet 3.8: To compare the current in wires of different thickness (P) <br> Worksheet 3.9: To show the heating effect of an electric current (P) <br> Worksheet 3.10: To show the effect of passing different currents through a strand of steel wool (P) <br> Worksheet 3.11: To show the action of a fuse (P) |
| **7** Quizboard | Worksheet 3.12: Making a quizboard (P) <br> Worksheet 3.13: Questions for a game (E) |
| **8** The hazards of electricity | |
| Review | Worksheet 3.14: Test on electricity |

# ➡ *Chapter plan*

| | Demonstration | Practical | ICT | Activity | Word play | Time to think | Ideas and evidence |
|---|---|---|---|---|---|---|---|
| **Lesson 1** | | Making circuits | Using a CD-ROM | | | What do you know? | |
| **Lesson 2** | | Building circuits | | Game: Electrical dominoes | Circuits | | |
| **Lesson 3** | | Building parallel circuits | | | | | |
| **Lesson 4** | | Measuring current with an ammeter | | Creative thinking: Using models | | Using key words | |
| **Lesson 5** | | Changing the brightness of a bulb | | | | | |
| **Lesson 6** | | Altering the current in circuits <br><br> Action of a fuse | Using a spreadsheet | Evaluation: Changing current | | | Luigi Galvani and Alessandro Volta |
| **Lesson 7** | | Making a quizboard | | Revision: Loop card game | | Electrical quiz | |
| **Lesson 8** | Human conduction | | Internet search | Presentation: Uses of electricity | | | |

# ➡ *Expectations*

**At the end of this chapter**

**in terms of scientific enquiry**

**most pupils will:** select and use appropriate equipment to investigate circuits which include cells, bulbs and switches; measure current; identify patterns in their results and draw conclusions about series and parallel circuits; describe hazards associated with electricity and how to deal with them

**some pupils will not have made so much progress and will:** explore circuits using appropriate equipment; identify patterns in their results and use these to describe the behaviour of simple circuits; identify and report on hazards associated with electricity

**some pupils will have progressed further and will:** plan and carry out a systematic investigation of series and parallel circuits to obtain sufficient evidence to draw conclusions; give examples of the development of scientific ideas about electricity, for example, Galvani and Volta on electric current, and explain how electricity can be hazardous to humans

**in terms of physical processes**

**most pupils will:** construct a range of working electrical circuits and represent these in circuit diagrams; state that electric current is the same at all points in a series circuit and divides along the branches of a parallel circuit; use a flow model to describe resistance and to distinguish between electric current and energy transfer in a circuit; compare and contrast the advantages of series and parallel circuits in use, for example, fuses, ring main

**some pupils will not have made so much progress and will:** construct simple electrical circuits and represent these diagrammatically; give examples of useful circuits; state safety rules for use of electricity

**some pupils will have progressed further and will:** relate voltage of cells and batteries qualitatively to energy transfer in circuits; use a flow model to explain the difference between electric current and energy transfer; apply the idea that nerves are electrical conductors to explain electrical hazards

# ➡ *Links with CASE*

The chapter makes several references to the use of models for explaining the ideas of current flow in electrical circuits, and pupils are encouraged to relate the descriptive models used to the more abstract ideas of current flow. Explanatory models require formal operational thinking and, while many pupils will be able to describe circuit setups and predict brightness of lamps or whether circuits are formed or not, there is quite a leap in thinking level required to enable pupils to explain such events in terms of one or more model.

Proportionality is involved in the voltage–current relationship that occurs in circuits where the number of cells is increased.

Inverse proportionality, involving the relationship between two variables, is one of the reasoning patterns of formal operational thinking used in CASE. This particular relationship is referred to in the work on current and resistance using pencil leads and it may be further considered in other practical activities.

# → *Pupils' misconceptions*

| Misconception | Scientific understanding |
|---|---|
| Electricity is a substance kept in the battery. | The battery is the source of energy for the circuit. |
| Current is the same thing as electrical energy. | Electric current is the flow of charge round the circuit. |
| Current gets less as it goes round the circuit. | Current is the same all round a series circuit.<br>What does diminish is the amount of energy that the charge possesses. |
| In circuits current flows out of both terminals of the battery (the clashing currents model) and meets in the bulb to make it light. | The conventional current flows round the circuit from positive (+) to negative (−). The actual charges are carried by moving electrons (which flow in the opposite direction). |
| Only one wire is needed to connect from the battery to the bulb. | A complete circuit is needed for the current to flow. |
| The voltage flows round the circuit. | The greater the voltage of the battery, the greater the energy transferred to the circuit by the current flowing round the circuit. |
| Fuses are resistors and stop current. | Fuses are safety devices that break circuits when too great a current passes through them. |

# ➡ *Literacy, numeracy and other cross-curricular links*

At the start of and throughout this topic pupils should be encouraged to work collaboratively, discussing and explaining their ideas to each other. This topic has often been dealt with in a superficial manner, whereby pupils carry out circuit board work with the teacher giving them a few statements about circuits. This, however, does not equip pupils to deal with novel circuits nor explain results with clarity, so discussion of the various circuits and models used is an essential part of the learning in this topic.

## Numeracy

There is a section discussing the use of prefixes and their symbols including multiples and submultiples and the convention adopted by the 'Système International d'Unités' (SI units). Pupils describe how to present results effectively in a table. They identify errors in recorded data. They learn how to interpret results presented in a line graph. They describe the relationship between the variables and are introduced to drawing lines of best fit.

## Language for learning

By the end of this chapter pupils will be able to understand, use and spell correctly words and phrases relating to:

- circuit components – battery, cell, bulb or lamp, connecting wire, switch, power supply, fuse
- electrical concepts – current, resistance, energy transfer.

Pupils should use skimming, scanning, highlighting and note making as appropriate to different texts. For example, at the end of the chapter there is a scientific passage requiring the comprehension of the historical links between the work of Volta and Galvani and modern electro-physiology.

# 1 *What do you know about electrical circuits?*

## Learning outcomes

Pupils:

- support their predictions by demonstration circuits
- explain that the bulb(s) light because electricity travels round the circuit

This first lesson is designed to allow teachers to establish the pupils' prior knowledge about electricity and electrical circuits. The reason for using a festoon bulb is to help clarify in the pupils' minds that the electric current passes into the bulb through the filament and out of the bulb at the other end.

If pupils are clearly familiar with the concepts and they have few misconceptions then this work can be covered quickly. The use of a CD-ROM providing circuits for discussion is a possible approach that teachers may wish to use. Such software includes Crocodile clips and Edison4.

## *Activity* Practical: Making circuits

➡ *Worksheet 3.1: What do you know? (S)*

Some teachers may wish to introduce the topic with a class demonstration or through a series of class practicals. Although pupils will almost certainly be familiar with setting up simple circuits, they may find the equipment provided is quite different from that which they have used before. Some pupils will need to be told to strip the plastic covering off the wire if they are constructing the circuits without using kits such as UNILAB 'yellow' electricity kits or Worcester circuit boards. (These use leads with 4 mm plugs already attached.) Points to emphasise are that it does not matter which way round the bulb, cell or switch is connected in the circuit. However, two or more cells must be connected in the 'same direction', +ve to −ve. A few pupils may think that the colour of the wire is important and some may fail to recognise that two circuits constructed using different equipment – a UNILAB kit and a Worcester circuit board, for example – are essentially the same circuits.

As far as possible ensure that the bulbs used are bought from the same supplier and preferably are from the same batch, so that they all glow with approximately the same brightness under the same conditions. Also, if the kits have not been used for some months, ensure that the connections are not corroded and that the batteries are not 'flat'.

Worksheet 3.1 is designed to support pupils who are less familiar with the work than might be expected.

### Equipment

Each group will need the equipment available within your school for constructing simple circuits:

- two cells and cell holders
- two bulbs and bulb holders
- push switch
- four 4 mm plug leads

CD-ROMs can be obtained from:
Crocodile clips
11 Randolph Place
Edinburgh
EH3 7TA
Scotland
Tel: 0131 226 1511

Edison4:
Quickroute Systems Ltd
Regent House Heaton Lane
Stockport SK4 1BS
Tel: 0161 476 0202
Fax: 0161 476 0505

Schools that are members of CLEAPSS School Science Service (or SSERC in Scotland) can obtain further useful advice (see Appendix for details). A useful reference for teachers for whom physics is not their speciality is the Primary School Teachers and Science PSTS Project Pack 7 *Current understanding, Electricity concepts and practice for primary and non-specialist secondary teacher education*, published by Oxford University Department of Educational Studies and Westminster College, 1996.

## Answers

1 Pupils should mark the direction of the conventional current round the circuit from the positive terminal of the left-hand cell back to the negative terminal of the right-hand cell. Many pupils have the 'clashing currents' misconception of electricity and this question will allow teachers to identify these pupils.

2    1   C          5   B
     2   F          6   E
     3   A          7   D
     4   G

3

| Bulb | Lights up? |
|------|------------|
| a | ✗ |
| b | ✗ |
| c | ✓ |
| d | ✗ |
| e | ✓ |
| f | ✗ |
| g | ✗ |
| h | ✓ dim |
| i | ✓ dim |
| j | ✓ |
| k | ✓ |
| l | ✓ dim |
| m | ✓ dim |

# What do you know?
## Answers

➡ *Pupil's Book page 58*

1 This question is designed to ensure that pupils are familiar with simple electrical components that they used at Key Stage 2.
**a** = leads; **b** = bulb/lamp; **c** = batteries.

2 The important point is that pupils should realise that electric current passes in at one end of the bulb, through the fine filament and out at the other end, and that there must be a complete electrical circuit for the bulb to light.

3 In the first picture both wires are connected to the same terminal of the cell. In the second picture both wires are connected to the same terminal of the bulb holder. In the third one, the wire is missing between the cell and the bulb. The bulb will not light in any of these circuits because a complete electrical circuit has not been made.

4 In the second circuit both bulbs are less bright. The current flowing is less because there is greater resistance to its flow.

# 2 Circuits and symbols

## Learning outcomes

Pupils:

- support their predictions by demonstration circuits or circuit diagrams
- show their understanding of circuit ideas by successfully finding faults
- identify a cell or battery as a source of energy
- describe why cells have positive and negative terminals and connect them correctly in circuits
- know that current does not change in a simple series circuit, that it is not 'used up' as it travels round the circuit

This lesson could be combined with the first lesson if pupils are already confident in using series circuits.

The cross-section through a dry cell on page 60 of the Pupil's Book serves to emphasise that the energy is transferred from chemicals stored in the cell.

The session introduces (or revises) the use of electrical symbols in circuits (page 61).

It is worth clarifying the use of the words 'cell' and 'battery'. A cell is a single cylinder or box containing chemicals that produce about 1.5 volts of electricity, whereas a battery is the term used when several cells are connected together (possibly inside the same packaging) to produce more volts. Such a battery is the PP3 9 volt battery.

Note also the two symbols used for an indicator or light source. They are often used interchangeably.

*Activity* ## Game: Dominoes

➡ *Worksheet 3.2: Electrical dominoes (S)*
Worksheet 3.2 provides suggestions for an electrical dominoes game that pupils could construct. This will reinforce their knowledge of the symbols and the devices that the symbols represent. This could be used as a homework activity.

*Activity* ## Practical: Building circuits

If pupils have not used buzzers or motors, it is worth allowing them to set up circuits with these devices and for them to note which devices are polarity sensitive.

### Equipment

Each group will need the equipment available within your school for constructing simple circuits:

- two cells and cell holders
- two bulbs and bulb holders
- push switch
- four 4 mm plug leads
- buzzer
- motor

## Circuits
## Answers
→ *Pupil's Book page 62*
**1**

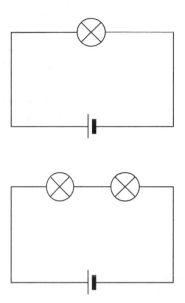

2 Bulbs **b**, **c** and **d** are all very dim. Bulbs **e**, **f** and **g** are all at normal brightness. Bulb **h** is brighter than normal.
3 A – bulb is lit at normal brightness.
  B – bulbs are lit equally but dimly.

### Attainment targets
Work in the previous sections should provide evidence that pupils are working towards the following attainment levels.

| Use circuit diagrams to construct circuits | Level 3 |
|---|---|
| Describe and explain how to connect devices such as buzzers into electric circuits for them to work | Level 4 |
| Explain that electric current transfers electrical energy from the cell to the bulb | Level 6 |

# 3 *Series and parallel circuits and switches*

## Learning outcomes
Pupils:

- explain how connecting bulbs in parallel allows each to shine equally brightly

Any of the first three lessons could be expanded or shortened to accommodate the pupils' existing knowledge and understanding. Even if pupils have done work using switches and bulbs they are less likely to be familiar with parallel circuits. While pupils can usually manage to set up circuits they often have limited knowledge to recognise different circuits and to describe the properties of each. Teachers will probably want to demonstrate parallel circuits or give pupils opportunities to set up the circuits themselves.

*Activity* Practical: Building parallel circuits

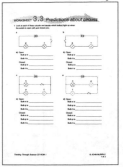

➡ *Worksheet 3.3: Predictions about circuits (S)*

Pupils should see that bulbs connected in parallel across a cell glow with equal brightness. (This assumes that the bulbs are identical.) Also they should see that the brightness is about the same as when just one bulb is connected to one cell. (In practice they may see that the single bulb is slightly brighter – especially if the cells are not new. This is due to the internal resistance of the cell or in the case of zinc-chloride or zinc-carbon cells it could be due to polarisation.)

Pupils should be clear that this circuit diagram:

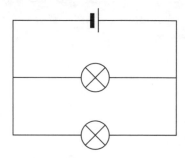

shows an identical circuit to this:

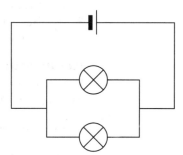

or even this:

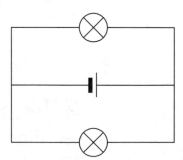

**Equipment**

Each group will need the equipment available within your school for constructing simple circuits:

- two cells and cell holders
- two bulbs and bulb holders
- push switch
- four 4 mm plug leads
- additional bulbs and connectors

## Answers

**1 a)** Open: **p** is off, **t** is off.
Closed: **p** is on, **t** is on.

**b)** Open: **p** is off, **t** is off.
Closed: **p** is on, **t** is on.

**c)** Open: **n** is off, **p** is on, **t** is on.
Closed: **n** is on, **p** is on, **t** is on.

**d)** Open: **n** is on, **p** is on, **t** is off.
Closed: **n** is on, **p** is on, **t** is on.

**2 a)** No bulb is lit.

**b)** Both bulbs **p** and **t** are lit.

**c)** No bulbs are lit.

**d)** Bulb **p** is off, bulb **t** is lit.

**3 a)** **A**

**b)** **D**

**c)** **F**

**d)** **G** and **H** are the same.

**4**

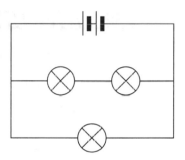

**5 a)** i) ✗   ii) ✓   iii) ✓   iv) ✗   v) ✓   vi) ✗

**b)** i) ✓   ii) ✗   iii) ✗   iv) ✓   v) ✓   vi) ✗

**c)** i) ✗   ii) ✓   iii) ✗   iv) ✓   v) ✓   vi) ✗

## Answer

➡ *Pupil's Book page 63*

**4** Series circuit: both bulbs lit at normal brightness.
Parallel circuit: both bulbs will be bright.

If room lights were connected in series, and the filament in one bulb breaks, all the bulbs would go out because the circuit would be broken.

## Two switch circuits

➡ *Pupil's Book page 64*

The theoretical circuits are related to practical situations including two-way switches on stairs and circuits using two switches for safety purposes. Reference can be made to the diagram of a torch in the Pupil's Book on page 64. Extension work could include asking pupils to design and draw up a list of components needed to build a lighting system for a model house.

## Answers

**5** When both switches are in the 'up' position, there is a complete circuit through the top wire and the bulb lights. If one switch is in the 'up' position and one is in the 'down' position, there is a break in the circuit and the bulb does not light.

6 Pupils should explain the action of the switch; that the cells must be inserted the same way and the need for a complete conducting path.

7 **b** is normal; **c** and **d** are normal; **e** and **f** are normal; **g** and **h** are normal, **i** is bright; **j** is bright, **k** and **l** are out because the wire between them acts as a short circuit.

8 In diagram A when the switch is open, only the top bulb is lit at normal brightness. When the switch is closed, it makes no difference, as the bottom bulb is still short-circuited by the wire.

In diagram B, with the switch open, both bulbs are dim; closing the switch short-circuits the right-hand bulb and so it goes out. The other bulb is now at normal brightness.

In diagram C, the bulb is lit before the switch is closed; closing the switch short-circuits the battery.

9 Pupils should be reminded not to connect up this circuit as it will flatten the battery and possibly make the wires very hot!

# 4 Measuring current using ammeters

## Learning outcomes

Pupils:

- use an ammeter with care
- measure and record current in simple series circuits
- know that current does not change in a simple series circuit, that it is not 'used up' as it travels round the circuit
- distinguish between current and energy, for example current just circulates back to the battery, energy is used to light a bulb
- explain current in terms of a model
- explain how connecting bulbs in parallel allows each to shine equally brightly
- predict and explain measurements of current in different parts of parallel circuits
- explain these observations using a model
- identify strengths and weaknesses of a model for electricity

Pupils have difficulty connecting ammeters and will need to be taught that the red (+ve) terminal on the ammeter must eventually go to the +ve end of the battery.

Reading ammeters accurately is a common problem. Analogue meters give an easy visual feel for the strength of the current but pupils often have difficulty interpreting the minor scale divisions, especially on dual scale meters. There are many computer programs available to give pupils practice at reading such scales. Nowadays digital meters are much more common than analogue meters but they also present problems as pupils can often struggle to interpret the relative magnitude of readings after the decimal point (0.175, 0.3, etc.).

In this section there is an opportunity to introduce analogies of electric circuits to help with the pupils' understanding.

*Activity* Practical: Measuring current with an ammeter

➡ *Worksheet 3.4: Measuring electric current (P), Worksheet 3.5: True/false? (S)*

Pupils can perform a number of experiments using ammeters to establish that the current in a series circuit is the same all round the circuit. They can also place the ammeter at different positions in parallel circuits to establish the general rule that the current leaving the battery is equal to the sum of the currents through each branch of a parallel circuit. Less able children may find it difficult to connect the ammeter at different points in the circuit and it may be worth demonstrating a circuit that contains three or four ammeters in it.

### Equipment

Each group will need the equipment available within your school for constructing simple circuits:

- two cells and cell holders
- two bulbs and bulb holders
- push switch
- four 4 mm plug leads
- ammeter (preferably digital)

## Answers

➡ *Worksheet 3.4: Measuring electric current*

1 Pupils should conclude that the readings on ammeters at X, Y and Z are approximately the same because the current in a series circuit is the same all round the circuit.

2 Pupils should conclude that the readings on ammeters at P and Q are the same, the readings on ammeters at R and S are approximately the same, and that the reading at R plus the reading at S equals the reading at P or Q.

➡ *Worksheet 3.5: True/false?*

1 Position 2 reads 1 A ✗
Position 2 reads 2 A ✓
Position 3 reads 1 A ✗
Position 3 reads 2 A ✓

2 Position 2 reads 1 A ✓
Position 2 reads 2 A ✗
Position 3 reads 1 A ✓
Position 3 reads 2 A ✗
Position 4 reads 1 A ✗
Position 4 reads 2 A ✓

3 Position 2 reads 0.2 A
Position 3 reads 0.2 A
Position 4 reads 0.2 A
Position 5 reads 0.6 A

4 Position 1 reads 1.5 A
Position 4 reads 1.5 A

5 Position 4 reads 4 A (because the total current flowing in is 3 A + 2 A = 5 A and it must be the same as the total current flowing out). The current flow though position 4 is away from the junction.

## Measuring electric current
## Answers
➡ *Pupil's Book page 68*

**10** Full scale deflection is 1 A. Reading on left-hand meter is 0.6 A and reading on right-hand meter is 0.2 A.

**11** A digital clock gives a numerical display, and does not need to be interpreted. It often uses the 24-hour system. With an analogue clock it is easier to judge how long it will be for a certain period of time to elapse. An example could be sitting an exam, which finishes at 12:15 p.m. Looking at an analogue clock, which shows 20 minutes to 12, it is easy to see how long you have left.

**12** With an analogue ammeter, it is easy to see from a glance at the dial whether the current is large or small. It is difficult to work out the exact reading between divisions. Dual-reading dials can be confusing – using a multiplication factor is difficult when the dial reads from 0–10 but the full scale deflection is only 1 A. With a digital meter it is easy to read off the value directly. Sometimes the decimal points cause confusion.

## Thinking about models in electricity
## Answers
➡ *Pupil's Book page 70*

**13** Wire – plastic tubing
   Current – moving chain
   Battery – cotton reel

*Activity* ## Creative thinking: Using models
➡ *Pupil's Book page 70*

There has been a lot of research over the last 20 years or so into children's understanding of science. Two well known projects are the secondary Children's Learning in Science Project (CLIS) and the Science Process and Concept Exploration (SPACE) project for primary age children. Children have their own ideas which they use to explain electric circuits. These mental models do not necessarily match up with our accepted scientific model. To help children take on board the scientific model we need to introduce analogies to assist them in their understanding. A number of analogies are suggested in the Pupil's Book. These are by no means exhaustive and teachers may well wish to use their own. Another popular analogy is the sweets circuit, where pupils move around the circuit and as they pass the teacher they receive a sweet, which they consume as they climb on to a chair placed in the circuit. The purpose of these physical models is to reduce the complexity of the phenomena so that pupils will more readily understand the key features.

Models are used particularly to explain abstract features, so helping the pupils' understanding of the concept. We will come across the use of these models in various topics, such as in explaining the particulate nature of matter and in describing the Solar System.

## Using ammeters in circuits
## Answers
➡ *Pupil's Book page 71*

**14** The readings on X and Y will be the same.

**15** The current passes through Z, splits and some goes through X and some through Y and then joins up again to return to the battery.

**16** Always 0.5 A.

**17 a)** Ammeter **4**.
    **b)** Ammeters **2** and **3**.
    **c)** Ammeters **1** and **4**.

### Attainment targets
Work in the previous sections should provide evidence that pupils are working towards the following attainment levels.

| | |
|---|---|
| Make elementary observations and measurements using ammeters | Level 3 |
| Communicate what they have discovered about current in series and parallel circuits | Level 3 |
| Connect ammeters in circuits and take a series of readings | Level 4 |
| Record the observations using tables | Level 4 |
| Use simple models to explain the effects caused by an electric current flowing around a circuit | Level 5 |
| Select apparatus and use it effectively in constructing electric circuits | Level 5 |

# 5 *Varying current in a circuit*

## Learning outcomes
Pupils:

• use the term resistance in describing circuit effects

In this section pupils will recap on work from Key Stage 2 in Years 4 and 6 where they constructed simple circuits to test whether materials are electrical conductors or insulators. They will extend this to discuss the size of the current and how the size of the current varies with the amount of resistance in a simple circuit. The example provided in the textbook (page 73) is for an experiment using a carbon rod. You may wish the pupils to perform a similar experiment using the equipment you have available in your school.

*Activity* ## Practical: Changing the brightness of a bulb
➡ *Worksheet 3.6: Changing resistance (P)*

Pupils can use a length of nichrome or eureka wire taped to a metre rule. The circuit should always have a bulb so that the current is not too great when the length of the wire is reduced to zero. Pupils can use a spreadsheet to enter their results and plot a graph. With less able pupils you may wish to give them a less demanding experiment using a variable resistor (rheostat) and ammeter. They observe the variation in brightness of the lamp and the changes in the current reading. They may also perform a similar experiment with an electric motor.

**Equipment**
Each group will need the equipment available within your
school for constructing simple circuits:

- two cells and cell holders
- bulb and bulb holder
- push switch
- four 4mm plug leads
- length of eureka wire (approx. 32 swg) mounted on 1 metre
  baton
- rheostat

## Answers

**1** Yes, the bulb lights.
**2** As the length of eureka wire gets longer, the bulb gets
dimmer.
**3** As the length of eureka wire increases, the ammeter reading
decreases.
**4** For the greatest current the lead should be on the left with
the least amount of eureka wire in the circuit.
**5** For the bulb to be dim, put the lead at the right-hand end
with all the eureka wire in the circuit.
**6** The eureka wire reduces the flow of electricity.
**7** As the length of the eureka wire increases, the current
decreases; the longer the wire, the smaller the current.
**8** The shorter the eureka wire, the faster the motor.

# **6** *Resistance, fuses and voltage*

## Learning outcome
Pupils:

- explain how a fuse protects a circuit

This work follows on closely from varying currents in a circuit
and some teachers may wish to incorporate the work on
resistance into the previous lesson.

## Resistance and fuses
## Answer
➡ *Pupil's Book page 73*
**18** It is important that pupils distinguish between the object
and the material. Any valid objects and materials may be
chosen.

*Activity* ## Evaluation: Changing current
Spreadsheet 'Current.xls' on the CD-ROM can be used for this
activity.
## Answers
➡ *Pupil's Book page 73*
**1** Pupils should suggest ordering the results in the table.
**2** 0.67 is incorrect.

**3** Input variable is the length of pencil lead. The outcome variable is the current in amps, A.

**4** Vertical (*y*) axis the current in amps, A. Horizontal (*x*) axis the length in cm.

**5** Pupils should suggest a sentence with a clear relationship between the length and the current, such as 'the longer the pencil lead, the smaller the current' or 'the longer the pencil lead, the greater the resistance and the smaller the current'.

**6** Pupils should realise that this allows a greater current to flow because there are two parallel routes through which the current flows.

*Activity* ## Practicals: Altering the current in circuits

➡ *Pupil's Book page 75*

➡ *Worksheet 3.7: To investigate the action of a rheostat (P), Worksheet 3.8: To compare the current in wires of different thickness (P), Worksheet 3.9: To show the heating effect of an electric current (P), Worksheet 3.10: To show the effect of passing different currents through a strand of steel wool (P)*

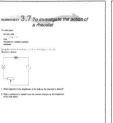

An approach that leads logically through these topics is to develop the concept of resistance from the previous lesson; teachers could either demonstrate or allow pupils to investigate the action of a variable resistor (rheostat) (Worksheet 3.7) and develop the idea that different materials show different amounts of resistance. Teachers could then introduce the idea that wires made from the same material but of different thickness have different resistances even though they are the same length (Worksheet 3.8).

Teachers can further show that the current in a circuit can be increased by increasing the voltage of the circuit. This will lead to a demonstration of connecting a coil of nichrome wire to a low voltage supply and gradually increasing the voltage (Worksheet 3.9). Not only will the current increase but also the wire will begin to glow. The teacher can demonstrate how a thin wire will melt if the current is too great (Worksheet 3.10). Alternatively pupils could perform the experiment themselves. It is important to choose wire that melts before the bulb blows! This then leads on to the idea of fuses (Worksheet 3.11, see notes on page 75).

Teachers may prefer to demonstrate some of these activities, in particular the practical described in Worksheet 3.9.

➡ *Worksheet 3.7: To investigate the action of a rheostat*

**Equipment**
- two dry cells
- connecting wires
- bulb
- ammeter
- rheostat (or variable resistor)
- ammeter

## Answers

**1** The brightness of the bulb changes.

**2** As the current decreases the bulb gets dimmer.

➡ *Worksheet 3.8: To compare the current in wires of different thickness*

**Equipment**
- two dry cells
- connecting wires
- bulb
- ammeter
- three eureka wires of different thickness fixed to a 1 metre baton

**Safety**
Pupils should avoid touching the eureka wires as they can get very hot when current is passing through them.

## Answers

1 When the same lengths of wire are used but they are of different thickness, the bulbs have different brightnesses.
2 The thicker the wire, the brighter the bulb.
3 The thinnest wire has the smallest current.
4 As the bulb gets brighter the current is greater.

➡ *Worksheet 3.9: To show the heating effect of an electric current*

**Equipment**
- low voltage power supply
- mounted coil of nichrome wire
- connecting leads with crocodile clips

**Safety**
Pupils should avoid touching the nichrome wire as it can get very hot when current is passing through it.

## Answers

1 It begins to glow more and more brightly.
2 Electric fires, toasters.

➡ *Worksheet 3.10: To show the effect of passing different currents through a strand of steel wool*

**Equipment**
- two dry cells
- switch
- connecting wires
- four bulbs
- ammeter
- strands of steel wool

**Safety**
Pupils should avoid touching the strands of steel wool as they can get very hot when a current is passing through them.

## Answers

1 The steel wool burns and melts.
2 This will vary depending on the amount of steel wool.
3 It melts.
4 The bulb is short-circuited. The current flowing is greater and it causes the steel wool to become hot and to melt.

*Activity*  ## Practical: Action of a fuse

➡ *Worksheet 3.11: To show the action of a fuse (P)*

### Equipment
- two or three dry cells or a low voltage power supply
- switch
- connecting wires
- bulb
- ammeter
- 1 A fuse in holder

## Answers
**1** The fuse melts or 'blows'.
**2** To ensure that the current flowing is not too large.

## Answer
➡ *Pupil's Book page 76*

**19** A kettle needs a large current to flow through it; however it should not be greater than 13 A and the fuse is designed to 'blow' or melt if the current becomes greater than this.

## Ideas and evidence: Luigi Galvani and Alessandro Volta
## Answers
➡ *Pupil's Book page 76*

**1** Alessandro Volta has the volt named after him.
**2** In the nerve cells.
**3** It records and displays the pulses of the heart.
**4** If the person's heart does not give regular pulses the pacemaker helps to ensure that the heart pulses are maintained regularly.
**5** Galvani thought the source of the electricity was inside the frog's nerves. Volta thought that the electricity was produced because the two metals, copper and iron, together with the liquid inside the frog, made a battery.
**6** The frog's leg twitched because the nerves were stimulated by an electrical impulse. This was produced by the battery that was formed from the copper, iron and salty liquid inside the frog.
**7** Copper, iron and acid.

### Attainment targets
Work in the previous sections should provide evidence that pupils are working towards the following attainment levels.

| | |
|---|---|
| Describe and explain how and why a fuse is connected in an electrical circuit | Level 4 |
| Explain that there are a number of ways of altering the current in a circuit | Level 5 |
| Explain the glowing of a nichrome wire in terms of the size of the electric current | Level 5 |

# 7 *Quizboard*

## Learning outcome

Pupils:

• consolidate the work covered so far

## Time to think

➡ *Pupil's Book page 77*

This activity encourages pupils to reflect upon their own learning. Lesson outcomes will be differentiated because of this. The practical construction of the quizboard requires pupils to put their knowledge into action as well as provide revision questions for others to try.

## *Activity* Practical: Making a quizboard

➡ *Worksheet 3.12: Making a quizboard (P)*

This is suggested as a fun way of allowing pupils to use their knowledge of electric circuits, both in a practical way and also theoretically. Pupils use their knowledge of electric circuits to construct a quizboard and they also provide the questions and answers (see page 77 of the Pupil's Book). They then test each other's knowledge. They use a bulb and holder, paper fasteners, connecting wires and card. The details are described on the worksheet.

### Equipment

Each group will need:

• bulb and holder
• connecting wire
• wire strippers
• at least 10 paper fasteners
• cell and holder
• stiff card

## *Activity* Revision: Loop card game

➡ *Worksheet 3.13: Questions for a game (E)*

A further activity to test pupils' knowledge is to use this loop card game in which about 30 questions are prepared on cards. Each card has a question on the left and a key word answer on the right. The questions and answers should be photocopied onto card and then cut up and distributed. If there are any spare cards some pupils will need to be given more than one. A pupil starts off by reading out the question on their card. The rest of the class look at their cards and the pupil with the correct answer reads it out and then reads the question on the back of their card. This continues until all the questions have been answered. To add further challenge the activity can be timed and then repeated later to see if the pupils have improved.

# 8 *The hazards of electricity*

## Learning outcomes

Pupils:

- associate high voltage with electrical hazards
- provide descriptions and/or explanations of the effects of electric current on the human body
- describe in a clear sequence the work of scientists in developing ideas and applications of current

Safe working should pervade the whole of this topic. Risk assessments are required for any hazardous activity. Pupils must not experiment with mains equipment. All practical activities in science must comply with the requirements of the Health and Safety at Work Act 1974. Specifically, teachers must carry out risk assessments of any hazards and are required to meet the demands of COSHH Regulations 1999 and/or the Management of Health and Safety at Work Regulations 1992. Employers (LEAs, school governors, and so on) generally use model (general) risk assessments for science activities normally carried out in schools. These are found in the following publications:

*Be safe! Some aspects of safety in science and technology for key stages 1 and 2* (ASE, second edition, 1990)
*Safeguards in the school laboratory* (ASE, tenth edition, 1996)
*Topics in safety* (ASE, second edition, 1998)
*Safety reprints* (ASE, 1998 edition)
*Safety in science education* (DfEE, 1996, HMSO)
*Hazards* (CLEAPSS, 1995 or 1998 update)
*Laboratory handbook* (CLEAPSS, 1997 or later)
*Risk assessments for technology* (CLEAPSS, 1994)

Teachers should check which safety regulations are recommended by their employers and ensure these are used. In addition, teachers are responsible for risk assessment of any modifications appropriate to their own classroom situation.

The Science National Curriculum for England and Wales provides the following guidance on Health and Safety in science:

*When working with tools, equipment and materials, in practical activities and in different environments, including those that are unfamiliar, pupils should be taught:*

**a** *about hazards, risks and risk control*
**b** *to recognise hazards, assess consequent risks and take steps to control the risks to themselves and others*
**c** *to use information to assess the immediate and cumulative risks*
**d** *to manage their environment to ensure the health and safety of themselves and others*
**e** *to explain the steps they take to control risks.*

## _Activity_ Demonstration: Human conduction

The human body as a conductor can be linked to the experiments on frogs described by Galvani and written about in the Pupil's Book. Teachers could introduce the idea of the human body as a conductor using a circuit. A volunteer grips the two copper handles to complete the circuit. The teacher shows that the current is very small. The size of the current depends on the resistance in the circuit (the person) and the battery voltage.

### Equipment
- mounted copper handles constructed from copper pipe
- digital 0–100 µA meter
- cell and holder
- connecting leads

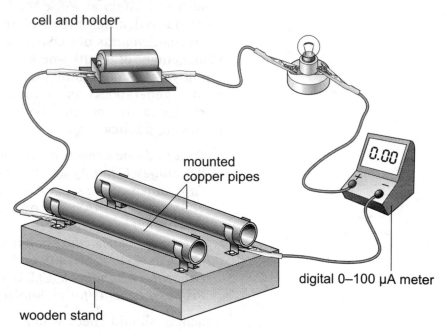

cell and holder

mounted copper pipes

0.00

digital 0–100 µA meter

wooden stand

Teachers can discuss the factors affecting the resistance of the body, such as the moistness of the skin. (Reference could be made to lie detectors.) Teachers should emphasise that the mains at 230 V is potentially fatal. The further information below is for teachers but may prove of interest to pupils.

### The effects of electric shock
- The level of current producing the shock in milliamps is called the shock intensity.
- The product of shock intensity and its duration in seconds is called the shock severity.
- The threshold of sensation is about 0.5 mA. Much smaller currents at high voltages can cause a prickling feeling but they have no effect otherwise.
- Shock currents above 50 mA, unless of extremely short duration, will probably start ventricular fibrillation. The average shock at which men are unable to release themselves has been established as 16 mA; for women it is 10.5 mA. This is sometimes known as the 'no let go current'.
- Following an electric shock quick action is essential. First of all the electricity must be switched off. Respiration can

cease; this can be restored by the use of cardiac pulmonary resuscitation (CPR).

- Body resistance occurs predominately in the skin and it can vary considerably according to conditions. Hard dry skin may have a resistance of more than 10 kΩ, but wet or contaminated skin, or skin that is broken, may have a resistance of only a few hundred ohms.

*Activity*  ## Presentation: Uses of electricity

Pupils can use the Internet to research this area and prepare a presentation on their topic. Topics could include the dangers of mains electricity, the use of electric fences, pacemakers, the historical developments in producing light bulbs, and so on.

## Review

➡ *Worksheet 3.14: Test on electricity*
This worksheet provides a 20–30 minute test to check pupils' understanding of electricity.

## Answers

**1 a)**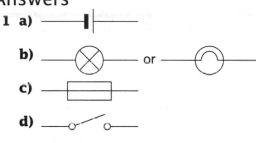

   **b)** ⊗ or ◯

   **c)**

   **d)**

   **e)** (A)

   (5 marks)

**2 a)**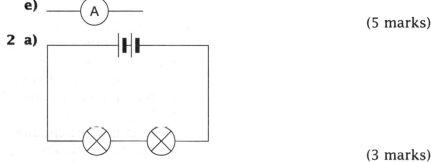

   (3 marks)

   **b)**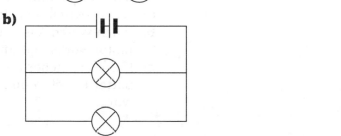

   (3 marks)

   Note. Cells are in series, bulbs are in parallel.

**3** 500 kV.    (1 mark)
**4** 1/1000 A.    (1 mark)
**5** Current (in amps) and voltage (in volts).    (2 marks)
**6 a)** Conductor.    (1 mark)
   **b)** Insulator.    (1 mark)
**7 a)** It glows less brightly with second bulb in series.    (1 mark)
   **b)** When a second bulb is added in parallel, it makes no difference to the brightness.    (1 mark)

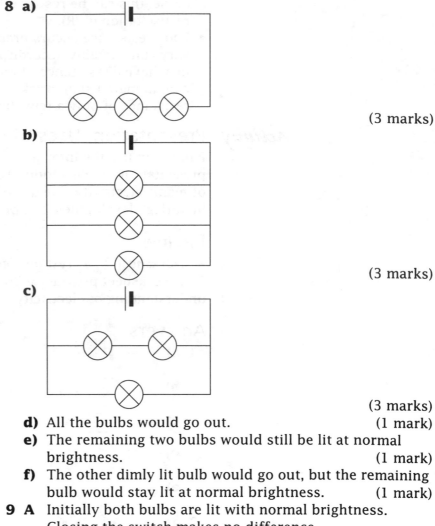

**8 a)** (3 marks)

**b)** (3 marks)

**c)** (3 marks)

**d)** All the bulbs would go out. (1 mark)

**e)** The remaining two bulbs would still be lit at normal brightness. (1 mark)

**f)** The other dimly lit bulb would go out, but the remaining bulb would stay lit at normal brightness. (1 mark)

**9 A** Initially both bulbs are lit with normal brightness. Closing the switch makes no difference.

**B** Initially neither bulb is lit. Closing the switch lights both bulbs normally.

**C** With the switch open, both bulbs are at normal brightness. When the switch is closed, the left-hand bulb is short-circuited and so goes out, and the right-hand bulb shines brighter than normal. (6 marks)

**10 a)** When switch A is closed, the motor works. (1 mark)

**b)** When switch A is opened and switch B is closed, the motor works, but turns in the opposite direction. (1 mark)

**c)** If both switches are closed at the same time the batteries act in opposition and the motor does not work. (1 mark)

# 4 Solids, liquids and gases

## ➡ Rationale

This chapter provides up to 6 hours of teaching materials. The first part builds on the Key Stage 2 work on solids, liquids and gases. The pupils will have identified solids, liquids and gases using characteristic properties such as retention of shape and volume and ease of flow. They should also have looked at the similarities between powders and liquids, explained in terms of the small grains in powders flowing over each other. The key scientific idea in this chapter is particles.

The main aim of the chapter is to introduce the particle theory. Most pupils will find difficulty with the abstract ideas introduced by the particle theory. Many will simply retain the knowledge presented and not yet be able to transfer ideas to other phenomena. They learn how the particle model can be used to explain differences between solids, liquids and gases, and explore how experimental evidence relates to the models. The phenomena of diffusion and gas pressure are examined and explained in terms of particle theory. Discussion of ideas and explanations plays an important role in accessing the knowledge in this topic.

The topic underpins many concepts in Sc2, Sc3 and Sc4 but particularly 'Solutions' in Year 7, 'Atoms and elements', 'Compounds and mixtures' and 'Heating and cooling' in Year 8, and 'Pressure and moments' and 'Using chemistry' in Year 9.

## ➡ Overview

The textbook sections, activities and worksheets have been arranged into 1 hour blocks to aid lesson planning. Clearly several of the activities and worksheets could form part of a homework session. The planning includes reading time for individual sections but some teachers may prefer to organise this as homework preparation for the following lesson. Five types of worksheet – extension (E), support for an activity (S), practical (P), key skills (K) and developmental (D) – allow for differentiation and flexibility to accommodate teachers' preferred practice. The actual timing and emphasis on different sections will depend on the current knowledge base of the pupils, the ability of the teaching group and the preferences of the teacher.

| Lesson | Worksheet |
|---|---|
| **1** Solids, liquids and gases: uses and classification | |
| **2** Evidence for the particle theory | |
| **3** Applying the particle theory | Worksheet 4.1: Applying the particle theory (S)<br>Worksheet 4.2: Pupils as particles (D) |
| **4** Diffusion in liquids and gases | |
| **5** Gas pressure | Worksheet 4.3: Air pressure (P) |
| **6** Reviewing the particle theory | Worksheet 4.4: Review of solids, liquids and gases (S) |
| Review | Worksheet 4.5: Test on solids, liquids and gases |

# ➡ *Chapter plan*

| | **Demonstration** | **Practical** | **ICT** | **Activity** | **Word play** | **Time to think** | **Ideas and evidence** |
|---|---|---|---|---|---|---|---|
| **Lesson 1** | Frying onions<br><br>Solids, liquids and gases | | | Reasoning: What is it? | | What do you know? | |
| **Lesson 2** | The proximity of the particles<br>**1** Solid → liquid<br>**2** Gas<br><br>Marbles in a tray | | | | | | Brownian motion and the kinetic theory |
| **Lesson 3** | | | Using a CD-ROM | Role play: Pupils as particles<br><br>Reasoning: Using models | | Explaining expansion | |
| **Lesson 4** | Diffusion in a solid, a liquid and a gas<br><br>Bromine diffusion in a vacuum<br><br>Ammonia and hydrogen chloride | | | Reasoning: Why does this happen? | | | |
| **Lesson 5** | Collapsing can | Air pressure | | | Scientific meanings | | |
| **Lesson 6** | | | | Discussion: Review of solids, liquids and gases | | Reviewing the particle theory<br><br>Solids, liquids and gases | |

# ➡ *Expectations*

**At the end of this chapter**

**in terms of scientific enquiry**

**most pupils will:** describe and explain observations, using the particle model

**some pupils will not have made so much progress and will:** describe observations and try to offer explanations for them

**some pupils will have progressed further and will:** compare explanations of a phenomenon and evaluate whether evidence supports or refutes them

**in terms of materials and their properties**

**most pupils will:** classify materials as solid, liquid or gas; explain their classification of some 'difficult' materials; describe materials as being made of particles and describe the movement and arrangement of these, and begin to use the particle model to explain phenomena, for example, diffusion in liquids, how a gas exerts a pressure

**some pupils will not have made so much progress and will:** classify materials as solid, liquid or gas and recognise that materials are made of particles

**some pupils will have progressed further and will:** use the particle model to explain a range of phenomena

# ➡ *Links with CASE*

The idea of sorting things into groups and subgroups developed in chapter 2 will be further developed in this chapter because pupils are asked to classify a range of common substances. The introduction of substances such as sand and toothpaste, which do not fit easily into the normal classification system used, creates conflict which the pupils have to resolve. This involves thinking that incorporates and tests class inclusion and exclusion, forcing the learner to look in detail at similarities and differences.

The pupils are introduced to the 'particles in a box' model and use it to explain various phenomena of solids, liquids and gases. The imposition of a model plus the difficulty of relating a two-dimensional model to three-dimensional phenomena can cause difficulties here and many pupils will withdraw from the challenge of explaining phenomena using the model. They revert to a descriptive mode, so lowering the thinking level at which they approach this work.

# ➡ *Pupils' misconceptions*

| Misconception | Scientific understanding |
|---|---|
| There are more than three states of matter, for example powders, 'soft solids'. | Matter exists in three states: solid, liquid and gas. |
| Matter is not permanent – if it 'disappears' (in dissolving), it ceases to exist. | Matter is permanent. |
| Matter is continuous, not particulate. Matter is particulate but the bulk properties are due to the particles changing their form – expanding, shrinking, and so on. | Matter is made up of incredibly small component particles (atoms, ions or molecules). |
| The space between particles in a gas is occupied by air; dirt; germs; oxygen. | There is nothing in the space between the particles. |
| Pressure in gases and liquids acts downwards. | Pressure acts equally in all directions at a given point. Pressure is caused by the impacts of moving particles. |
| Air is weightless. | Air has low density but it does have mass. |

# ➡ *Literacy, numeracy and other cross-curricular links*

There is scope in this chapter to develop pupils' speaking and writing skills. Discussion of evidence and articulating ideas will play an important part in accessing and working with this conceptually difficult topic. Pupils are also encouraged to look carefully at language in scientific and everyday usage. Writing skills are encouraged, especially through imaginative writing where pupils explain phenomena as though they were the particle experiencing it. Numeracy skills are developed through consideration of quantitative experimental results.

## Language for learning

By the end of this chapter pupils will be able to understand, use and spell correctly:

- words with a precise meaning in scientific contexts – evidence, theory, model
- words and phrases relating to the particle model – particle, diffusion, gas pressure, vibration
- words relating to scientific enquiry – evidence, data
- words that have different meanings in science and everyday language – particle, pressure, model.

# 1 *Solids, liquids and gases: uses and classification*

## Learning outcomes
Pupils:

- classify materials as solid, liquid or gas
- offer explanations for the observed differences in some properties of solids, liquids and gases, by linking their existing knowledge to observations
- work together as a team in group discussions to create a solution to a problem which is consistent with the evidence
- use a key to classify materials as solid, liquid or gas
- justify their classification of materials in terms of properties of solids, liquids and gases
- explain why some materials are difficult to classify

The child's view of matter has developed over many years of childhood, making it difficult to break down misconceptions and promote logical thinking even though the child may be equipped with the necessary skills. Even at the age of 14, many children think that there are more than three states of matter (see the section 'Classifying solids, liquids and gases' below). Gases cause particular problems because the common gases are invisible. Air is frequently thought to be weightless. Similarly, when matter disappears from sight (for example when salt dissolves in water) it is thought that it no longer exists.

*Activity* ## Demonstration: Frying onions
One way to begin the topic would be to bring in a frying pan, a bottle of cooking oil and an onion:

- Look at the bottle of cooking oil.
  *What is the shape of the oil in the bottle?*
- Pour some oil into the frying pan.
  *What is the shape of the oil now?*
- Start to cook the sliced onion over a tripod and Bunsen burner. Mention that you love the smell of fried onions.
  *Can anyone else smell it yet? Put your hands up when you can smell it.*
- While the cooking proceeds and the smell diffuses, ask for an example of a solid, a liquid and a gas from the demonstration. Mention that the 'fried onion smell' is a gas. Note that it travelled across the room quite quickly.
  *Why can gases travel across a room but liquids and solids stay where they are?*
  *Why does a liquid spread out when poured but a solid keeps its shape?*

It might be best to keep these two questions rhetorical at the moment. Say that they should be able to give scientific explanations by the end of the topic.

### Safety
Stress that pupils should never eat or drink in the laboratory, no matter how tempting.

## What do you know?

→ *Pupil's Book page 78*

Set the two exercises from the textbook for group work as a timed task (say 10 minutes). Get feedback from the groups to check the level of understanding.

*Activity* ## Demonstrations: Solids, liquids and gases

These simple demonstrations can be used to consolidate this Key Stage 2 work.

- Using three plastic syringes filled with approximately 20 cm³ sand, water and air, show that only the gas can be squashed (**compressed**).
- Using a block of wood, water and a gas jar of carbon dioxide, show that a liquid and a gas can be poured but a solid cannot. For the gas, light a short candle and pour the gas on to it to put it out.
- Pour some orange juice into different containers to show that a liquid takes up the shape of its container.

### Equipment
- three plastic syringes filled with approximately 20 cm³ of sand, water and air
- block of wood, beaker of water and a gas jar of carbon dioxide
- short candle
- orange juice (approximately 150 cm³)
- an assortment of containers such as measuring cylinder (250 cm³), beaker (250 cm³), conical flask (250 cm³)

## Uses of solids, liquids and gases

→ *Pupil's Book page 79*

Refer to the examples in the textbook showing how the uses of solids, liquids and gases are related to their properties.

## Answers

**1 a)** Air is a gas. It can be squashed, giving a more comfortable ride than solid tyres.

**b)** Air-filled tyres can be punctured and the air escapes.

**2** Example answers:

| State | Material | Use | Reasons for use |
|-------|----------|-----|-----------------|
| solid | steel | chassis | strong, hard, rigid |
| liquid | petrol | fuel | can be pumped, takes up the shape of its container |
| gas | air | to inflate tyres | can be pumped, squashy, takes up the shape of its container |

## Classifying solids, liquids and gases

→ *Pupil's Book page 80*

Up to the age of 14, many children think that there are more than three states of matter. For example, powders can be poured, but they are obviously not liquids so children believe that they must belong to another type of matter; and that a substance that is not hard and rigid, such as a lump of rubber, is not a solid and must be something else.

*Activity* Reasoning: What is it?

➡ *Pupil's Book page 81*

**Equipment**

- two beakers (250 cm³), one half-filled with sand (or an hour glass)
- an eraser
- a jelly
- a tube of toothpaste
- rubber gloves
- a piece of sandstone

It is useful for pupils to see a demonstration of the five objects: pour the sand from one beaker to another (or use an hour glass), bend the eraser, shake the jelly, squeeze the toothpaste and the rubber glove. The pupils then work through Q1–3 in groups.

This activity links with the CASE Reasoning pattern: Classification, TS6 and TS7, and it is likely that they will have been covered before this activity. Key points are:

- there can be several ways of classifying a group of objects
- classifications are abstractions and a scientist must learn to stand outside the classification process and observe the nature of the process itself
- the five substances will cause varying difficulty to fit into the key. This should cause some cognitive conflict about the process of classification
- classification systems are a convenience for their creators. They do not necessarily have absolute right or wrong values, they are not laws of nature.

All five materials will create some discussion and give the pupils opportunities to modify their ideas in the light of new evidence.

In the feedback, encourage the pupils to 'think about their thinking' by asking questions to get them to explain their decisions.

**Discussion points**

Sand can be poured and does not have a fixed shape. This is because it is in the form of small grains. Show a piece of sandstone – this cannot be poured.

You could also pour some sand into a measuring cylinder containing some water. Note the bubbles of gas. What is the gas? Does the sandstone contain the gas? In one sense, sand is a mixture with air in between the grains. This can be used to make small grains behave as a liquid (see the questions in the Pupil's Book).

Some pupils may say that the eraser can be squashed, whereas it just temporarily changes shape.

If we think of how jelly is made (with lots of water), then maybe jelly and, similarly, toothpaste are difficult materials to classify because they are mixtures. You could show a lump of jelly from the packet – it behaves like the eraser.

Rubber gloves are made from the same material as the eraser, but this certainly does not have a fixed volume. Again, this is because it is not a single substance. It contains air which is easily squashed/expelled.

## Answers

1 Sand is a solid but with some liquid properties. Rubber gloves and an eraser can be squashed but are solid. Jelly and toothpaste are solid.

2 **a)** All of the examples.

**b)** Because they showed some properties of other groups.

3

4 **a)** It can be easily and quickly fed into the furnace through pipes.

**b)** A powder burns more quickly than lumps.

5 **a)** Solids and liquids are not squashable, but gases are.

**b)** The flour is slightly squashable because it is a fine powder with air trapped between the grains.

## Attainment targets

Work in the previous sections should provide evidence that pupils are working towards the following attainment levels.

| Classify materials into solids, liquids and gases | Level 3 |
| --- | --- |
| Explain why different materials have been classified as solids, liquids or gases | Level 4 |
| Explain why some 'difficult' materials have been classified into solids, liquids or gases | Level 5 |
| Explain the 'unusual' behaviour of some solids | Level 5 |

# 2 *Evidence for the particle theory*

## Learning outcomes

Pupils:

- explain that theories are based on experimental data and that sometimes new evidence results in changes to theories
- describe in writing and by drawing the arrangement, the proximity and motion of particles in solids, liquids and gases

Some children persist in thinking that matter is continuous and not particulate. Their view is based on the 'seeing is believing' principle. Particles cannot be 'seen', so they are not needed to explain the behaviour of matter. Other children who appreciate that matter is particulate find it difficult to completely let go of their naive view and ascribe the bulk properties of matter to the particles themselves, for example that particles can change their form and colour, explode, expand or shrink. Pupils of all ages find it difficult to imagine that there is nothing in the spaces between particles and intuitively fill it with something – air, dirt, germs, oxygen.

It is thought that children are reluctant to use particle ideas because their own theory of matter that they have developed from sensory experiences works perfectly well for them. Even if pupils use particle ideas in lessons, they may not apply them in everyday situations or some may use a primitive model, for example some think that particles expand when they are heated.

In order to overcome these barriers, teachers should not impose a 'scientist's view' directly on to the children but try to involve them as active learners. This is best achieved by a 'cognitive conflict' strategy to encourage children to discuss their ideas and to construct new ones when faced with problems that cannot be solved with their current way of thinking. Feedback should be used to encourage pupils to 'think about their thinking'. Particle theory is a key idea in Key Stage 3 Science and teachers should use bridging whenever the opportunity presents itself throughout the course.

## Ideas and evidence: Brownian motion and the kinetic theory

➡ *Pupil's Book page 82*
This section could be done with pairs of pupils, followed by a whole-class session.

## Answers

1 He had assumed that pollen from a living flower could move because it was also living. This was not expected with a plant that had been dead for 100 years.
2 Movement due to heat currents would be a rising and falling cycle rather than in random directions.
3 Inputs: size of pollen grains and how runny the liquid. Outcome: speed of movement of the pollen grains. Temperature will also affect the speed of the grains.
4 The particles of the liquid were colliding with the pollen grains and making them move in random directions. These particles move faster if they are smaller or if the liquid is more runny.

## The 'particles in a box' model

➡ *Pupil's Book page 83*
This work links with the CASE Reasoning pattern: Formal models. It leads on to 'Explaining states of matter' which are Year 8 CASE lessons focusing on changes of state (TS23–25) and is also part of the Year 8 scheme in *Thinking Through Science 2* ('Heating and cooling').

Some texts show considerable spaces between the particles of a liquid. A reasonable guide is that a pupil's drawing is correct if there is less than a particle diameter gap between the particles and roughly 50% of the particles are touching. A liquid can be viewed as a 'disordered solid'. The particles are very close together unless the liquid is approaching its boiling point. The particles move by swapping places rather than moving freely as in a gas.

As indicated in the 'Pupils' misconceptions' section, page 84, pupils find this key idea very difficult. By the end of Key Stage 3, it is intended that a significant number of pupils have the following understanding of the particle theory:

- Solids: the particles are held in fixed positions by strong attractions in a regular arrangement. They are in contact with each other and they can only vibrate from side to side. They cannot move around.
- Liquids: the particles are still very close together but they are arranged randomly. They are changing positions because they are not as strongly held together.
- Gases: the particles are very far apart, moving very quickly in a totally random way. There is only weak attraction between the particles. They are colliding with each other and with everything around them.

*Activity* ## Demonstrations: The proximity of the particles

These two demonstrations are intended to present the pupils with some evidence concerning the proximity of particles in a solid, a liquid and a gas.

**Demonstration 1: Solid → liquid**

This demonstration is to show that the particles of a liquid are virtually as close as they are in a solid. It uses a boiling tube containing approximately 5 cm depth of either salol or stearic acid that has previously been melted and allowed to solidify (if you use a powder, you may find that the volume of the liquid produced on melting is less than that of the powdered solid).

- Measure the height of the solidified stearic acid in the boiling tube (or mark the level on the side).
- Ask the pupils to predict the resulting level on melting and explain their prediction. Most are likely to predict that the level will rise significantly because of the greater space between the particles.
- Melt the sample – many are surprised to see that the level does not change.

Ask pupils to discuss what this tells us about liquids and solids.

**Equipment**
- one boiling tube with approximately 5 cm depth of melted and solidified stearic acid
- heating equipment
- eye protection
- tongs or boiling tube holder

**Demonstration 2: Gas**

This is to show that the particles of a gas are *very* far apart. It involves vaporising a very small volume of a liquid (methanol) and measuring the volume of the gas (vapour).

- Seal approximately 5 cm$^3$ of air in a glass gas syringe (100 cm$^3$) with a rubber self-sealing cap. Stand this in a beaker containing boiling water.

- Leave for at least 5 minutes so that the syringe becomes very hot.
- Show the pupils the methanol and explain that you are going to turn 0.2 cm³ (say 2 drops) into a gas. Ask for predictions of the resulting volume of gas.
- Draw 0.2 cm³ of methanol into a hypodermic syringe fitted with a long needle (CARE: methanol is flammable and toxic).
- Remove the gas syringe with a towel and clamp securely (but not too tightly) in a horizontal position and inject the methanol through the self-sealing cap (again CARE!).
- If the syringe is hot enough, the methanol will fully vaporise and occupy approximately 80 cm³. If not, replace in the hot water.

Ask pupils to discuss what this dramatic increase in volume tells us about the proximity of the particles in a gas.

### Equipment
- large, tall form beaker
- methanol (approximately 1 cm³) (CARE: highly flammable and toxic)
- glass gas syringe (100 cm³) with rubber self-sealing cap
- hypodermic syringe (1 cm³) plus needle (CARE: keep close control)
- towel

### Mechanical/animated models
The main problems with the diagrammatic versions of the 'particle in a box' model are that they are two-dimensional and static. Animated models should be used at this point to develop the particle theory. For example:

- there are mechanical models that can show a three-dimensional picture of a gas (particularly to visualise gas pressure, which is covered in a later lesson)
- the vibrating particles in a solid can be demonstrated with a three-dimensional cubic model which has weak springs connecting polystyrene spheres
- the use of marbles in a tray can demonstrate the movement of particles (see below).

The use of ICT, video or role play for this purpose is covered in the next lesson.

*Activity* ## Demonstration: Marbles in a tray
The movement of the particles can be shown by shaking some marbles in a shallow tray.

For a solid, tilt the tray slightly so that the marbles run down to one end. Show that the particles are packed closely together and take up a fixed volume and shape. Slight movement can show the vibrations about fixed points. (This model produces the generally more correct close-packing of spheres rather than the open-packing picture that is sometimes presented in texts and exam papers.)

For a liquid, more vigorous movement of the tray causes the particles to swap positions and 'flow' around the tray. They are still very close together but they no longer occupy a fixed shape.

For a gas, remove most of the marbles and vigorously rock the tray. The particles are far apart and moving very quickly, colliding with each other and the sides of the tray (useful to show gas pressure later on).

### Equipment
• one tray, roughly one-third full of same-size marbles

### Attainment targets
Work in the previous sections should provide evidence that pupils are working towards the following attainment levels.

| | |
|---|---|
| Recognise that materials are made up of particles and begin to describe the movement and arrangement of the particles | Level 5 |
| Describe the movement and arrangement of the particles and begin to use this model to explain some properties of solids, liquids and gases | Level 6 |

# 3 Applying the particle theory

## Learning outcomes
Pupils:

• describe in writing and by drawing the arrangement, the proximity and motion of particles in solids, liquids and gases
• state that the particle model is used to explain phenomena which cannot be observed
• describe how particle theory can explain some phenomena

### Use of ICT, video or role play
In addition to physical models of movement such as the 'marbles in a tray', movement of particles can also be shown by using ICT, video or role play:

• use of ICT: for example the CD-ROM *Multimedia Science School*: 'States of matter'
• use of video: for example *Science in Action*: 'States of matter' or 'Air'; *Scientific Eye*: 'Changing state'
• The use of role play with pupils as particles.

*Activity*

## ICT: Visualising
➡ *Worksheet 4.1: Applying the particle theory (S)*
For schools that have the New Media *Multimedia Science School*: 'States of matter', there is a short slideshow ('Solid, liquid and gas') on the CD-ROM. Worksheet 4.1: Applying the particle theory is designed to accompany this slideshow. It helps those pupils who have difficulty visualising the action of particles, which will be most pupils at this stage.

## Answers

**1**

| State | Behaviour of the particles | | |
|-------|---------|-------------|----------|
| | Spacing | Arrangement | Movement |
| solid | very close together | regularly arranged | vibrating |
| liquid | slightly further apart | quite disordered | changing positions with frequent collisions |
| gas | very far apart | totally randomly arranged | fast moving with occasional collisions |

**2 a)** In a solid, the particles are very close together in fixed positions, therefore the solid keeps its shape.

**b)** In a gas, the particles are far apart, therefore they can be pushed closer together.

**c)** The particles in a liquid are constantly changing position, therefore they can easily flow over each other when poured.

*Activity* ## Role play: Pupils as particles

➡ *Worksheet 4.2: Pupils as particles (D)*

This activity allows pupils to demonstrate their understanding of the particle theory for some contexts. It may be advisable to organise this as a lesson away from the laboratory for some classes.

A solid can be represented by pupils tightly linking arms in rows. When pushed, they cannot get much closer together. They can only sway from side to side.

On entering a 'container' made by three benches, the row keeps its shape. The tightly linked arms represent the strong attractions between particles.

A liquid can be represented by pupils holding hands at their sides in a row and occasionally swapping positions (weaker attractions). When pushed, they cannot get much closer together but can change places and shape, for example from a row into a square.

For a gas, the pupils are far apart and moving around, bouncing into each other. There are no attractions between them.

*Activity* ## Reasoning: Using models
## Answers

➡ *Pupil's Book page 84*

**1 a)** A solid keeps its shape because the particles are packed closely together and held in fixed positions by strong attractions.

**b)** In a liquid, the particles are free to move. A liquid does not keep its shape because the particles are not held in fixed positions.

**c)** A gas is easily squashed because the particles are very widely spaced and can be forced closer together.

**d)** A liquid is easy to pour because the particles are free to move past each other. In a solid, the particles are held in fixed positions by strong attractions.

**e)** This question is included here as a lead-in to the next section. It requires application of knowledge to a new situation. The smell of frying onions is a gas. The particles are free to move around in the air which is also a gas.

**2** This is a difficult question. The pupils may choose an answer intuitively, such as 'A liquid is more like a gas', and supply some observational evidence. They may then experience cognitive conflict when they try to use the particle model to back up their answer.

**a)** Supporting Tom's comment, you can also pump a gas and a liquid through a pipe, and a gas and a liquid take up the shape of the container.

**b)** Using the particle theory, a liquid is more like a solid – the particles are very close together with strong attractions between them and with relatively little movement (in a liquid they are changing positions and in a solid they are just vibrating). A liquid can be described as a 'disordered solid'.

## Time to think

➡ *Pupil's Book page 85*

**1** Natasha's answer is the most correct one.

**2** Tom: the particles remain the same size whatever the physical state.

Mira: the balloon would just contain camping gas particles.

Rashid: there should be no dust in the camping gas and it would make no difference if it were there.

Neil: this is not an explanation.

### Attainment targets

Work in the previous sections should provide evidence that pupils are working towards the following attainment levels.

| | |
|---|---|
| Explain why different materials have been classified as solids, liquids or gases | Level 4 |
| Recognise that materials are made up of particles and begin to describe the movement and arrangement of the particles | Level 6 |
| Describe the movement and arrangement of the particles and begin to use this model to explain changing states | Level 7 |

# 4 *Diffusion in liquids and gases*

## Learning outcomes

Pupils:

- describe gas particles as moving all the time and pushing against surfaces
- describe liquid particles as changing positions
- explain observations in terms of particles
- evaluate their own explanations and those of others

Random particle motion in liquids and gases is difficult to understand. In one study involving about 100 undergraduates, none of them attributed dye diffusion to random motion of particles. In another example, students aged 16 and above accepted that gas particles are uniformly distributed in a vessel, but when asked, 'Why don't the particles fall to the bottom?', only around half thought that the particles were in constant motion.

*Activity* ## Demonstration: Diffusion in a solid, a liquid and a gas

The experiments shown on page 86 of the Pupil's Book compare the rate of diffusion in a solid, a liquid and a gas. They could be set up at the beginning of the lesson and changes examined from time to time.

- The water/orange cordial demonstration is set up by placing water in a gas jar or measuring cylinder and then adding the cordial carefully using a bulb pipette.
- The gas jar of bromine vapour is prepared by adding a few drops of liquid bromine to a gas jar and leaving it to vaporise with a lid on. (CARE: bromine is corrosive and toxic. Use eye protection, gloves, fume cupboard.) Note that bromine is a dense liquid and tends to spurt out of a pipette. Any spillages should be treated with a 25% solution of sodium thiosulphate.

### Equipment
- three gas jars or measuring cylinders and one lid
- bulb pipette (25 cm$^3$)
- orange cordial
- liquid bromine and a dropper (CARE: corrosive and toxic)
- eye protection
- protective gloves
- 25% solution of sodium thiosulphate

*Activity* ## Reasoning: Why does this happen?
## Answers

➡ *Pupil's Book page 87*

1 The orange cordial slowly mixes with the water because the particles of a liquid are free to move by changing positions. The bromine gas diffuses quite quickly because the particles of gases are far apart and move freely between collisions.

2 The bromine gas moves rapidly into the vacuum because there are no gas particles in the way for the bromine particles to collide with. It is much slower diffusing into air because of the collisions with the air particles.

3 This question presents an opportunity for some extended, creative writing. Early attempts at this may produce a wide variation in quality. Teachers can exemplify their expectations before the exercise by reading out some 'selected pieces of work of other pupils' and can give model answers after the exercise by reading out some good attempts.

*Activity* ## Demonstration: Bromine diffusion in a vacuum

The bromine diffusion experiments in the Pupil's Book (page 87) could be demonstrated if the apparatus is available. Emphasise that a vacuum contains nothing. Pupils often talk about a vacuum 'sucking' something into it (see the next lesson on 'Gas pressure'). This is an opportunity to overcome that misconception.

- To fill a flask with bromine vapour, place two drops of liquid bromine into the flask, stopper and leave to evaporate. (CARE: use eye protection, gloves, fume cupboard.)
- Connect up to the other flask and turn the three-way tap so that the second flask can be connected to the vacuum pump.
- Evacuate the flask (CARE: use eye protection and safety screen).
- Turn the tap to connect the two flasks.
- Note that the bromine diffuses in a fraction of a second.

### Equipment
- vacuum pump
- safety screen
- glassware as shown in the Pupil's Book, page 87
- liquid bromine and a dropper (CARE: corrosive and toxic)
- eye protection
- protective gloves
- 25% solution of sodium thiosulphate

*Activity* ## Demonstration: Ammonia and hydrogen chloride

The following experiment could also be demonstrated here.

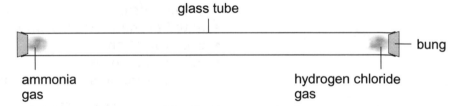

glass tube

ammonia gas

hydrogen chloride gas

bung

The cotton wool plugs are soaked in concentrated ammonia solution to supply the ammonia gas and concentrated hydrochloric acid for the hydrogen chloride gas. (CARE: both are corrosive and toxic.)

The two gases are colourless but where they meet, a white solid (ammonium chloride) is formed as a ring on the inside of the tube. The ring is not formed at the half-way point but more towards the hydrogen chloride end of the tube. This is because hydrogen chloride molecules are heavier than ammonia and therefore travel more slowly.

- If you work quickly, this can be carried out in a well-ventilated laboratory, but it is better to handle the concentrated ammonia and hydrochloric acid solutions in a fume cupboard.
- Soak a cotton wool plug in the hydrochloric acid solution. (CARE: use eye protection, gloves and tweezers.)
- Insert into one end of the tube and seal in with a bung.
- Repeat the procedure as quickly as possible with the ammonia solution. (CARE: use eye protection, gloves and tweezers.)

**Equipment**

- concentrated ammonia solution (CARE: corrosive and toxic)
- concentrated hydrochloric acid (CARE: corrosive and toxic)
- cotton wool
- eye protection
- protective gloves
- plastic tweezers
- long glass tube (approximately 3 cm diameter and at least 60 cm long)
- two bungs to fit into the ends of the tube
- two clamps and stands

# 5 *Gas pressure*

## Learning outcomes

Pupils:

- describe gas particles as moving all the time and pushing against surfaces
- explain that the can collapses because there are fewer air particles on the inside pushing out than on the outside pushing in

Some 11–13 year olds think that only *moving* air (wind) exerts a pressure. Others tend to think that in a gas (or a liquid) the pressure acts mainly downwards rather than in all directions. A common explanation for experiments with drinking straws or syringes involves a vacuum 'sucking' in air or water.

## Gas pressure

## Answer

➡ *Pupil's Book page 88*

**3** Evidence for the existence of air will have probably been covered at primary school and the pupils should readily give examples such as: the washing on a line or leaves on a tree blowing in the wind, feeling the air on your face when riding on a bicycle or waving a hand in front of your face.

*Activity* ## Demonstration: Collapsing can

The collapsing can experiment shown in the textbook can be demonstrated. If you find difficulty in obtaining a cheap supply of cans to collapse, the Gatsby SEP project (www.sep.org.uk) sell a simple attachment that can be used to collapse drinks cans.

**Equipment**

- vacuum pump
- metal can to collapse

*Activity* Practicals: Air pressure

➡ *Worksheet 4.3: Air pressure (P)*

### Experiment 1: Suction pad

When the pad is pressed on to a smooth surface, all of the air is expelled and the rubber forms a seal. Air particles in the atmosphere bombard the pad, holding it in position. Eventually air finds its way between the pad and the surface, resulting in bombardment on both sides and the pad loses its 'suction'.

If the rubber pad is wet, it forms a better seal with the surface and the 'suction' lasts longer.

**Equipment**

Each group will need:

• suction pad or child's toy with suction pad on a spring

### Experiment 2: Yoghurt pot

Most pupils (and adults) would expect the water to pour out of the pot when the force holding the card in place is released. Pupils find this result particularly puzzling because even if they have some grasp of air pressure, they generally believe that it acts *down* on something and not equally in all directions.

The air particles are bombarding the piece of card but there is no balancing air pressure on the other side – only the pressure due to the water. While surface tension keeps the card in place, air pressure pushes upwards balancing the weight of the water.

**Equipment**

Each group will need:

• one yoghurt pot (the type with a wide brim is best)
• one piece of card to cover the top of the yoghurt pot

### Experiment 3: Collapsing can

This is a difficult problem. The partial vacuum is created by condensing the water vapour in the can. The pupils are applying knowledge to an unfamiliar situation and it links together several of the ideas that have been covered (and one that hasn't!).

• Gas particles are far apart, whereas liquid particles are very close together.
• The gas particles in the air are constantly bombarding us.
• A small volume of liquid produces a large volume of gas (and vice versa).
• If a gas (vapour) is cooled down, it will eventually condense to a liquid.
• The result is few gas particles inside the can producing a low pressure and the normal atmospheric pressure on the outside crushes the can (as for the evacuated can at the beginning of the lesson).

**Equipment**

Each group will need:

• eye protection for each pupil
• one empty drinks can
• one clamp
• one bowl for the cold water

## Word play

➡ *Pupil's Book page 88*

Example answers include:

*Particle*

1 I found a small particle of glass in my finger.
2 Each particle of a solid is surrounded by other particles and held in a fixed position.
3 In everyday use, a particle means a 'small piece of' but in scientific use it means 'the smallest possible part of'.

*Pressure*

1 I am under a lot of pressure to get this finished.
2 The air pressure on the can is due to the air particles hitting it.
3 In everyday use, pressure usually has a similar meaning to scientific usage but in the above example there is more a meaning of 'compulsion'.

*Model*

1 The model wore some brightly coloured clothes.
2 The particle model is used to explain why a gas can be compressed.
3 There are very different meanings of the word model even within the two separate categories of everyday usage and scientific usage.

### Attainment targets

Work in the previous sections should provide evidence that pupils are working towards the following attainment levels.

| | |
|---|---|
| Explain why different materials have been classified as solids, liquids or gases | Level 4 |
| Recognise that materials are made up of particles and begin to describe the movement and arrangement of the particles | Level 6 |
| Describe the movement and arrangement of the particles and begin to use this model to explain air pressure | Level 7 |

# 6 *Reviewing the particle theory*

Because of the difficult nature of this concept, pupils need to review their understanding and identify areas of uncertainty. It is intended that about 60 minutes of lesson time is spent on this. Various approaches are available:

- group discussion work using the revision questions in the 'Time to think' section (see below).
- peer-assessment group work using Worksheet 4.4: Review of solids, liquids and gases.
- revision test using Worksheet 4.5: Test on solids, liquids and gases.

## Time to think

➡ *Pupil's Book page 89*

Some of these questions are very similar to earlier ones, but pupils require practice in articulating their ideas in a range of contexts. In the feedback session it would be helpful to highlight the following:

- The particles in a liquid are free to move around and take up the shape of the container. The particles in a solid are held in fixed positions, maintaining a fixed shape.
- When the nitrogen gas is changed into a liquid, the volume decreases dramatically because the particles are far apart in a gas but they are touching in a liquid.
- The dust particles are being hit by particles of air which are moving around freely.
- This is extension work. The particles move more slowly at the low temperature and there is less space between them so the balloon becomes smaller and softer.

*Activity*

## Discussion: Review of solids, liquids and gases

➡ *Worksheet 4.4: Review of solids, liquids and gases (S)*

This is an exercise in peer-assessment. The emphasis should be on 'helping each other to understand'. Also emphasise that the usual rules of group discussion work apply, particularly that all comments should be objective (focused on the two targets) and not subjective (focused on the individual).

### Attainment targets

Work in the previous sections should provide evidence that pupils are working towards the following attainment levels.

| | |
|---|---|
| Recognise that materials are made up of particles and begin to describe the movement and arrangement of the particles | Level 5 |
| Describe the movement and arrangement of the particles and begin to use this model to explain some phenomena such as diffusion in gases and gas pressure | Level 6 |

## Review

➡ *Worksheet 4.5: Test on solids, liquids and gases*

This test should take about 20 minutes to complete.

## Answers

**1 a)**   A = solid; B = gas; C = solid; D = liquid.          (4 marks)
  **b) i)**   metal or plastic                                           (1 mark)
      **ii)**   glass (or plastic if the answer to **i)** is metal)   (1 mark)

**2**

| Solid | Liquid | Gas | |
|---|---|---|---|
| ✓ | | | (If more than one box is ticked award no mark.) |
| | ✓ | ✓ | (If three boxes are ticked award one mark.) |
| | | ✓ | (If more than one box is ticked award no mark.) |

(4 marks)

**3 a)** A is a liquid. (Accept 'A' in the liquid box instead of a tick. If more than one box is ticked award no mark.) (1 mark)
A = petrol **or** oil **or** diesel. (Accept a brand name or paraffin or kerosene.) (1 mark)

  **b)** B is a gas. (Accept 'B' in the gas box instead of a tick. If more than one box is ticked award no mark.) (1 mark)
B = gas **or** natural gas **or** calor (Accept a brand name, gas or butane or propane. Do not accept 'hydrogen' or methane or camping gaz.) (1 mark)

  **c)** C is a solid. (Accept 'C' in the solid box instead of a tick. If more than one box is ticked award no mark.) (1 mark)
C = coal **or** coke **or** wood **or** charcoal (Accept a brand name or 'peat'.) (1 mark)

**4 a)** gas (1 mark)
  **b)** liquid (1 mark)
  **c)** solid (1 mark)

**5 a)** **B** further apart than those in the liquid. (1 mark)
**F** the same size as those in the liquid. (1 mark)
(If more than two answers are given, deduct one mark for each incorrect one (minimum mark zero.))

  **b)** By hitting **or** colliding with the inside of the cylinder. (1 mark)

# 5 Acids and alkalis

## → Rationale

This chapter provides up to 7 hours of teaching materials. At Key Stage 2 pupils will have mixed different materials to show that changes occur; some of these, such as melting, freezing and dissolving, can be reversed but in other cases new materials are produced as a result of a permanent chemical change. Acids are not part of the Key Stage 2 curriculum except when the process of tooth decay is studied but pupils do have preconceptions about acids.

The chapter builds on Unit 6C More about dissolving, and Unit 6D Reversible and irreversible changes. It is helpful if pupils are aware that solids can dissolve and form solutions.

Pupils are introduced to the scientific terms relating to acids and alkalis, safety, and action of acids and alkalis. The work provides them with a range of indicators and opportunities to explore indicator use practically and/or through data. The approach taken encourages pupils to see the use of acids and alkalis in everyday contexts.

This chapter lays the foundation for work taught in chapter 11: Simple chemical reactions and in Year 9, Unit 9E Reactions of metals and metal compounds. It touches upon chemical weathering due to acids, which is covered in Year 8, Unit 8G Rocks and weathering. Acid rain and its effects are included in chapter 11.

## → Overview

The textbook sections, activities and worksheets have been arranged into 1 hour blocks to aid lesson planning. Clearly several of the activities and worksheets could form part of a homework session. The planning includes reading time for individual sections but some teachers may prefer to organise this as homework preparation for the following lesson. Five types of worksheets – extension (E), support for an activity (S), practical (P), key skills (K) and developmental (D) – allow for differentiation and flexibility to accommodate teachers' preferred practice. The actual timing and emphasis on different sections will depend on the current knowledge base of the pupils, the ability of the teaching group and the preferences of the teacher.

| Lesson | Worksheet |
|---|---|
| **1** What do you know about acids? | Worksheet 5.1: What do you know? (D) <br> Worksheet 5.2: Passing its fizzical (P) |
| **2** Introducing alkalis, using indicators | Worksheet 5.3: Colours of indicators (P) |
| **3** Extracting and comparing indicators | Worksheet 5.4: Choosing the best indicator (P) |
| **4** How strong? Use of universal indicator | Worksheet 5.5: How acidic or alkaline? (P) <br> Worksheet 5.6: pH dominoes game (S) |
| **5** Neutralisation | Worksheet 5.7: Getting the balance right (P) |
| **6** Using neutralisation | Worksheet 5.8: What's the plan? (S) |
| **7** Assessment | |
| Review | Worksheet 5.9: Test on acids and alkalis |

# ➡ *Chapter plan*

| | Demonstration | Practical | ICT | Activity | Word play | Time to think |
|---|---|---|---|---|---|---|
| **Lesson 1** | | Acid attack | | Discussion: Acid display <br><br> Evaluation: Testing different liquids on limestone | Corrosive | What do you know? |
| **Lesson 2** | Alkali display | Using indicators | | | | Uses of acids and alkalis |
| **Lesson 3** | | Choosing the best indicator | | Reasoning: Plant indicators <br><br> Evaluation: Orange indicator | | |
| **Lesson 4** | | Universal indicator | | Enquiry: Testing acid <br><br> Game: Playing dominoes | Neutral | pH scale |
| **Lesson 5** | | Neutralisation | Using a pH probe | | | |
| **Lesson 6** | | Applications of neutralisation | | Creative thinking: Neutralisation | | |
| **Lesson 7** | | | | | | Acids and alkalis |

# Expectations

**At the end of this chapter**

**in terms of scientific enquiry**

**most pupils will:** obtain and present qualitative results in a way which helps to show patterns; describe how to deal with hazards relating to acids and alkalis; suggest how to investigate a question about acids and alkalis, planning and making a fair comparison; complete a variables table and identify key errors in an experimental procedure; construct a pH graph with axes provided

**some pupils will not have made so much progress and will:** obtain and present qualitative results; describe some hazards of acids and alkalis; explain how they made a fair comparison in their investigation into acids and alkalis; identify the input and outcome variables, and with help construct a simple variables table

**some pupils will have progressed further and will:** explain how their conclusions match the evidence obtained and suggest ways in which the data collected could be improved; construct their own variables table; construct a pH graph and interpret its shape

**in terms of materials and their properties**

**most pupils will:** name common acids and alkalis and classify solutions as acidic, alkaline, or neutral, using indicators and pH values; describe what happens to the pH of a solution when it is neutralised; describe some everyday uses of acids, alkalis and neutralisation; use their developing ideas of particles to show the difference between dilute and concentrated solutions

**some pupils will not have made so much progress and will:** name some common acids and alkalis; state some everyday uses of acids and alkalis and classify solutions using indicators

**some pupils will have progressed further and will:** explain how a neutral solution can be obtained and relate the pH value of an acid or alkali to its hazards and corrosiveness

# Links with CASE

There are a number of opportunities for pupils to develop the process of recognising variables and controlling and manipulating variables within investigations. The values encountered are both qualitative and quantitative. Dilution of acids requires ideas on proportionality. Classification is also used to group chemicals as acids, alkalis or neutral solutions, and this system evolves and is refined through the use of a variety of indicators, pH and contexts.

# → *Pupils' misconceptions*

| Misconception | Scientific understanding |
|---|---|
| An acid is something that eats material away or that can burn you. | Acids that are strong are corrosive and will burn your skin. Weak acids are not as corrosive as strong acids of the same concentration. Concentrated ethanoic acid is corrosive. Pupils will need a lot of support in differentiating between strong/weak and concentrated/dilute. |
| Neutralisation is the breakdown of an acid or something changing from an acid. | Acids and alkalis are chemical 'opposites' that when mixed form a product that is neutral. |
| Alkali/base is a substance that inhibits the corrosive properties of an acid rather than having corrosive properties of its own. | Strong alkalis such as sodium hydroxide are actually more corrosive because they dissolve protein. |
| Testing for acid can only be done by trying to make it eat something away. It is the acid that is changing colour. | Indicators are special chemicals that change colour in acids or alkalis. |

# → *Literacy, numeracy and other cross-curricular links*

There is scope in this chapter to develop children's speaking and writing skills. Whenever possible, pupils should be encouraged to compare their ideas and discuss their reasoning about the properties of acids and alkalis. Symbolic representation is involved in this topic both in consideration of hazard signage and in word equations.

The chapter contributes to the development of numeracy skills through analysing data, selecting ranges for measuring instruments, and with proportionality in dilutions.

## Language for learning

By the end of this chapter pupils will be able to understand, use and spell correctly:

- words that have different meanings in scientific and everyday contexts – neutral, indicator, equation
- words that are synonyms – corrosive and caustic
- words and phrases related to acids and alkalis – indicator, neutralisation, pH scale, salt
- names of laboratory acids and alkalis – hydrochloric acid, sodium hydroxide, sulphuric acid, ethanoic acid.

## Drawing scientific/chemical apparatus

Pupils often find it difficult to draw apparatus accurately and to switch between three-dimensional drawings in textbooks and two-dimensional images on worksheets or in examination papers. Many of the experimental setups shown in the Pupil's Book have been drawn in 2D and in 3D to show pupils the difference, and these are a useful point of reference to help pupils develop this key skill. Worksheet 0.1 provides an opportunity for pupils to identify and draw two-dimensional apparatus and symbols (see page 2 for notes).

# 1 *What do you know about acids?*

## Learning outcomes

Pupils:

- identify some common acids and their uses
- identify main laboratory acids, and common hazard symbols, for example corrosive
- are able to work safely with acids and explain how to dilute a concentrated acid to make it less hazardous
- compare a range of acids' reactions with magnesium and present their results in a way that makes it easier to recognise a pattern.

## What do you know?

➡ *Pupil's Book page 90*

➡ *Worksheet 5.1: What do you know? (D)*

It is essential to establish pupils' prior knowledge at this stage. Worksheet 5.1 can be used to flag up what they know and also their misconceptions. There is an opportunity to analyse data and pupils are asked to evaluate an experiment. Use of models is important in this lesson as pupils try to visualise dilute and concentrated acids by developing their ideas about particles.

Many schemes would allow a pupil to taste the diluted acid but this is at the discretion of the teacher. If it is done great care must be taken. Make sure that the acid is very dilute and that the apparatus is clean.

There are strong links with the early CASE lessons (TS1 to 5) which focus on the control of and relationships between input and outcome variables.

## Answers

➡ *Worksheet 5.1: What do you know?*

Teachers may find it helpful to refer to the misconceptions table on the previous page. Acids and alkalis are chemical opposites and both can be strong or weak. Alkalis are certainly dangerous.

## *Activity* Discussion: Acid display

Although many acids in the display will be familiar, many pupils believe that acids are all corrosive and this issue needs addressing immediately. Some of the displayed items will be products or reagents with corrosive and other labels. It is useful to build up a collection of different CLEAPSS Student Safety Sheets and pupils can be encouraged to design their own.

### Equipment

- access to a range of household acids, such as vitamin C, vinegar, fruit juices (different brands), fizzy drinks (including cola), aspirin, tea, coffee, washing up liquid
- hazard labels, which can be collected from packaging of chemicals as they arrive in school from suppliers

## Answers

→ *Pupil's Book page 91*

1 and **2** depend on pupils' previous knowledge.

3 Bacteria change trapped food into acid. This acid attacks our teeth causing decay.

4 It produces saliva, which removes the acid. Chewing also helps remove plaque.

## *Activity* Practical: Acid attack

→ *Worksheet 5.2: Passing its fizzical (P)*

The activity allows pupils to look at the effect of different acids on magnesium.

### Equipment

Each group will need:

- magnesium ribbon
- a range of weak and strong acids: hydrochloric (0.4 M is low hazard), citric, ethanoic (0.4 M is low hazard), carbonic (fizzy water), nitric and sulphuric (both at 0.4 M, nitric acid would be irritant only)

### Safety

Eye protection should be worn whenever acids or alkalis are used, including when washing up. Note: safety spectacles are not adequate if solutions are TOXIC and/or CORROSIVE.

This table is intended to assist in the choice of solution concentrations.

| Reagent | Low hazard | Irritant | Corrosive |
|---|---|---|---|
| Hydrochloric acid | < 2 M | 2 M < 6.5 M | 6.5 M or more |
| Nitric acid | < 0.1 M | 0.1 M < 0.5 M | 0.5 M or more |
| Sodium hydroxide | < 0.05 M | 0.05 M < 0.5 M | 0.5 M or more |
| Sulphuric acid | < 0.5 M | 0.5 M < 1.5 M | 1.5 M or more |
| Ammonia | < 3 M | 3 M < 6 M | 6 M or more |

## Answers

1 Corrosive.

2 No, the different lengths of magnesium means this is not a fair test. Check the temperature.

3 Pupil is not wearing eye protection. Bubbles are not visible in the test tubes.

4 Input variable – type of acid.
  Outcome variable – rate of bubbling or amount of bubbling.

5 Probably 2–5 cm of magnesium ribbon and a fixed depth of acid.

6 Bubbling, some tubes get warm/hot. Magnesium gets smaller. Pupils should not use the term 'dissolves'.

7 Probable order: sulphuric, nitric, ethanoic, citric, carbonic. Carbonic acid is carbonated water which will produce bubbles anyway.

8

| Weak acid | Strong acid |
|---|---|
| ethanoic | nitric |
| citric | sulphuric |
| carbonic | |

*Activity* Evaluation: Testing different liquids on limestone
## Answers
→ *Pupil's Book page 92*

1 Input variable – type of acid/liquid.
   Outcome variable – rate of bubbles released.
2 Amount of limestone, volume of liquid, temperature of liquid.
3 Worn eye protection, used small amounts of liquid.
4 It shows that even rainwater is slightly acidic, which may be surprising although people talk about acid rain these days.
5 Most likely answer will be: stomach acid, vinegar, white wine, orange juice, rainwater, pure water. The wording of vinegar, wine and orange juice results makes them more difficult to rank.
6 Count the bubbles, count how quickly bubbles are produced (bubble rate).

## Laboratory acids
## Answers
→ *Pupil's Book page 92*

1 Concentrated hydrochloric acid.
2 All except stomach acid.

## 999: An emergency
## Answers
→ *Pupil's Book page 93*

3 That it is corrosive.
4 More economical, can carry more acid.
5 Other acids, flammables, toxic chemicals, harmful chemicals.

## Diluting acids
## Answers
→ *Pupil's Book page 93*

6 Work slowly, adding the acid a small amount at a time. Use a thermometer for monitoring, control the temperature. Wear protective clothing, eye protection. Have the CLEAPSS Student Safety Sheets available for reference.
7 How to carry bottles of acids, pouring/pipetting into test tubes, dealing with spills of acids.
8 Flag up eyewash station and have a Student Safety Sheet available. (Wash thoroughly with water as indicated on the Safety Sheet. This should be for at least 10 minutes and longer for alkalis.)
9 The 'concentrated' beaker should have a greater number of acid particles in the same volume as the 'dilute' acid beaker.

# 2 Introducing alkalis, using indicators

## Learning outcomes

Pupils:

- identify the range of alkalis and know that many are corrosive
- know that litmus is an indicator which shows a different colour in acids and alkalis
- use their results to identify acids, alkalis and neutral solutions

In this lesson pupils are introduced to a wide range of alkalis and, as with acids, they need to realise that they vary considerably in strength from soap to caustic soda. The term alkali will be less familiar to them and a common misconception is that alkalis are not as harmful as acids. The maximum concentration of sodium hydroxide recommended for use in the laboratory for Key Stage 3 is 0.5 M and the procedure for irrigation of the eye after being splashed with this reagent is very specific. Point out that this chemical feels soapy to the touch because it is hydrolysing skin cells. Sodium hydroxide has a greater effect on wooden benches when spilled and leaves a very stubborn dark stain.

The term indicator is introduced here as a safe method for detecting acid and alkali solutions.

*Activity* ## Demonstration: Alkali display

**Equipment**

- variety of antacids
- cleaning solutions/creams
- toothpaste
- oven cleaners/drain cleaners (should not be handled by pupils and must be used only by the teacher)
- Cif (or similar cleaner)
- Ajax (or similar cleaner)
- ammonia (1 M, if fresh, is a low hazard)
- sodium hydroxide (0.4 M is an irritant)
- CLEAPSS Student Safety Sheets for strong alkalis in the display

**Safety**

This is intended as a classification and observation exercise. If pupils are allowed to handle these items then eye protection should be worn.

## Time to think
## Answers

➡ *Pupil's Book page 95*

1 Nitric, sulphuric, hydrochloric acid.
2 Three from: antacid, cleaners, soap, shampoo, toothpaste.
3 Corrosive chemicals attack and destroy most materials including metals and living tissues – including eyes and skin which have to be protected.
4 CLEAPSS Student Safety Sheets (or Hazcards) tell us the hazards and some of the consequent *risks* associated with the chemicals we use in the laboratory, as well as suitable control measures to reduce the risks from these hazards.

**5** They are strongly alkaline and would harm your skin and eyes. They may have a corrosive sign depending on the concentration. An able group might wish to produce a poster explaining the different risks presented by different concentrations of different reagents.

**6** Weak, since strong alkalis are very corrosive and would be harmful to take.

**7** Use a large volume of water to safely dilute the concentrated acid.

*Activity* Practical: Using indicators

➡ *Worksheet 5.3: Colours of indicators (P)*

The worksheet can be used to help the pupils collate data on the effect of a range of acids and alkalis on litmus indicator. It also helps them realise that indicators change colour in different acid and alkali solutions and that it is not the acid or the alkali that changes.

**Equipment**
Each group will need:

- litmus paper/solution
- selection of acids and alkalis from displays (use the specified concentrations, see below)
- salt water
- sugar solution
- distilled water
- some samples just labelled acid, alkali and neutral

**Safety**
Using solutions with 0.4 M will eliminate any contact with corrosive solutions. Reagents will be irritant or low hazard. Eye protection is essential. Remember that goggles would be essential if any corrosive solutions were used. See table on page 107.

# Answers

| Indicator | Acid | Alkali | Neutral |
| --- | --- | --- | --- |
| red litmus | red | blue | red |
| blue litmus | red | blue | blue |

**Attainment targets**
Work in the previous sections should provide evidence that pupils are working towards the following attainment levels.

| | |
| --- | --- |
| Recognise two different sorts of materials as acidic or alkaline | Level 2 |
| Recognise a wider variety of ways of sorting things into groups (strong acid, weak alkali) | Level 3 |
| Use indicators to classify substances as acidic or alkaline | Level 4 |

# 3 *Extracting and comparing indicators*

## Learning outcomes

Pupils:

- learn how to extract the dyes from different plants
- assess the usefulness of different plant extracts as indicators

In this lesson, pupils are allowed to investigate a range of plant materials and assess their suitability for use as an indicator. Pupils develop their reasoning skills by studying some data on red cabbage. Fresh red cabbage and pickled cabbage on display would provide a good starting point. An account of an extraction of orange juice provides an opportunity for evaluation. Pupils should be encouraged to bring in as many different plants as they can to provide a rich variety for analysis.

*Activity* ## Practical: Choosing the best indicator

➡ *Worksheet 5.4: Choosing the best indicator (P)*

### Equipment

Each group will need access to some of the following:

- red cabbage
- blackberries
- blackcurrant jam
- hydrangea
- fuchsia
- bilberries
- raw beetroot
- elderberries
- rose petals
  (Some items will be seasonal but red cabbage and blackcurrant or blackberry jam should be easily available)
- selection of acids and alkalis such as vitamin C, vinegar, fruit juices (different brands)
- fizzy drinks (including cola)
- aspirin
- tea
- coffee
- washing up liquid
- antacids
- cleaning solutions/creams
- toothpaste
- Cif (or similar cleaner)
- Ajax (or similar cleaner)
- ammonia (1 M)
- sodium hydroxide (0.4 M)
- oven cleaner and drain cleaner (should not be used by pupils, teacher demonstration only)
- CLEAPSS Student Safety Sheets for strong acids and alkalis
- strips of filter paper for pupils to make their own indicator paper

**Safety**
- Wear eye protection.
- Ethanol used to assist in extraction is highly flammable: no naked flames.

## Answer
The choice of indicator will depend upon which plant extract shows clearly as a different colour in each of the three types of solution.

*Activity* ## Reasoning: Plant indicators
## Answers
➡ *Pupil's Book page 96*
1 The indicator changed colour to red in acid and yellow/green in alkali.
2 Milk is neutral.

*Activity* ## Evaluation: Orange indicator
➡ *Pupil's Book page 96*
Improvements should include using smaller pieces of orange, using less than 200 ml of water and using hot water to extract the juice from the peel.

Groups of pupils should produce instructions for the experiment that include clear steps for the method and sensible equipment.

## Comparing different indicators
## Answers
➡ *Pupil's Book page 97*
10 Marigold.
11 Red cabbage, hydrangea, fuchsia.
12 They are difficult to keep fresh and are not always easy to get hold of.
13 **a)** Red. **b)** Red. **c)** Green. **d)** Black. **e)** Red.

# 4 *How strong? Use of universal indicator*

## Learning outcomes
Pupils:

- identify the pH of a solution from a pH chart
- classify solutions as weak/strong acids/alkalis or neutral
- link the use of common acids/alkalis to their strength (for example antacids are weak alkalis)

In this lesson pupils quantify the strength of acids and alkalis using the pH scale. pH actually stands for 'potenz Hydrogen', meaning hydrogen power. Pupils can understand the difference between dilute and concentrated with guidance. The concept of acid/alkali *strength* is much more demanding and it is way beyond the scope of Key Stage 3. It depends on the degree of ionisation of the acid. Hydrochloric acid is fully ionised into hydrogen ions whereas ethanoic acid is only very slightly ionised. This produces vastly different numbers of acid particles (ions) in solution. It is best to link strength at this stage to how corrosive acids are. A major misconception is that acids are more corrosive than alkalis and this issue must be addressed.

There is a worksheet for the pupils to help them organise their work on universal indicator. It is best to say that universal indicator is a man-made indicator and also a mixture of a number of different indicators.

A useful homework activity is a survey of toiletry products such as soaps, shower gels and shampoos with any reference to pH. The pH value is becoming an increasingly popular label on many brands of toiletries.

## Universal indicator
## Answers
➡ *Pupil's Book page 98*
**14 a)** E. **b)** C. **c)** B. **d)** C. **e)** Two.
**15 a)** Potato: acid; rhubarb: acid; radish: acid; hydrangea: alkali.
  **b) i)** Hydrangea.   **ii)** Potato and rhubarb.
  **c)** Indicator.

*Activity* ## Practical: Universal indicator
➡ *Worksheet 5.5: How acidic or alkaline? (P)*

**Equipment**
Each group will need:

- universal indicator paper/solution plus pH scale cards
- range of solutions to include sulphuric acid, hydrochloric acid and ethanoic acid (both at 0.4 M: low hazard), citric acid (1 M: low hazard), lemonade, distilled water, baking soda solution (sodium hydrogen carbonate), potassium hydroxide
- CLEAPSS Student Safety Sheets for strong acids and alkalis

**Safety**
Wear eye protection.

*Activity* ## Enquiry: Testing acid
➡ *Pupil's Book page 99*
Pupils are given the opportunity to plan an investigation into the effect of dilution on the pH of an acid. They are encouraged to use a variables table and this is a key feature of all Sc1 work.

## Answers
**1**

| Variable – what will change | Type of variable – input, outcome, fixed | Values |
|---|---|---|
| concentration of acid | input | strong, medium, dilute |
| volume of acid tested | fixed | 50 cm³ |
| pH of acid tested | outcome | between 1 and 6 |

**2** Use universal indicator.

**3** Possible extra readings could be:

| Volume of acid (cm²) | Volume of water (m³) | Total volume (cm³) |
|---|---|---|
| 10 | 40 | 50 |
| 0 | 50 | 50 |

**4** To keep the volume constant and make it a fair test.
**5** Add a small amount of acid to a large volume of water.

*Activity* ## Game: Playing dominoes

➡ *Worksheet 5.6: pH dominoes game (S)*
Pupils can use the dominoes game to reinforce their understanding of the pH scale.

### Attainment target
Work in the previous sections should provide evidence that pupils are working towards the following attainment level.

| Describe the pH scale to sort substances into different categories of acidity/alkalinity (strong/weak) | Level 5 |
|---|---|

# 5 *Neutralisation*

## Learning outcomes
Pupils:

- explain how to obtain a neutral solution
- describe the change in pH when an acid neutralises an alkali

It is important to establish how pH changes during neutralisation and that a temperature change occurs. At the end of the lesson pupils must be clear that the product is neutral – neither acid nor alkali. Here the emphasis is on chemical opposites reacting with each other. (Link with chapter 11 Simple chemical reactions.)

*Activity* ## Practical: Neutralisation

➡ *Worksheet 5.7: Getting the balance right (P)*
The worksheet can be used to aid the practical and also to assist in constructing the graph to show both pH change and change in temperature. Since both acid and alkali are weak the curve will not correspond to the graph in the Pupil's Book (on page 102) but the general shape will be typical of a neutralisation reaction.

### ICT opportunity
A pH probe can be used to monitor changes taking place.

### Equipment
Each group will require:

- dilute colourless ethanoic acid (1 M)
- powdered calcium hydroxide (could also be labelled gardener's lime)
- thermometer
- stirring rod

ICT link: if available, a pH probe connected to computer. *Insight 2* is an excellent software package and is compatible with most dataloggers.

**Safety**
Wear eye protection.

## Answers

1 pH 3/4, weak.
2 This will depend upon the graph – where it shows the pH at 7, pupils will need help to read the amount off the graph. This is a good opportunity for estimating.
3 pH of dissolved gardener's lime = 10.5, making it weak.
4 The temperature increases and will drop once the reaction is complete. This can be a point for discussion with more able pupils.

## Making use of acids and alkalis
## Answers

➡ *Pupil's Book pages 100–101*
16 Weak alkali.
17 Neutralisation takes place.
18 They help neutralise the acid produced by bacteria in our plaque.
19

| Variable – what will change | Type of variable – input, outcome, fixed | Values |
|---|---|---|
| toothpaste | input | different brands |
| pH | outcome | 1–14 |
| amount of toothpaste | fixed | 1 g |

20 Strong: its pH is between 1 and 2.
21 Weak alkalis.
22 It is a strong alkali and very corrosive.
23 It is neutralised.
24 Extra acid in their stomach.

# 6 *Using neutralisation*

## Learning outcomes
Pupils:

* know the uses of acids and alkalis in a range of everyday situations
* understand the importance of neutralisation in: soil treatment, curing acid indigestion, pH balanced skin products and toothpaste pH.

There is a good choice of activities, which extend pupils' knowledge and understanding of neutralisation. The choice of reagents in neutralisation is crucial so that the use of weak acids or alkalis in these situations can be discussed.

It may be useful to demonstrate the neutralisation of acid using antacid tablets at this point, either using litmus to track the changing pH or by incorporating datalogging using a pH probe.

*Activity* Practical: Applications of neutralisation

→ *Worksheet 5.8: What's the plan? (S)*

If lessons are 1 hour or less then an extra lesson should be allowed for this extended enquiry. A variety of tasks is suggested. The toothpaste and soil tasks are more straightforward than the other two and may be more appropriate for groups of pupils who have not done much laboratory work.

The emphasis is on the applications/uses of neutralisation in familiar situations. The worksheet helps pupils to consolidate the skill of planning a fair test.

The class can be divided into teams, each carrying out a different investigation and producing a report for the class. This could be in the form of a poster, talk, OHP transparency, PowerPoint presentation, or leaflet.

**Equipment**

1 For the toothpaste survey, each group will need:
   • access to a variety of toothpaste brands
   • test tubes with stoppers
   • pH paper and pH charts
2 For the soil analysis, each group will need:
   • access to loamy soil, chalky soil, sandy soil, clay-based soil, plus one soil pretreated with calcium hydroxide to produce a pH of 8/9
   • filter papers and funnels
   • test tubes with bungs
   • pH papers and charts
3 For the dock leaves analysis, each group will need:
   • pestle and mortar
   • sharp sand
   • ethanol (highly flammable label)
   • pH paper and charts
4 For the shampoo/skin product survey, each group will need:
   • pH paper charts
   • test tubes and bungs
   • a range of shampoo/skin product brands (include the Johnson pH 5.5 range, if possible)

*Activity* Creative thinking: Neutralisation

Answers

→ *Pupil's Book page 102*

1 pH 7.
2 25 cm³.
3 Strong alkali.
4 This is an opportunity for some creative thinking!
5 Since the pH changes from about 12 (alkali) to 2 (acid) a new chemical must have been produced.
6 It has a better calibration. Each 10 cm³ is divided into ten whereas on the measuring cylinder only whole numbers are given.

**Attainment target**

Work in the previous sections should provide evidence that pupils are working towards the following attainment level.

| Identify and describe similarities between some chemical reactions | Level 6 |
|---|---|

# 7 *Assessment*

## Time to think

➡ *Pupil's Book page 103*

Pupils should complete Q1 before starting the test to revise and consolidate what they have learnt in the chapter. Pupils who finish the test early may like to do Q2. Alternatively, Q2 could be done as a homework task.

## Review

➡ *Worksheet 5.9: Test on acids and alkalis*

The test should take about 20 minutes to complete.

## Answers

1 **a)** alkali; **b)** neutral; **c)** alkali; **d)** neutralisation;
   **e)** sour; corrosive.           (1 mark each)

2 **a)** red; **b)** blue; **c)** red; **d)** blue.    (1 mark each)

3 **a)** orange; **b)** yellow; **c)** blue; **d)** violet.   (1 mark each)

4 **a)** neutralisation;                   (1 mark)
   **b)** bee: acid (baking soda: alkali); wasp: alkali (lemon juice: acid).                (1 mark each)
   **c)** alkali.                     (1 mark)
   **d)** Chop into small pieces.
      Place into pestle and mortar.
      Add a few drops of alcohol.
      Crush until all the colour has been removed.
      Use a dropping pipette to place extract into a test tube.
                     (1 mark each)

5 **a)** purple; **b)** green; **c)** neutral.    (1 mark each)
   **d)** The alkali: 25 cm³ of alkali needed 100 cm³ of acid to neutralise it.             (2 marks)

6 NaOH is a strong alkali;
  harmful to soil;
  needs a weak alkali;
  neutralises acid;
  without harming creatures in the soil.    (1 mark each)

# 6 Forces and their effects

→ ## *Rationale*

This chapter provides up to 8 hours of teaching materials. Pupils should already have done quite a lot of work on forces at Key Stage 2 and this chapter builds on their earlier work on forces of attraction and repulsion. They will have covered friction and air resistance in Unit 4E Friction, and other forces in Unit 6E Balanced and unbalanced forces. They should have used forcemeters to measure forces. They should know that forces are measured in newtons, and that weight is a force. They should have been introduced to diagrams illustrating forces acting on objects. Nevertheless, confusion can very easily arise between the forces acting on an object which is in equilibrium and the action and reaction forces of Newton's Third Law where two equal and opposite forces act on *different* bodies. This chapter consolidates their earlier work, and attempts to present the material in a fresh way, with quite an emphasis on opportunities for using ICT. Work on forces is an important part of the Key Stage 3 curriculum.

The chapter covers three main ideas. The first part (lessons 1 to 4) looks at forces and their effects, identifying types of forces and what they do. There is an introduction to forces and motion, including reaction times, and to handling data and interpreting graphs. The work on reaction time links to road safety and stopping distances of vehicles. The second part of the chapter (lessons 5 and 6) looks at floating and sinking, density, and the difference between mass and weight. The third part covers stretching and the use of forcemeters (lesson 7), and frictional forces and air resistance (lesson 8).

Throughout the chapter there is an emphasis on interpreting graphs. Numerical calculations are introduced on speed and also on density.

The work on forces lays the foundations for future work on gravity (Unit 9J Gravity and space); the relationship between forces and motion (Unit 9K Speeding up); and the relationship between force and area and the action of levers (Unit 9L Pressure and moments).

# ➡ Overview

The textbook sections, activities and worksheets have been arranged into 1 hour blocks to aid lesson planning. Clearly several of the activities and worksheets could form part of a homework session. The planning includes reading time for individual sections but some teachers may prefer to organise this as homework preparation for the following lesson. Five types of worksheet – extension (E), support for an activity (S), practical (P), key skills (K) and developmental (D) – allow for differentiation and flexibility to accommodate teachers' preferred practice. The actual timing and emphasis on different sections will depend on the current knowledge base of the pupils, the ability of the teaching group and the preferences of the teacher.

| Lesson | Worksheet |
|---|---|
| **1** Introduction | Worksheet 6.1: What do you know about forces? (P) Worksheet 6.2: Balanced and unbalanced forces (S) |
| **2** Reaction time | Worksheet 6.3: Measuring reaction time (P) (alternatives: with and without IT) |
| **3** Measuring speed | Worksheet 6.4: Calculating speed (K) Worksheet 6.5: Measuring the speed of a trolley running down a slope (P) (alternatives: with and without IT) |
| **4** Interpreting graphs | Worksheet 6.6: Using a motion sensor (P) Worksheet 6.7: Time to think (S) |
| **5** Floating and sinking | Worksheet 6.8: Floating and sinking (D) |
| **6** Density | Worksheet 6.9: Density, volume and mass (P) (Excel version as alternative) |
| **7** Stretching a spring | Worksheet 6.10: An experiment to stretch a spring (P) (Excel version as alternative) |
| **8** Friction and air resistance | Worksheet 6.11: Parachute (P) Worksheet 6.12: Pulling shoes on different surfaces (P) Worksheet 6.13: Investigating a paper spinner (P) |
| Review | Worksheet 6.14: Test on forces |

# Chapter plan

| | Demonstration | Practical | ICT | Activity | Word play | Time to think | Ideas and evidence |
|---|---|---|---|---|---|---|---|
| **Lesson 1** | | Forces | | | Forces | What do you know?<br><br>Types of forces | |
| **Lesson 2** | | | Using spreadsheets | Information processing: Reaction time | | | |
| **Lesson 3** | | Measuring speed | Using a spreadsheet<br><br>Datalogging using light gates | Numerical: Calculating speed<br><br>Information processing: Animal speed | | | |
| **Lesson 4** | | Motion | Using a motion sensor<br><br>Using spreadsheets | Reasoning: Train travel<br><br>Information processing: Road safety | | Road safety<br><br>Time to think | |
| **Lesson 5** | Floating and sinking | Floating | | Enquiry: Upthrust | | | Upthrust and Archimedes |
| **Lesson 6** | | Finding density | Using a spreadsheet | | Weight | | |
| **Lesson 7** | | Stretching | Using a spreadsheet | Information processing: Stretching springs<br><br>Reasoning: Stretching elastic bands | | | |
| **Lesson 8** | Guinea and feather | | Simulations of terminal velocity | Reasoning: Friction<br><br>Investigation: Friction<br><br>Simulations: Terminal velocity | | Concept map | Bicycles |

# Expectations

**At the end of this unit**

**in terms of scientific enquiry**

**most pupils will:** make predictions about upthrust, test these and relate their findings to scientific knowledge; make suitably precise observations, including repeats to check reliability, and use these to plot graphs; investigate friction, identifying and controlling key factors

**some pupils will not have made so much progress and will:** make predictions about upthrust, test these and identify patterns in their results; with help plot graphs of their results; make relevant observations using appropriate equipment

**some pupils will have progressed further and will:** explain how they made a fair comparison in their investigation of friction; interpret their results on floating, using knowledge of balanced forces to explain conclusions; explain how the scales they chose and lines they drew on graphs enabled them to show data effectively

**in terms of physical processes**

**most pupils will:** identify directions in which forces act and describe situations in which forces are balanced; distinguish between mass and weight, giving examples; describe some ways of reducing friction and some situations in which friction is useful; describe what is meant by speed

**some pupils will not have made so much progress and will:** identify forces, for example, friction, upthrust and weight; recognise that friction opposes motion, upthrust pushes upwards and weight pulls downwards; compare speeds qualitatively

**some pupils will have progressed further and will:** show how forces can combine to give a resultant effect which depends on both the sizes and directions of the forces; describe how weight is caused by gravity; explain contact friction in simple terms

# ➡ *Links with CASE*

The main thinking skills promoted are those related to variables and relationships. The approach to variables in this chapter is designed to promote problem solving as well as focusing on forces and their effects. When stretching a spring, pupils look at the relationships between two variables. This links with the CASE activity TS3 'What sort of relationship?'. Interpreting the distance–time graphs is a further opportunity for pupils to develop their visualisation of relationships between two variables.

The work on floating and sinking leads to an appreciation of Archimedes' principle and is associated with compound variables. The work on speed also involves the use of compound variables.

The work on reaction time where pupils plot scatter graphs provides a simple introduction to the idea of correlation which is one of the reasoning patterns identified in CASE lessons. Ideas of proportionality and scale are also used in the representation of forces through the size of arrows in diagrams.

# ➡ *Pupils' misconceptions*

| Misconception | Scientific understanding |
|---|---|
| Non-scientific use of the word force relating to ideas of compulsion, or to living things. | A force has two characteristics: size and direction. |
| When a moving object stops, it runs out of 'force'. | There is a clear distinction between force and energy. |
| Pupils often only consider one of a pair of forces. | There are often two or more pairs of forces acting. |
| When something is moving at a steady speed there is a steady force acting on it. | No resultant force is needed to keep an object moving at a steady speed. |
| Friction acts all the time. | If an object is at rest, then the forces acting on it must be balanced. |
| The words weight and mass can be interchanged. | Weight is the force of gravity on an object and is measured in newtons. Mass is measured in kilograms and does not change even if gravitational pull varies. |

# ➡ *Literacy, numeracy and other cross-curricular links*

This chapter provides opportunities for developing children's speaking and writing skills. At the start of the chapter pupils are encouraged to share ideas about forces by discussing a number of pictures to help them to organise their thoughts and to make sense of their own ideas. There is an emphasis on the correct use of everyday words in a scientific context with particular reference to the word force.

The chapter has extensive opportunities to consolidate numeracy skills in producing and interpreting information in the form of line graphs as well as practice at performing numerical calculations. Pupils build on their Key Stage 2 experience of finding averages and ranking numbers.

## Language for learning

By the end of this chapter pupils will be able to understand, use and spell correctly:

- words that have different meanings in scientific and everyday contexts – force, pressure, weight
- words relating to forces and their effects – density, upthrust, repulsion, attraction
- words and phrases related to graphing skills – line of best fit.

## ICT opportunities

This chapter provides a variety of opportunities for ICT development. Pupils can use the Internet or CD-ROMs to find relevant information, for example on bicycles. ICT skills in presenting data will be developed through production of bar graphs and line graphs. Pupils will also have an opportunity to use spreadsheets to present data from an experiment on reaction times. A different use of spreadsheets is provided by using the *Multimedia Science School* CD-ROM on terminal velocity. Often pupils get 'bogged down' with the calculations. Using a spreadsheet allows pupils to easily perform the calculations and this allows additional time for analysis of results.

Calculations on speed are done through the use of light gates to measure time. This speeds up the experiments on speed–time measurements. Software such as *Insight* presents the results quickly and effectively.

There are many computer simulations available to model reaction times and stopping distances. Pupils find them fun and they are at the same time instructive.

A different type of datalogging is achieved using a motion sensor where the pupils' motion is displayed directly on screen as they move.

# 1 *Introduction*

## Learning outcomes

Pupils:

- identify different types of forces including gravity, electrostatic, magnetic, twisting
- describe forces as 'pulls' or 'pushes'
- distinguish between forces of attraction and forces of repulsion
- understand that forces can deform an object
- measure forces using forcemeters

The time spent on this section depends on pupils' prior knowledge.

## What do you know?

➡ *Pupil's Book page 104*

The introductory activity is designed to find out pupils' understanding of friction; of terminal velocity; their ability to draw force diagrams and represent both the magnitude and direction of the force (the difference between force and direction of the football); their understanding of the difference between weight and mass, and how gravity effects the weight of an object; and of balanced forces and upthrust. Several misconceptions, such as the Moon has no gravity, may occur.

## Answers

1 Curling stone is sliding at an almost constant speed. There must be little friction between the ice and the stone to allow this. The small amount of friction acts to gradually slow the curling stone down.
2 The parachutist would speed up until a high terminal velocity had been reached. She could have spread out her body to present the maximum air resistance. The astronauts would continue to speed up because the parachutes would be ineffective, due to the fact that there is no air resistance

on the Moon. However, the gravitational pull of the Moon is about one-sixth of that on Earth so the astronauts' increase in speed per second (acceleration) would be less. This means that, falling from the same height on both the Earth and the Moon, the astronauts would take longer to reach the surface of the Moon but the impact velocity would be less.

3 Air resistance and gravity. Pupil's drawing should show a downward arrow to indicate gravity and an arrow pointing right to indicate air resistance. The coloured arrow to indicate direction should point left (in the exact opposite direction to air resistance).

4 Measuring weight of potatoes. The reading would be reduced by one-sixth, i.e. 1.2.

5 Gravity acting downwards and water pushing upwards. It would not float. Polystyrene, balsa wood, cork, etc.

## *Activity* Practical: Forces

➡ *Worksheet 6.1: What do you know about forces? (P)*
Teachers may wish to reinforce this introduction with a practical session. Some suggestions include:

- pupils weigh objects using a forcemeter
- use a variety of forcemeters to exert forces to open a drawer
- look at forces between two balloons electrostatically charged by rubbing
- look at the forces of repulsion between two cylindrical magnets (as described in the Pupil's Book, page 107)
- use a chest expander
- measure the force they can exert with their hands using bathroom-type scales
- look at the force required to move an object horizontally across a table.

Pupils should produce a diagram for each example with an arrow showing the direction of the force.

### Equipment
This will depend on the range of equipment available in the school. The activities are only suggestions. Teachers may substitute and add their own activities depending on the equipment available.

*Activity 1:* The drawer can be pulled open with a range of forcemeters.

*Activity 2:* Bathroom-type scales are used. Pupils squeeze them between thumb and finger to obtain the measurement.

*Activity 3:* This is best performed with the scales held vertically against the wall and the pupil sitting on the floor pushing against the scales.

*Activity 4:* This activity is designed to highlight the difference between frictional force and the weight of the brick (activity 5). Teachers may wish pupils to compare the forces needed to pull the brick on different surfaces or to use different objects of similar mass.

*Activity 5:* This requires a spring balance with a range appropriate to the object being lifted.

*Activity A:* The two balloons should be suspended by long nylon threads from the ceiling. They can be charged by rubbing with a duster. As with all statics experiments, this works best on a dry day.

*Activity B:* If ring magnets are not available, you can use two bar magnets in a wood or plastic track.

*Activity C:* An alternative to a chest expander is to use the retaining cords designed for car roof-racks.

*Activity D:* The 'model hovercraft' could be a simple polystyrene cylinder with a balloon attached on top, or made more sophisticated with a simple motor, fan and small battery.

*Activity E:* If the school does not possess an 'Eclipse' magnet, an alternative is to use an electromagnet.

## Balanced and unbalanced forces

➡ *Worksheet 6.2: Balanced and unbalanced forces (S)*
The worksheet could be used as homework or for work in class.

## Answers

1 Forces are balanced – bent plank is pushing back on the boy with a force equal to the boy's weight. The ends of the plank are pushing down on the boxes, which also push back.
The plank does not keep bending because the forces are balanced.
With two people, the plank bends downwards about twice as much.
The plank pushes back with a force equal to the weight of the the two people.

2 Arrow should be pointing to the back of the sail. The boat moves forwards.

The force pushing the sail is equal to the drag on the boat by the water.

3 Gravity. It causes the ball to speed up (accelerate).

4 Gravity down and air resistance up. They are equal, otherwise the parachutist would be speeding up or slowing down.

## Forces, forces everywhere
## Answer

➡ *Pupil's Book page 108*
1 Magnetic force.

## Showing forces
## Answers

➡ *Pupil's Book page 109*

**2** With no net the ball would carry on at a constant speed. With a brick wall the ball would bounce back at almost the same speed.

**3** Examples could include the following:
kicking a ball, pushing a shopping trolley, catching a ball, whirling a conker on a string, squashing modelling clay.

### Attainment target

Work in the previous sections should provide evidence that pupils are working towards the following attainment level.

| | |
|---|---|
| Make generalisations about physical phenomena such as how forces can affect the motion, position or shape of an object | Level 4 |

# 2 *Reaction time*

## Learning outcomes

Pupils:

* recognise that when measurements are repeated, the same result may not be obtained; but repeating readings allows them to get closer to the true value and gives a more reliable result
* identify that, for a given vehicle, the stopping distance depends on its speed, the reaction time of the driver, the weather conditions and the road surface
* use a spreadsheet to present data in a scattergraph
* enter formulae into a spreadsheet and use it to draw a scattergraph (higher ability)
* interpret information gained from a CD-ROM or the Internet

Worksheet 6.6: Using a motion sensor links closely with the work in this lesson, so depending on time available you may interchange or combine parts of lessons 2 and 4. (For details on Worksheet 6.6, see page 130.)

*Activity* ## Information processing: Reaction time

➡ *Pupil's Book page 110*

➡ *Worksheet 6.3: Measuring reaction time (P)*

The material in the Pupil's Book gives an example of calculating reaction time. Pupils use the graph to read off their reaction time having measured the distance fallen by a ruler. The importance of repeated measurements to get greater reliability is a feature of this section. Worksheet 6.3 provides two possible approaches to measuring reaction time, one using Excel and the other without the aid of ICT. The first part of the worksheet instructs pupils to collect their own data and enter their results into a table or the spreadsheet 'Reactiontm1.xls' on the CD-ROM, which will calculate the average distance fallen by the ruler automatically. Pupils can then work out their own reaction time using the graph in the Pupil's Book, page 111.

The second part can be used to explore patterns in data by adding additional columns for variables such as height, weight, eye colour, etc. Spreadsheets 'Reactiontm2.xls' and 'Reactiontm3.xls' are provided for this part of the activity. Only one computer is needed, but if more than one computer is available pupils can pool their results and so increase their sample size. They can then plot scatter graphs to look at the relationship between reaction time and another variable.

**Equipment**
- 0.5 m ruler
- computer with Excel (optional)

## Answers
➡ *Pupil's Book page 111*

**1** 0.19 s.

**2** Vesna 0.24 s.

**3** Lesley.

**4** Some had noticeably different reaction times with their left and right hands. This could be because they were left or right handed. More evidence would be needed.

**5** 19 cm.

**6** 4.5 cm.

**7** Less than 0.17 s. Nathalie and Lesley are the only ones who would have been likely to frequently catch the note with either hand.

**8** An average of the four readings will be more likely to give a typical value for that person.

## Road safety
➡ *Pupil's Book page 112*

The rest of this lesson may be combined with the following lesson or left until lesson 4. There is an opportunity to discuss the importance of reaction time in calculating the stopping distance of a car. The other factors involved in affecting the stopping distance of cars could be discussed, including drugs and the speed of the vehicle. There are a number of computer simulations which pupils can use involving reaction time and thinking distance.

## Answers
**4**

| | |
|---|---|
| Thinking time | The greater the thinking time, the further the stopping distance. |
| Type of car | Different cars will have different quality brakes. An old car may have poor brakes, a modern car may have an automated braking system (ABS). |
| Weight of car | The heavier the car, the harder it is to stop. |
| Weather | Wet weather or ice will increase the stopping distance. |
| Speed of car | As the speed of the car increases, the stopping distance becomes much further. |
| Type of road surface | A poor road surface would increase the stopping distance. |

**5** 70 m.p.h. is about 112 km/h.

# 3 *Measuring speed*

## Learning outcomes

Pupils:

- explain the various units in which speed is measured including m.p.h., km/h and m/s
- know that speed = distance/time
- understand that as an object moves down a slope its speed increases
- use light gates to measure time intervals (some pupils)

### *Activity* Numerical: Calculating speed

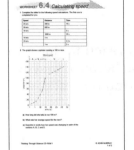

➡ *Pupil's Book page 113*
➡ *Worksheet 6.4: Calculating speed (K)*

This follows on closely from the previous lesson and introduces how speed is calculated. Two calculations are provided in the Pupil's Book, and Worksheet 6.4 has further numerical problems for practice.

## Answers

➡ *Worksheet 6.4: Calculating speed*

**1**

| Speed (m/s) | Distance (m) | Time (s) |
|---|---|---|
| 20 | 200 | 10 |
| 30 | 600 | 20 |
| 10 | 50 | 5 |
| 50 | 1000 | 20 |
| 10 | 5 | 0.5 |
| 20 | 10 | 0.5 |
| 0.5 | 1 | 2 |

**2 a)** 15 s
  **b)** 6.7 m/s
  **c)** A almost steady speed, B going faster, C going even faster, D slowing down.
  **d)** In the middle of section C.
  **e)** 40 m
**3 a)** 30 km
  **b)** 5 h
  **c)** 3.00 p.m.

**d), e)**

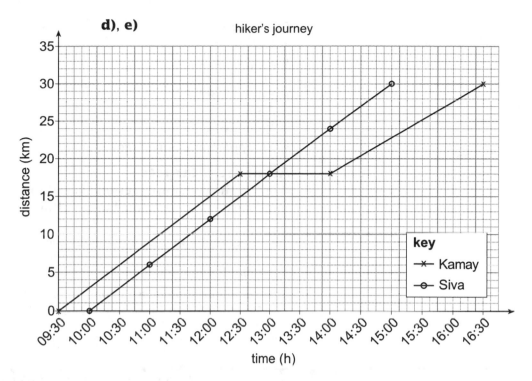

hiker's journey

*key*
- ✕ Kamay
- ⊸ Siva

distance (km) / time (h)

**f)** 1.00 p.m.
**g)** 18 km

## *Activity* Information processing: Animal speed

➡ *Pupil's Book page 114*

If computers are available, the pupils could do the work on the speeds of animals using Excel. Spreadsheet 'Animalspeed.xls' on the CD-ROM can be used for this activity. They could also research other animals and enter those results.

### Answers

**1** The names of the animals.
**2** The speed.
**3** Swift.
**4** Tiger shark.
**5** Four.

## *Activity* Practical: Measuring speed

➡ *Worksheet 6.5: Measuring the speed of a trolley running down a slope (P)*

Weather permitting, pupils could go outside and measure their own speeds for running 50 m, or hopping 50 m. Again results could be entered into a spreadsheet, particularly useful for weaker pupils who might find the calculations tedious.

Inside the laboratory, pupils could measure the time taken for a trolley to run down a slope by timing it over a fixed distance. If you have a computer and light gate available then pupils can use these to explore the way in which the speed changes as the trolley runs down the slope. They measure the speed at different distances from its release point. It is important that they understand how the computer calculates the speed from the time measurement and the length of the card. Worksheet 6.5 gives two possible alternatives for carrying out the practical, one using ICT and one without.

**Equipment**
• trolley
• long runway
• stop clock
• pile of books
*optionally:*
• light gates
• computer and interface

**Attainment targets**
Work in the previous sections should provide evidence that pupils are working towards the following attainment levels.

| Make generalisations about physical phenomena such as how forces can affect the motion, position or shape of an object | Level 4 |
| --- | --- |
| Use some quantitative definitions, for example speed, and perform calculations using the correct units | Level 7 |

# 4 *Interpreting graphs*

## Learning outcomes
Pupils:

• describe the journey shown in a distance–time graph

*Activity* ## Practical: Motion

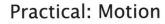

➡ *Worksheet 6.6: Using a motion sensor (P)*
As an introduction to this lesson, a very effective approach is to use a motion sensor and computer. A 'volunteer' pupil moves towards and away from the sensor and the motion is displayed interactively on the monitor as a distance–time graph. Worksheet 6.6 suggests a possible approach. It may need altering, depending on the type of motion sensor you possess.

*Activity* ## Reasoning: Train travel
Spreadsheets 'MidlandMetro.xls' and 'Lift.xls' on the CD-ROM can be used for this activity.

## Answers
➡ *Pupil's Book page 115*
1 About 40 km.
2 20 min.
3 150 min.
4 The trains will not travel at a steady speed; they will slow down, stop and accelerate.
5 The tram is moving when the trace on the graph produces an upward slope.
6 Nine times.
7 About 26.5 min.
8 It stops on the way up to let people in or out. It moves at the same speed throughout its motion.

**9** No.

**10** Ten.

**11** Steep downwards slope.

*Activity* Information processing: Road safety

Spreadsheet 'Roadsafety.xls' on the CD-ROM can be used for this activity.

## Answers

➡ *Pupil's Book page 118*

**1** The time that elapses before the brake is applied.

**2** The time taken for the car to stop once the brakes have been applied.

**3** A straight-line graph.

**4** As the speed increases, the thinking distance increases in proportion.

**5** Input variable is the speed, outcome variable is the braking distance.

**6** The shape is a curve (a parabola).

**7** As the speed increases, the braking distance increases by greater amounts. (Pupils should realise that this is not a linear relationship like the answer to Q4.)

## Time to think

➡ *Worksheet 6.7: Time to think (S)*

This is a convenient point to consolidate the work covered so far. Worksheet 6.7 provides a range of questions.

## Answers

**2 c)** 12 m.

   **d)** 24 m.

   **e)** At 60 km/h it is 24 + 12 = 36 m.

   **f)** Increase the stopping distance.

   **g)** Road surface, size of vehicle, brakes, driver's alertness.

**3** Car stops in 36 m at 60 km/h. To ensure that the car stops within 25 m it would need to travel at below 50 km/h.

# 5 *Floating and sinking*

## Learning outcomes

Pupils:

- state that all objects weigh less in water than in air
- explain their observations in terms of an upward force from the water 'cancelling out; some of the downward force of the weight
- recognise that when an object floats it shows a zero weight reading
- state that an object that is less dense than water will float in water
- state that some liquids produce a greater upthrust on an object than others

*Activity* ## Demonstration: Floating and sinking

➡ *Pupil's Book page 120*

The experiment with the two cola cans is simple but makes a good discussion point.

It is worthwhile demonstrating the upthrust on an object such as a ball (which floats) when it is pushed below the surface in a bucket of water.

**Equipment**
- full can of diet cola
- full can of ordinary cola (same brand)
- bowl of water
- bucket of water
- ball

*Activity* ## Practical: Floating

➡ *Worksheet 6.8: Floating and sinking (D)*

You may wish to do the practical suggested in the activity *Enquiry: Floating* (Pupil's Book, page 120). Worksheet 6.8 provides a possible approach. Weighing the object in a liquid other than water reinforces the idea of different upthrust in different liquids (floating in the Dead sea, the Plimsoll line on ships etc.).

**Equipment**
- regular blocks
- thread
- scissors
- beaker
- water
- forcemeter
- clamp and stand

## Answers

1 The readings are lower.
2 The readings in cooking oil would be less than those in air but more than those in water.
3 They float more easily.
4 To check that the ship is not overloaded.
5 If the object is a regular shape, measure its dimensions; or, for any object, immerse it in water and measure the volume of water displaced.

## Ideas and evidence: Upthrust and Archimedes

## Answers

➡ *Pupil's Book page 121*

1 When an object is placed in a fluid an upward force acts on it; this is the upthrust.
2 Archimedes was the first person known to have understood the ideas of upthrust and applied them.
3 Lift water.
4 (Sensible discussion expected to do with the application of science.)

*Activity* ## Enquiry: Upthrust

## Answers

➡ *Pupil's Book page 121*

1 The weight in water is zero.
2 Zero.

### Attainment targets

Work in the previous sections should provide evidence that pupils are working towards the following attainment levels.

| | |
|---|---|
| Describe physical phenomena such as objects weigh less in water than in air | Level 4 |
| Apply abstract ideas in explanations of the relationship between upthrust and weight of liquid displaced | Level 7 |

# 6 *Density*

## Learning outcomes

Pupils:

- know the relationship between volume, mass and density
- use the formula Density = mass/volume to perform simple calculations
- use a spreadsheet to calculate density and volume
- construct a spreadsheet and insert a formula (higher ability)

*Activity* ## Practical: Finding density

➡ *Worksheet 6.9: Density, volume and mass (P)*

This is a further opportunity to use ICT and spreadsheets in particular. The lesson could be split into two halves; one half for the practical measurements and the second half for entering the results into the spreadsheet. Pupils use regular blocks and measure their height, width and length. They use a top pan to find their mass. They also test whether the blocks will float or sink. In the second half of the lesson they enter their results into the spreadsheet. Differentiation can be achieved with this and many spreadsheet activities by producing different templates for different groups of children. The most able could enter their own formulae into the template, while others would be presented with the template with the formulae already embedded. Spreadsheet 'Density.xls' on the CD-ROM can be used for this activity.

The Extension activity allows pupils to simulate density/volume experiments using Internet Explorer and the website: www.bigchalk.com/cgi-bin/WebObjects/WOPortal.woa/961/wa/HWCDA/file?flt=GA&fileid=192611.

### Equipment
- top pan balance
- regular cubes of different materials
- centimetre rule
- bowl of water

## Density
## Answers

➡ *Pupil's Book page 124*
 **6** Oak, ice.
 **7** 8.9 g/cm³, 270 g, 20 cm³.
 **8** Lead.
 **9** Copper.
**10** Lead.

# 7 *Stretching a spring*

## Learning outcomes

Pupils:

- present experimental data in a graphical form
- describe and explain relationships shown by graphs

*Activity* ## Information processing: Stretching springs

➡ *Pupil's Book page 125*

This presents an opportunity to discuss the shape of graphs, lines of best fit and reliability of results.

## Answers

**1** Load.
**2** Stretch.
**3** Graph C.
**4** If you increase the size of the load you increase the stretch of the spring.

*Activity* ## Practical: Stretching

➡ *Worksheet 6.10: An experiment to stretch a spring (P)*

This could be introduced by a demonstration, or pupils could perform the standard experiment of stretching a spring using a mass hanger. As a variation to this experiment they could use ICT to enter their results into a spreadsheet and the graph could be presented interactively as the results are entered. Spreadsheet 'Stretching.xls' on the CD-ROM can be used for this activity.

### Equipment

Each group will need:

- some 100 g masses and a mass hanger
- a spring
- a stand and clamp
- a ruler
- a strip of card

*Activity* ## Reasoning: Stretching elastic bands
## Answers

➡ *Pupil's Book page 126*

**1**

| Load (g) | Length (cm) | Extension (cm) |
|---|---|---|
| 0 | 10 | 0 |
| 100 | 16 | 6 |
| 200 | 22 | 12 |
| 300 | 28 | 18 |
| 400 | 34 | 24 |
| 500 | 37 | 27 |
| 600 | 39 | 29 |

**2** Load on horizontal axis, extension on vertical axis.
**3** The bigger the load, the greater the extension of the elastic band.

**4** They would both stretch by smaller amounts and so the extension would be less.

**5** Each rubber band would stretch as much as the single rubber band, and so the total extension would be twice as much. In the second case, the same load is acting on each rubber band. (In the first case, the two rubber bands are sharing the load.)

# **8** *Friction and air resistance*

## Learning outcomes

Pupils:

- describe and set up a fair test
- use their scientific knowledge and understanding to explain and interpret observations and measurements
- identify factors that might affect the frictional force between two surfaces

Pupils will already have done some work on this topic at Key Stage 2 (Unit 4E Friction).

If time is available, this could be extended over two or even three lessons.

*Activity* ## Reasoning: Friction
## Answers

➡ *Pupil's Book page 127*

**1** It is the same as the pulling force.

**2**

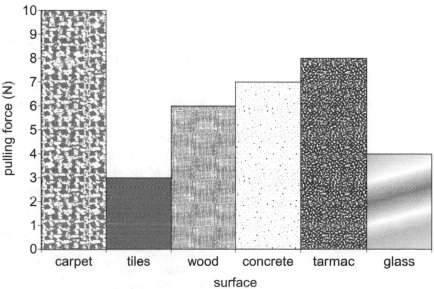

**3** Carpet.

**4** Tiles, glass, wood, concrete, tarmac, carpet.

**5** It would be low, perhaps 4N.

**6** Glass and tiles have low friction force and the plastic surface would behave similarly.

**7** Make the friction even less.

**8** Oil makes the surface slippery by reducing the friction. Sand mixes with the oil to make it less slippery and so increase the friction.

**9 Useful**

soles of shoes
rubber tyres
sandpaper
bath mat
brake pads
grit on the road

**Nuisance**

causes wear between the surfaces in machines
carpets wear out
parts of an engine, for example, rubbing together creates heat
causes friction burns from a rope
water, ice or oil on the road causes skidding

*Activity* Investigation: Friction

➡ *Worksheet 6.11: Parachute (P), Worksheet 6.12: Pulling shoes on different surfaces (P), Worksheet 6.13: Investigating a paper spinner (P)*

This topic provides a number of opportunities for pupils to design and perform simple investigations. Pupils could investigate the factors affecting the rate of fall of a parachute; the slowing down of a paper spinner with paper clip weight; the sliding of an object on different types of surface (this could be a shoe or a wooden block).

**Equipment**

➡ *Worksheet 6.11: Parachute*
- range of materials (for example, paper, cotton, silk, plastic)
- thread
- scissors
- Plasticine
- stopclock
- metre rule or tape measure
- top pan balance

➡ *Worksheet 6.12: Pulling shoes on different surfaces*
- range of surfaces (for example, carpet, wood, plastic flooring)
- shoe or wooden block
- long runway
- pile of books
- forcemeter or pulley and 100 g masses

➡ *Worksheet 6.13: Investigating a paper spinner*
- different thicknesses of card
- scissors
- paper clips
- stopclock
- metre rule or tape measure

These three worksheets provide opportunities for developing investigative skills. In Worksheet 6.11 pupils make a parachute and are then offered three investigations to choose from. Pupils complete a variables table for the investigation chosen – this supports development of planning. Worksheet 6.12 also develops planning of investigations but is more open ended than Worksheet 6.11. Worksheet 6.13 gives the outline for an investigation for the pupil to carry out, and write a report in which they explain how they ensure it is a fair test. Help is given in this worksheet to prompt pupils to include all aspects in their planning and write-up of the investigation.

## Ideas and evidence: Bicycles

➡ *Pupil's Book page 128*

Pupils could use the Internet for this activity. It is an opportunity to take a wider view of science; to consider the relative merits of using a bicycle, the introduction of cycle paths all over Britain; and to look at the type of bicycles available and the reasons for their design. It could be a homework or mini project.

## Answers

1 One wheel was very large and one was very small. The coins at that time included a large penny and a small coin, the farthing.
2 The bike would move a large distance for one rotation of the wheel because the circumference of the wheel was large.
3 The old tyres were solid.
4

| beginning eighteenth century<br>first bicycle, Hobby Horse,<br>with no pedals | **1839**<br>pedals<br>introduced | **1880s**<br>safety<br>bicycle<br>invented | **1899**<br>derailleur<br>gear<br>invented | **1950s**<br>steel frame<br>Raleigh<br>bicycle |
|---|---|---|---|---|

1700 1720 1740 1760 1780 **1800** 1820 1840 1860 1880 **1900** 1920 1940 1960 1980 **2000**

| | **1870s**<br>first all-metal<br>machines;<br>penny-farthing<br>bicycle invented | **1890**<br>pneumatic<br>tyre<br>invented | | **present day**<br>aluminium,<br>titanium,<br>carbon-fibre<br>bicycles |
|---|---|---|---|---|

5 Increased stability; comfort; gears made them easier to ride up a slope; different materials made them lighter.
6 Comfort, cost, colour, size of frame, number of gears, weight, size of wheels, type of seat, thickness of tyres, position of handle bars, and so on.

*Activity* ## Demonstration: Guinea and feather

If you have the equipment available you could demonstrate the traditional 'Guinea and feather' experiment.

**Equipment**
• vacuum pump
• wide glass tube
• rubber bung
• 'guinea' and 'feather'

## Air resistance

## Answers

➡ *Pupil's Book page 129*

11 An Italian astronomer and physicist.
12 Galileo constructed the first astronomical telescope to gain knowledge about the stars and planets.
13 There were no accurate timing devices.
14 To increase the air resistance and reduce the terminal velocity.

*Activity* Simulations: Terminal velocity

There are a number of useful simulations available for use with this topic. The *Multimedia Science School* CD-ROM 'Terminal velocity' offers two scenarios: a parachutist and three different types of bicycle travelling on the level and up and down different slopes.

## Time to think

➡ *Pupil's Book page 129*

As consolidation of work, pupils could be asked to produce a concept map to draw together the key ideas presented in this topic.

## Review

➡ *Worksheet 6.14: Test on forces*

This worksheet provides a 20 minute test to check on understanding of this chapter.

## Answers

**1** Force.                                                    (1 mark)

**2** Current.                                                  (1 mark)

**3 a)–d)**   Suitable examples, 1 mark each.        (4 marks)

**4 a)**  Bar chart rather than line graph.
    Axes correct orientation.
    Axes labelled.
    Suitable scale chosen for speed.
    Accuracy of bars.                                  (5 marks)

  **b)**  Type of animal.                                (1 mark)

  **c)**  Three.                                        (1 mark)

  **d)**  12 minutes = $\frac{1}{5}$ hour.
    Travels $\frac{1}{5}$ distance it would do in 1 hour
    50/5 = 10 km.                                      (3 marks)

**5** Upward force
  of water/liquid
  balances/counteracts gravity.          (Any 2 for 2 marks)

**6 a)**  Concrete.                                       (1 mark)

  **b)**  Sand grains allow box to roll over them/sand
    grains do not resist motion as much as wood.     (1 mark)

# 7 Cells

## → Rationale

This chapter provides around 8 hours of teaching materials. Through Key Stages 1 and 2, children will have dealt with the science of whole organisms and so, in Key Stage 3, cells are introduced as a new topic and area of conceptual development. Cells may have been touched on in the reproduction of flowering plants at Key Stage 2, and specific human organs may have been looked at in terms of nutrition and circulation (Unit 5 Keeping healthy) and human life cycle. Bacteria and yeast may have been referred to as single celled in Unit 6B Micro-organisms at Key Stage 2. The key science idea in this chapter is cells, but the respiration work also links with the energy theme.

Cells are introduced through a historical context by looking at the work of Robert Hooke. The text moves quickly on to the role that cells play. Respiration is introduced early in the chapter to help pupils link cells and energy and realise that this reaction underpins 99.99 per cent of all life on this planet. The idea that all organisms are made of cells and that these cells respire, releasing energy for synthesis of new cell parts, enzymes and other chemicals, and for the workings of the cell, is a new and difficult idea for pupils to take on.

The emphasis in this chapter is on structure and function. This approach is taken with the introduction of animal and plant cell structure and later when specialised cells are considered. Pupils are encouraged to exhibit their understanding of structure and function through making models of cells as well as considering models introduced in the text. This enables them to begin to build up a three-dimensional picture of cells, tissues and organs which forms a strong basis for future consideration of concepts, such as surface area and absorption rates. A further difficult idea tackled in this chapter is size and scaling in microscope work.

The work in this chapter feeds into many areas throughout Key Stage 3 but is particularly important in progression through chapter 8 Reproduction. In Year 8 the ideas link into Unit 8B Respiration and 8C Microbes and disease. In Year 9, the work on cells develops through Unit 9A Inheritance and selection and 9C Plants and photosynthesis.

## → Overview

The textbook sections, activities and worksheets have been arranged into 1 hour blocks to aid lesson planning. Clearly several of the activities and worksheets could form part of a homework session. The planning includes reading time for individual sections but some teachers may prefer to organise this as homework preparation for the following lesson. Five types of worksheets – extension (E), support for an activity (S), practical

(P), key skills (K) and developmental (D) – allow for differentiation and flexibility to accommodate teachers' preferred practice. The actual timing and emphasis on different sections will depend on the current knowledge base of the pupils, the ability of the teaching group and the preferences of the teacher.

| Lesson | Worksheet |
|---|---|
| 1 Introducing cells | |
| 2 Size of cells | Worksheet 7.1: The microscope (S) |
| 3 Looking at cells | Worksheet 7.2: Looking at plant cells (P) |
| 4 Review of cells | Worksheet 7.3: Looking at cheek cells (P) |
| 5 Body systems | Worksheet 7.4: The organ game (S) |
| 6 Specialisation | Worksheet 7.5: Specialised cells (S) |
| 7 New cells | Worksheet 7.6: Identifying cells (E) |
| 8 Consolidation | Worksheet 7.7: Give us a clue (D) |
| Review | Worksheet 7.8: Test on cells |

# ➡ *Chapter plan*

| | Demonstration | Practical | ICT | Activity | Word play | Time to think | Ideas and evidence |
|---|---|---|---|---|---|---|---|
| **Lesson 1** | *Amoeba* | | | Enquiry: Investigating yeast | | What do you know? | Observing cells |
| **Lesson 2** | | Using microscopes | | Information processing: What size is it? | -scopes | | |
| **Lesson 3** | | Looking at cells | | Evaluation: Model cell | | | |
| **Lesson 4** | | Looking at animal cells | | | | Plant and animal cells | |
| **Lesson 5** | | | CD-ROM/ Internet | Information processing: Organs

Information processing: Body parts | | | |
| **Lesson 6** | | | CD-ROM/ Internet | Note taking: Specialised cells

Research | | | Then and now – our knowledge of cells |
| **Lesson 7** | | | Using a spreadsheet | Revision: Cells

Reasoning: Bacteria

Evaluation: Investigating liquid soap | | | |
| **Lesson 8** | | | | Testing knowledge: Crossword clues | | Cells | |

# ➡ *Expectations*

**At the end of this chapter**

**in terms of scientific enquiry**

**most pupils will:** describe some earlier ideas about the structure of living things and relate these to evidence from microscope observations; make observations using a microscope and record them in simple drawings; interpret data from graphs and explain what these show; evaluate an investigation

**some pupils will not have made as much progress and will:** relate drawings to observations made using a microscope; identify points on a graph; recognise input and outcome variables in an investigation; identify relevant safety points

**some pupils will have progressed further and will:** explain how evidence from microscope observations changed ideas about the structure of living things; use ideas of ratio and modelling to begin to gain understanding of microscopic size and magnification; estimate sizes of specimens viewed under the microscope and justify the sample chosen in an investigation

**in terms of life processes and living things**

**most pupils will:** identify and name features of cells and describe some differences between plant and animal cells; explain the role of the different parts of the cell; explain that growth occurs when cells divide and increase in size; describe how cells are grouped to form tissues, and tissues are grouped to form organs and organs systems

**some pupils will not have made as much progress and will:** recognise that all organisms are made from cells and name some parts of a cell

**some pupils will have progressed further and will:** describe how some cells in an organism are specialised to carry out particular functions; explain that cells respire to release energy from sugars

# ➡ *Links with CASE*

Classification ideas will have been used by children at a descriptive level in primary school within science and other subject areas. The ability to classify in terms of grouping similar things is introduced in this chapter through decisions about whether cells are plant or animal and also in terms of levels of organisation of cells–tissues–organs–organ systems. Clearly observational skills, identification techniques and ability to group information will play important roles in developing these basic ideas into conceptual understanding.

Ratio and proportionality thinking is also developed through calculating real and observed sizes when using a microscope. This involves developing the skill of scaling. This type of thinking is also used when estimating the real size of microscope specimens from measuring the field of view. CASE users will recognise the links here with TS8 Activity 2 Scale Drawings.

Variable recognition and the articulation of relationships is again worked on in this chapter. Evaluation skills are developed in the investigation on liquid soap.

# Pupils' misconceptions

| Misconception | Scientific understanding |
| --- | --- |
| Cells occur only in some parts of animals and plants. | Animals and plants are made of cells. |
| Respiration is breathing and takes place in the lungs of mammals. | All living things respire and respiration takes place in cells. |

# Literacy, numeracy and other cross-curricular links

There is considerable scope within this chapter to develop speaking and writing skills. Wherever possible, discussion and comparison of ideas should be encouraged. Pupils are asked to do extended pieces of reading and produce notes using a writing frame. They are also asked to research and produce text for a specific purpose and audience.

This chapter develops numeracy skills through estimation, ratio and scaling. Both continuous and discrete data are collected, collated, presented and analysed. The work requires pupils to use calculators and ICT resources to solve mathematical problems.

## Language for learning

By the end of this chapter pupils will be able to understand, use and spell correctly:

- words and phrases relating to cells and tissues – cytoplasm, nucleus, membrane, chloroplast, epithelium
- words and phrases relating to microscopy – magnification, lens, focus
- words relating to scientific enquiry – data, reliable, variables, relationships, evaluation.

# 1 Introducing cells

## Learning outcomes

Pupils:

- describe Hooke's early microscope work
- explain how evidence from microscope observations led to new ideas
- state that all living things are made of cells
- identify the input and outcome variables
- recognise controls
- interpret results and decide on a relationship

- articulate a conclusion using key words supplied
- relate the ideas to an everyday context

## What do you know?

➡ *Pupil's Book page 130*

It is likely that pupils will come from Key Stage 2 with the knowledge of the names and functions of some human organs and the ability to label plant parts and ascribe functions for a typical plant. This activity will provide you with an idea of the breadth and depth of knowledge that pupils bring to their Key Stage 3 work, enabling you to plan the work in the chapter to plug gaps, if necessary, and build on the ideas already there.

## Ideas and evidence: Observing cells

➡ *Pupil's Book page 132*

This is a simple comprehension activity to introduce the idea of the cell and Hooke's important work in producing one of the first microscopes and the first book of microscope drawings.

## Answers

1 Hooke was born in 1635.
2 He lived to be 68.
3 Astronomers study the planets, stars and galaxies in space. Physicists study the properties of matter and energy. Naturalists are descriptive biologists, usually botanists or zoologists.
4 Biologist.
5 Hooke needed to understand light and have a working knowledge of lenses, which were already used in astronomical telescopes. He used this knowledge to help him study living materials.
6 Hooke's book contained the first microscope drawings of cells.
7 Hooke chose the name cell because the shape of cork cells reminded him of monks' cells in a monastery.

## What are cells?

➡ *Pupil's Book page 132*

Respiration is introduced right at the start of this chapter and should be emphasised whenever possible as the reaction that is unique to living things, in that energy is released from sugar to fuel all living chemical reactions.

*Activity* ## Demonstration: *Amoeba*

Single celled creatures such as *Amoeba* are mentioned in the textbook. It is possible to collect some single celled organisms to view with the microscope by placing broken straw stems in water for 4–6 days and decanting off the liquid which should contain some organisms. Alternatively, batches of single celled organisms can be ordered from Philip Harris Scientific, Novara House, Excelsior Road, Ashby Park, Ashby de la Zouch, Leicestershire LE65 1NG; tel: 0845 6040490; fax: 01530 419300; www.phscientific.co.uk. These could be shown to pupils using a Visiview or similar microscope camera as it is difficult for pupils to make up slides of their own.

There are several snippets of video showing single celled organisms.

*Activity* Enquiry: Investigating yeast

➡ *Pupil's Book page 134*

This is an investigation description; pupils have to identify the input and outcome variables and interpret the results. There are two outcome variables considered which may cause some cognitive conflict.

## Answers

1

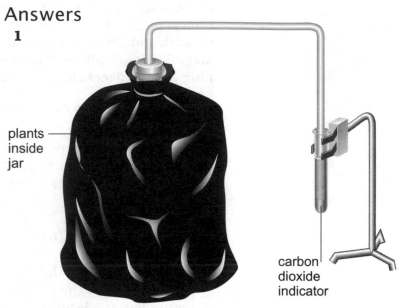

plants inside jar

carbon dioxide indicator

2 Time.
3 The temperature in the flask; and the volume of the balloon.
4 Red to orange.
5 If the air in the room changed temperature during the experiment, then this could increase or decrease the temperature inside the flask. She therefore could check that any increase in temperature resulted from the yeast.
6 It increased by 6 °C over the first hour and then more slowly by 4 °C over the next four hours.
7 It increased to 50 cm$^3$ by 5 hours.
8 Yeast respiration releases energy and produces a gas.
9 When yeast cells respire the temperature increases as they release energy from sugar and produce carbon dioxide gas.
10 No temperature increase or gas produced. Yeast needs sugar because sugar has energy locked in it.
11 It is used to inflate the bread dough (so the bread rises) by making tiny holes in the bread.
12 Yeast cells also make alcohol when they respire.

# 2 *Size of cells*

## Learning outcomes

Pupils:

• compare sizes that decrease by a factor of 10×
• name the parts of a microscope and state their function
• use ratios to compare real and observed size of objects
• compare modern microscopes with Hooke's one
• state the size of the field of view on a microscope
• use field of view to estimate size of microscope specimens

## Word play
## Answers
➡ *Pupil's Book page 135*
Stethoscope – to listen to heartbeat and lung movements.
Oscilloscope – to examine waves, such as sound waves.
Endoscope – to look inside the gut and other body organs.
Telescope – to view stars and planets.

*Activity* ## Practical: Using microscopes

➡ *Worksheet 7.1: The microscope (S)*
This worksheet provides a diagram of a typical microscope for pupils to label and annotate. They need to be shown the various parts and given the name and function of each part (see Pupil's Book page 138). Microscopes vary slightly in their light source and whether the platform is moved or the lens. They can practise setting up the microscope by either focusing on a small piece of newspaper print on a slide or on simple slides such as transverse sections (TS) of a dicotyledon stem.

## How big are cells?
➡ *Pupil's Book page 136*
This section makes high demands on pupils' reasoning skills related to ratio and scaling. Some pupils will only be able to comprehend that the lenses in microscopes magnify the specimen so that it can be seen more clearly. Others will realise that the different magnifications of the objective lenses mean that less of the specimen can be viewed but in more detail. Formal thinkers will be able to explain scaling and work out either real size or observed size using different objective lenses.

Work is also provided at a more concrete level where pupils are asked to compare modern microscopes with the type used by Hooke.

## Answers
**1** 100×
  1 : 100
**2** 400×
  1 : 400
**3** 20 mm, 50 mm, 200 mm
**4** $\frac{8}{40} = \frac{1}{5}$ mm or 0.2 mm
**5** Both have an eyepiece lens, an objective lens, a microscope tube, a light source and a means of focusing.
**6** Two from:
  Hooke's microscope had a light source provided by a flame and lens while the modern one has a light and mirror. There are several objective lenses on the modern microscope. The modern microscope has a stage with clips for the slide.
**7** Microscopes magnify objects by scaling them up so that the objects look larger than their real size. Telescopes magnify objects that are large but far away, so that they appear nearer.

*Activity* Information processing: What size is it?

➡ *Pupil's Book page 138*

The field of view of microscopes can be measured by placing either a piece of graph paper or a transparent ruler on the platform of the microscope. Estimates of real size can be made by comparing with the measurement of the field of view. If you want to view and measure specimens such as moss plants, hairs, stamen, then it is best to stick a piece of graph paper measuring about 5 cm × 2 cm on a microscope slide with transparent tape and then place the specimen on top. Alternatively, hairs can simply be taped to the scale on the transparent ruler. Pupils are usually very interested in hairs from different ethnic groups and treated hair such as permed or coloured hair.

### Answers

**2** Just over a square with 1 cm (10 mm) sides (1 cm$^2$ or 10 mm$^2$).

**3** Field of view just under 30 mm (so magnification is 3×).
Ant's leg 45 mm (section of leg within one square only).
Real length of ant's leg = 45/3 = 15 mm.

**4** 20 grains = $\frac{1}{5}$ cm (2 mm)
∴ 1 grain = $\frac{1}{100}$ cm or 0.01 cm ($\frac{1}{10}$ mm or 0.1 mm).

# 3 *Looking at cells*

## Learning outcomes

Pupils:

- relate the parts of model cells to diagrams and pictures of animal and plant cells
- describe what plant and animal cells have in common
- state the difference between animal and plant cells
- make a slide of onion epidermal cells
- view a slide of onion epidermal cells with a microscope
- make a drawing of a plant cell as seen through a microscope
- identify the nucleus, cytoplasm and cellulose cell wall

*Activity* Evaluation: Model cell

➡ *Pupil's Book page 140*

It is important to give pupils a three-dimensional image of cells and using models provides a good way of achieving this. It is possible to make animal and plant cells using a variety of coloured modelling clays and allocating set colours to particular structures, but this is quite time consuming and fiddly. One advantage though is that the cell can be cut to show transverse sections (TS) and longitudinal sections (LS) which can help pupils make sense of the labels on slides produced by Philip Harris and other manufacturers. Videos and CD-ROMs are available on cell structure and can be used here.

### Answers

**1** Runny jelly = cytoplasm.
Small ball = nucleus.
Plastic bag = cell surface membrane.

**2** Various answers here will indicate pupils' thinking about structure and function of cell parts. They may, for example, suggest a material with tiny holes to represent the transport role of the cell surface membrane, or materials that have similar properties (for example wallpaper paste instead of runny jelly) to show they understand the nature of the cell part.

**3** Vacuole (for example another bag with sugar/salt solution in it).
Cellulose cell wall (tough box).
Chloroplasts (small green balls/solar cells).

*Activity* Practical: Looking at cells

➡ *Worksheet 7.2: Looking at plant cells (P)*

This worksheet gives the practical procedures for making temporary slides. It is a good idea for you or the technician to cut the squares of onion from the onion bulb to prevent pupils cutting themselves. This technique of collecting onion epidermal cells is better than cutting the onion in half as it is less smelly and the piece of epidermis is the correct size to fit under the coverslip.

If the slide has air bubbles (these have dark rims when viewed under the microscope) then these can be removed by placing a drop of water along one edge of the coverslip and then sucking the liquid underneath by placing a piece of tissue on the opposite edge of the coverslip.

It is difficult to see the cytoplasm but turning the focus knob on the microscope slightly may allow you to see this more clearly. The vacuole cannot be seen in these cells and they do not have chloroplasts.

It is useful to put some good examples of the slides on a Visiview or other microscope camera to help pupils focus on what they are looking at and to help them identify the different parts of the cell. It might be useful here to look at other plant slides such as sections through leaves and stems, so that pupils can see what features are found in plant cells and also the variety of shapes and size of cell that is found.

**Equipment**
Each group will need:

* microscope
* glass slide
* coverslip
* mounted needle
* iodine solution (potassium iodide)
* methylene blue solution
* disinfectant
* scalpel/sharp knife
* tissue
* pipette

# 4 *Review of cells*

## Learning outcomes

Pupils:

- make a slide of cheek cells
- view a slide of cheek cells with a microscope
- make a drawing of a cheek cell as seen through a microscope
- identify the nucleus, cytoplasm and cell surface membrane in a cheek cell
- name the parts of an animal and a plant cell and give the function of each part
- classify cells as plant or animal, giving reasons, and label parts of a cell
- use ratios to compare real and observed size of objects

## *Activity* Practical: Looking at animal cells

➡ *Worksheet 7.3: Looking at cheek cells (P)*

This worksheet gives the practical procedure for making temporary slides. The method has been approved by the British Medical Association and the Institute of Biology. Some schools and local education authorities (LEAs) have decided not to make any mounts of human cells and you need to check the regulations for your school. Prepared slides can be purchased from Philip Harris (see page 143 for contact details). If you do use the procedure described, there are two safety instructions that you need to adhere to:

- The cotton buds should be taken from a new pack that you open at the start of the practical and you give cotton buds individually to pupils.
- The used cotton buds are placed in disinfectant immediately after transferring the cheek cells to the slide and the cotton buds are later collected into a sealed bag and either autoclaved or disposed of with other biological waste materials. The slides and coverslips can be washed and used again.

## Time to think
## Answers

➡ *Pupil's Book page 140*

**1**

| Cell part | Job |
|---|---|
| cellulose cell wall | tough outer coat of cell |
| cell surface membrane | contains cytoplasm and allows materials in and out of cell |
| cytoplasm | fills cell and is the site of cell's reactions |
| vacuole | bag of salty/sugary water which helps support cell |
| nucleus | control centre for cell plus hereditary material |
| chloroplast | traps sunlight for food production |

**2** A = plant cell.
  B = animal cell.
  Decision could be because of cell wall, chloroplasts or vacuole.

**3** 15 mm.

**4** 150×.

**5** Observed size is around 50 mm so real size is 0.33 mm or $\frac{1}{3}$ mm, because 150× smaller than in picture.

**6** Observed size is around 30 mm so real size is 0.2 mm or $\frac{1}{5}$ mm, because 150× smaller than in picture.

**Attainment target**

Work in the previous sections should provide evidence that pupils are working towards the following attainment level.

| Describe simple cell structure and identify differences between animal and plant cells | Level 6 |
| --- | --- |

## How are cells organised?

➡ *Pupil's Book page 140*

Here levels of organisation, viz. at cell, tissue, and organ level, are looked at. Two models are used to try to explain these levels of organisation and it is useful for pupils to discuss these and decide which they believe explains the concept in the best way and the limitations of each model. Pupils will bring knowledge from Key Stage 2 to help them make sense of the information.

# 5  *Body systems*

## Learning outcomes

Pupils.

- match organs to their function
- state where various organs lie in the human body
- allocate living material to cell, tissue, organ, or body system level
- name some cell types, tissues and organs

There are numerous CD-ROMs and Internet sites to support the topics covered in lessons 5 and 6; examples include www.bbc.co.uk/science/humanbody and www.learn.co.uk.

*Activity*

## Information processing: Organs

➡ *Worksheet 7.4: The organ game (S)*

This worksheet provides cards with names of organs and others with functions on. Pupils match the organs with their function and stick these in their books in the order the organs appear in the body from head to toe. It provides an opportunity to build on Key Stage 2 knowledge and collates information for the following 'Body parts' activity.

Discussion of organ function during this activity will advance knowledge in this area.

*Activity* Information processing: Body parts
## Answers

➡ *Pupil's Book page 143*

| Cells | Tissues | Organs | Body systems |
|---|---|---|---|
| muscle | muscle | eye | excretory system |
| white blood cells | blood | pancreas | circulatory system |
| red blood cells | | brain | nervous system |
| | | lungs | |
| | | kidney | |
| | | bladder | |

| Cells | Tissues | Organs | Body systems |
|---|---|---|---|
| muscle | muscle | heart | circulatory system |
| red and white blood cells | blood | | circulatory system |
| neurones | nervous | brain eye | sensory system |
| | | kidney bladder | excretory system |
| epithelia | epithelial | lung | breathing system |
| | | pancreas | hormone system |

*Note:* there are gaps in this table because the answer required is too complex or inappropriate for pupils at Key Stage 3.

## Attainment targets
Work in the previous sections should provide evidence that pupils are working towards the following attainment levels.

| | |
|---|---|
| Use scientific names for some major organs of body systems and identify their position | Level 4 |
| Describe main functions of organs of the human body and how these are essential to the organism | Level 5 |

# 6 *Specialisation*

## Learning outcomes
Pupils can:

- explain that different types of cell can be found in animals and plants, and that these cells carry out specialised functions
- identify specialised features in different types of cell and relate these to the function of the cell
- identify specialised features in white blood cells and relate these to the function of the cell
- describe how earlier ideas about white blood cells have changed
- explain how an example of scientific knowledge has benefited medicine

## Why are some cells specialised?

➡ *Pupil's Book page 143*

Structure and function play an important part in the knowledge base of biological topics and many pupils will find it difficult to separate the two aspects. Trying to get pupils to think of function as the *job* that cells do is a start. An activity that helps here is providing them with drawings of four or five specialised cells on the board and asking them to write something about the structure of each one on separate sticky notelets, then giving them a second set of different coloured sticky notelets and asking them to write down the function of each cell. All the structure notelets for a cell are stuck on the left of the cell and all the functions on the right. The teacher then reads through each one with the class and they decide whether each notelet gives the correct information (incorrect ones can be taken off), but more importantly, have they got structure and function the right way round? Any notelets that are on the wrong side of the drawing of the cell are moved across to the correct side. Because these are a different colour they stand out and so it is easy for you to consolidate the ideas of structure and function using these.

*Activity*

## Note taking: Specialised cells

➡ *Worksheet 7.5: Specialised cells (S)*

The section in the textbook 'Why are some cells specialised?' is an extended reading piece and Worksheet 7.5 provides a writing frame to help pupils make their own notes from the text. They should be encouraged to skim read first, then read through the writing frame before a second, more careful read of the text, before they begin the writing task. This activity helps pupils understand, locate and use information from reading.

## Answers

➡ *Pupil's Book page 146*

**8** Palisade layer of cells. They contain lots of chloroplasts and are positioned near the upper surface of the leaf.

**9** Cells in layer beneath palisade cells. They are loosely packed, have air spaces between them and are positioned near the stomata.

## Ideas and evidence: Then and now – our knowledge of cells

➡ *Pupil's Book page 147*

Pupils often think that science is a fixed body of knowledge and any new knowledge is only acquired through space exploration or new inventions. This activity is to help them see that the knowledge of white blood cells has only been sorted out in the last century. The activity provides them with an explanation of white blood cell function from an old textbook. Their task is to research what we know today about white blood cells and present it as an article. They will need access to books and/or CD-ROMs or the Internet. This activity helps pupils understand, locate and use information from reading, and write for a specific audience and purpose. Pupils' paragraphs should focus on white cells fighting disease bacteria by engulfing bacteria and attacking with antibodies.

*Activity* Research

→ *Pupil's Book page 147*

This activity requires use of textbooks and/or the Internet to find and present information on Fleming's discovery of penicillin.

# 7 *New cells*

## Learning outcomes

Pupils:

- explain that different types of cell can be found in animals and plants and that these cells carry out specialised functions
- identify specialised features in different types of cell and relate these to the function of the cell
- explain that cells divide causing the organism to grow
- explain that all cells contain DNA which is a chemical that codes for new cells
- state that DNA is found in the nucleus of all cells
- draw a line graph of data
- estimate readings that are extrapolated points on their graph
- identify the question that an experiment is trying to solve
- identify safety measures in an experiment
- identify input and outcome variables
- recognise and articulate relationships
- explain why a control has to be used
- decide on how to collect and present results
- evaluate an experiment in terms of reliability

*Activity* Revision: Cells

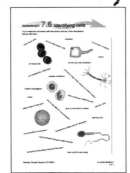

→ *Worksheet 7.6: Identifying cells (E)*

This is a revision worksheet to help pupils put together the knowledge they have been building on specialised cells and how cells are organised into tissues. Pupils cut out and then match drawings of cells with the name and function and other details, and then organise these into a table in their exercise books. The finished product should link the following functions/descriptions with these specialised cells.

**red blood cells**
- do not have a nucleus
- are tiny disc shaped cells
- contain haemoglobin

**white blood cells**
- produce antibodies
- fight bacteria
- give us immunity to disease
- can have a large single nucleus or a lobed nucleus

**neurones**
- have a long part called the axon
- are insulated by a fatty layer
- carry electrical messages called impulses

**pollen**
- are the sex cells of a flowering plant
- transport the hereditary material of the plant

**root hair cells**
- take in water for the plant
- increase the surface area for absorption

**sperm**
- are the sex cells of animals
- have a tail for swimming
- carry the DNA of one parent (this one could be placed with pollen also)

**Attainment targets**

Work in the previous sections should provide evidence that pupils are working towards the following attainment levels.

| | |
|---|---|
| Describe simple cell structure and identify differences between animal and plant cells | Level 6 |
| Use knowledge of cell structure to explain how cells are adapted to their functions | Level 7 |

## How are new cells made?

➡ *Pupil's Book page 148*

The idea of producing new cells is introduced in this section. Pupils find it difficult to understand that the DNA code is the same in all the body cells of a particular animal or plant. So, in the cells in their big toe are the genes that give them eye colour, skin colour, ear shape and so on. When new cells are made this whole code gets passed from cell to cell.

There is no need at this stage to use the term mitosis for cell division. While it could be useful to look at some slides of dividing cells to show that it is the material in the nucleus that brings cell division about, there is no need to look at the process in detail.

*Activity* ## Reasoning: Bacteria

➡ *Pupil's Book page 149*

Pupils will have been introduced to micro-organisms at Key Stage 2 and this activity looks at the rapid cell division that can occur with bacteria. Pupils are aided in selecting suitable scales for their graph, the orientation of their axes and the final shape of their slope. They then use estimating skills to extend the graph data. This develops numeracy skills. Calculators can be used but take care that these do not prevent the pupils from thinking through how they work out the answer. The cognitive conflict here is caused because pupils will expect the graph to demonstrate direct proportionality which this one does not. It may be helpful here to show pupils how the graph line could be extrapolated so that the number after 3 and 4 hours can be found by an alternative method. This will have to be done on the board or prepared OHT, as their piece of graph paper will not have enough space to contain this data extrapolation. Spreadsheet 'Bacteria.xls' on the CD-ROM can be used for this activity.

## Answer

1 Graph C fits the data.
2 There will be 512 bacteria after 3 hours and 4096 after 4 hours (most pupils will get this wrong and just double the 2 hours' total, rather than doubling every 20 minutes).

*Activity* Evaluation: Investigating liquid soap

➡ *Pupil's Book page 150*

This activity is intended to create a stimulus for discussion and thinking about whole investigations. By now, many of the atomistic skills have begun to develop but while planning often receives considerable attention the areas that are most difficult to focus on are the evaluations. Questions 10 and 11 in this activity are therefore the key ones to focus on. If pupils have not seen agar plates before it could be helpful to show them some and also to set up this investigation so that they can see the type of results that you do obtain.

## Answers

1 Whether Bactfree soap kills all the bacteria on your hands.
2 Various titles are possible – perhaps 'How effective is Bactfree soap at killing bacteria on our hands?'
3 Type of liquid added.
4 Growth of bacteria.
5 To see what the normal growth of bacteria was like (control).
6 Safety, to stop bacteria spreading.
7 Good conditions for bacteria to multiply.
8 They waited 3 days because bacteria are small and therefore they needed to wait for colonies of thousands of bacteria for results to be seen.
9 Put cotton buds in disinfectant and then into a sealed plastic bag before placing in a bin.
  Agar plates disposed of in an autoclave by the technician.
  Wiped surfaces with hot soapy water and washed hands.
10 There are a variety of ways of recording results from this experiment. The idea is to move pupils from qualitative descriptions (some, more, most colonies) to quantitative ones (2 colonies, 6 colonies, 9 colonies). Probably the best way of recording this data in a real experiment is to place the plates over graph paper and work out the area of bacterial colonies. This could be achieved here by tracing the colonies on to graph paper and then working out the areas on each plate.
11 Increase the number of each plate. Means might then be taken but as you may get a range of results, it is more common in biological experiments to take modes. In this way the results at either end of the range do not greatly affect those around the central distribution.

# 8 *Consolidation*

*Activity* Testing knowledge: Crossword clues

➡ *Worksheet 7.7: Give us a clue*

This worksheet provides a novel way of pupils testing their knowledge. The answers to the crossword are given and they have to write the clues. Pupils could compare clues and make decisions about which are good clues.

## Time to think

➡ *Pupil's Book page 151*

This is a reflective activity. By looking back at the first activity in this chapter and adding to it, pupils begin to gain a sense of their learning over the topic. By working individually and comparing their answers, they develop skills through peer assessment that will help them strengthen their self-assessment strategies. Pupils should be encouraged to improve their own answers after checking with one another to help develop classrooms as sites for improvement.

Pupils may be able to give actual measurements for the cheek cell (around 0.1 mm) with the red blood cell being some 100× smaller, or they may explain them in terms of the magnification that they have to use on the microscope. They should be encouraged to use more than the term microscopic or tiny for these.

Pupils should talk about lenses and magnification when explaining about cell size and microscopes. They may use the term 'scaling up' and some will be able to explain this in terms of ratios or specific objective lenses used.

Cells have cytoplasm, a nucleus and a cell membrane in common. Plant cells also have a cellulose cell wall, a vacuole of cell sap and chloroplasts.

Pupils should be able to explain two or three specialised cells and ascribe their function.

## Review

➡ *Worksheet 7.8: Test on cells*

This worksheet provides a 20 minute test to check on understanding of this chapter.

## Answers

| | | |
|---|---|---|
| **1** | Chloroplasts. | (1 mark) |
| **2** | Cell surface membrane. | (1 mark) |
| **3** | Chloroplasts. | (1 mark) |
| **4** | Vacuole. | (1 mark) |
| **5** | Nucleus. | (1 mark) |
| **6** | Cellulose wall/chloroplasts/vacuole. | (1 mark) |
| **7** | Red blood cells. | (1 mark) |
| **8** | Root hair cells. | (1 mark) |
| **9** | Pollen/sperm. | (1 mark) |
| **10** | Neurones. | (1 mark) |
| **11** | Red blood cells/white blood cells. | (1 mark) |
| **12** | White blood cells. | (1 mark) |
| **13** | Release of energy from sugar/glucose plus carbon dioxide produced. | (3 marks) |
| **14** | Eyepiece lens. Objective lens. Award 1 mark for lens only. | (2 marks) |
| **15** | Has a specific job. Example. Made up of tissue. | (3 marks) |

# 8 Reproduction

## Rationale

This chapter provides approximately 8 hours of teaching materials. It will extend pupils' ideas about human reproduction, including pregnancy and birth. In Key Stage 2 pupils will have been given the opportunity to describe the human life cycle in terms of infancy, childhood, adolescence, maturity and ageing (Unit 5B Life cycles). They will have learnt that plants and animals reproduce as part of their life cycle and that life cycles have distinct processes and stages. They will have begun to appreciate that reproduction is necessary for a species to survive. Most children should be able to name parts of a flower and their reproductive function. They may know about the stages of growth and development in a human but most will not know details of changes in puberty. They will have identified the risks of drugs, alcohol and tobacco, although this may not have been explicitly linked to the danger of these during pregnancy (Unit 2A Health and growth).

Check you are familiar with your school's policy on sex and drug education (usually part of the personal, health and social education programme) and that you have notified senior management in case there are reasons for any pupil's withdrawal.

The main science ideas fit within the interdependence theme. Pupils will learn the details of fertilisation, pregnancy, human development before birth, the first 2 years of life and through puberty. Human reproduction and development is compared and contrasted to that of fish, amphibians and birds. There is a lot of factual information so secondary research skills are developed, with pupils reading and interpreting information from annotated diagrams, tables and different types of graphs.

This topic links with Year 9 work in Unit 9A Inheritance and selection.

## Overview

The textbook sections, activities and worksheets have been arranged into 1 hour blocks to aid lesson planning. Clearly several of the activities and worksheets could form part of a homework session. The planning includes reading time for individual sections but some teachers may prefer to organise this as homework preparation for the following lesson. Five types of worksheet – extension (E), support for an activity (S), practical (P), key skills (K) and developmental (D) – allow for differentiation and flexibility to accommodate teachers' preferred practice. The actual timing and emphasis on different sections will depend on the current knowledge base of the pupils, the ability of the teaching group and the preferences of the teacher.

| Lesson | Worksheet |
|---|---|
| **1** Introducing reproduction | |
| **2** Sex cells | Worksheet 8.1: Comparing cell sizes (K) |
| **3** Egg production | |
| **4** Fertilisation | Worksheet 8.2: Survival rates (D) |
| **5** Development and birth in humans | Worksheet 8.3: Human development (S)<br>Worksheet 8.4: The growth of a human embryo (K) |
| **6** Pregnancy times and birth | Worksheet 8.5: Gestation in domestic and wild cats (K) |
| **7** Development | Worksheet 8.6: What is 'normal'? (K) |
| **8** Consolidation | Worksheet 8.7: Birth rates (K) |
| Review | Worksheet 8.8: Test on reproduction |

➡ ## *Chapter plan*

| | Demonstration | Practical | ICT | Activity | Time to think |
|---|---|---|---|---|---|
| **Lesson 1** | | | | Discussion:<br>Life cycles<br><br>Group discussion:<br>Human reproduction<br><br>Group discussion:<br>Men and women | What do you know? |
| **Lesson 2** | | | | Information processing:<br>Comparing male and female sex cells | Human reproduction |
| **Lesson 3** | | | | Debate:<br>Siamese twins | |
| **Lesson 4** | | | Video | Research:<br>Other life cycles | |
| **Lesson 5** | | | | Information processing:<br>Human embryo development<br><br>Data processing:<br>Human embryo growth<br><br>Group discussion:<br>Inside the womb | |
| **Lesson 6** | | | Using a spreadsheet<br><br>Internet<br><br>Video | Information processing:<br>Lifespans and pregnancy times<br><br>ICT: The birth of a baby | Concept map |
| **Lesson 7** | | | | Information processing:<br>Growth patterns<br><br>Data collection | |
| **Lesson 8** | | | | Information processing:<br>Birth rates<br><br>Enquiry: Looking at life cycles | Reproduction |

# ➡ *Expectations*

**At the end of this unit**

**in terms of scientific enquiry**

**most pupils will:** select information about reproduction from secondary sources; present and interpret data about growth in bar charts and graphs, indicating whether increasing the sample they used would have improved the work

**some pupils will not have made so much progress and will:** with help, find information from selected secondary sources and present data in tables and bar charts

**some pupils will have progressed further and will:** explain whether the sample size in their investigation of growth was sufficient for comparisons to be made with national data

**in terms of life process and living things**

**most pupils will:** identify and name the main reproductive organs and describe their functions; describe fertilisation as the fusion of two cell nuclei; describe egg and sperm cells; explain how the foetus obtains the materials it needs for growth; describe differences between the gestation periods and the independence of the young of humans and other mammals and describe the menstrual cycle

**some pupils will not have made so much progress and will:** identify and name the main reproductive organs; describe fertilisation as the fusion of egg and sperm and identify the importance of the placenta in supplying food for a developing foetus

**some pupils will have progressed further and will:** explain how egg and sperm cells are specialised, and describe how they carry the information for development of a new life

# ➡ *Links with CASE*

This chapter looks at the CASE reasoning pattern: variables and values, including ranking, sequencing and ordering. Most pupils can do this for numerical data but some pupils still find it difficult, and most pupils will need reminding that it is a good organising strategy when looking for relationships and correlation in sets of data.

Pupils also develop their reasoning using ratio, proportionality and inverse proportionality. A ratio is a constant number by which one set of data (scale drawing) may be multiplied to give a second set of data (real life size). Ratios describe constant multiplicative relationships between two variables while proportionality requires the comparison of two ratios. Inverse proportional reasoning relies on a sound concept of ratios and proportionality. The mathematical expression of inverse proportion requires formal operational thinking. This chapter gives several opportunities for pupils to calculate ratios and use scale drawings to estimate the real size of objects. These activities are at a concrete general level and do not require formal operations.

# ➡ *Pupils' misconceptions*

There is evidence that children in Britain have more misconceptions about human reproduction than those in North America, Australia and Sweden. This may be due to the many euphemisms and folklore tales surrounding the subject. Talking to the PSHE co-ordinator is essential to establish how open and frank discussions about sex can be encouraged.

| Misconception | Scientific understanding |
|---|---|
| It is not possible to get pregnant if standing up when having intercourse or if breast feeding or if menstruating. | Position of intercourse does not affect conception. Lactation may suppress ovulation in some women but not all. While ovulation rarely takes place during menstruation it can occur within a few days and sperm may still be in the oviducts. |
| Father has no role in the production of babies. | Egg and sperm are needed for fertilisation. |
| Human eggs hatch, like a bird. | A bird's egg is formed from an ovum and a sperm. Unfertilised ova are sometimes called eggs. They are sex cells. |
| Genes mix or blend. | Genes are discrete, each being one of a pair from male and female parents. |
| Babies are born down the same passage through which urine passes. | The urethra is separate from the vagina. In the man, both semen and urine pass down the same tube (urethra). |

# ➡ *Literacy, numeracy and other cross-curricular links*

This chapter offers opportunities to develop literacy skills through speaking and writing. Discussion has a major role to play in many of the activities and particularly those related to infertility and societal issues regarding separating Siamese twins. Pupils will continue to develop skills associated with literacy by: making their own notes and summaries to clarify ideas and thinking, which can be used later; planning and developing ideas and lines of thinking into continuous text, for example joining ideas within sentences, including using links of time (then, later) through sequencing activities, and cause and effect (so, because, since); collaborating with others to share information and ideas; and solving problems and answering questions using relevant evidence or reasons.

Numeracy skills will be developed through ratio, and through drawing and interpreting graphs, calculating means, other averages, scales and percentages.

This chapter makes a major contribution to PSHE, drugs and sex education. Through group discussions, research into secondary sources of information and data processing, pupils will be helped to develop a healthy, safer lifestyle. They will be taught to recognise the physical and emotional changes that take place at puberty and how to manage these changes in a positive way; to respect the differences between people as they develop their own sense of identity; and the basic facts and laws, including school rules, about alcohol and tobacco and illegal substances. They will learn that responsible sexual relationships take place within a loving, responsible context, for example marriage, about developing good relationships and respecting the differences between people. They will learn about the role and feelings of parents and carers, and the value of family life. They will have opportunities to communicate confidently with their peers and adults about sensitive issues such as infertility, puberty and human reproduction.

## Language for learning

By the end of this chapter pupils will be able to understand, use and spell correctly:

- names of reproductive organs – ovary, testis, oviduct, uterus
- specialised terms – menstruation, ovulation, fertilisation, placenta, mammary glands, sperm, gestation
- words with similar but distinct meanings – hereditary and inherited, baby and foetus, puberty and adolescence
- words with different meanings in scientific and everyday contexts – cell, fuse
- words relating to scientific enquiry – reliability, sample size, national data.

## 1 *Introducing reproduction*

### Learning outcomes

Pupils:

- name, locate and describe the functions of the reproductive structures: ovary, oviduct, uterus, vagina, penis, testes, sperm duct

### What do you know?

➡ *Pupil's Book page 152*

This is an opportunity to check pupils' knowledge from Key Stage 2 and their own experiences outside school. The last part asks what pupils already know about how a baby is made.

*Activity* ### Discussion: Life cycles

It might be useful to open the lesson by putting pupils in pairs or groups of four, to discuss what a life cycle is and list the ones they know. (They usually recall humans and flowering plants but some pupils may keep fish or have looked at frogs.

Remind them to think about their pets.) At the end of the groups' discussion check that the whole class hears good definitions of life cycle, reproduction and adolescence. Write these up for them to copy.

Many pupils may not know that living things grow by adding new materials to their bodies (new cells) or that energy from a food source is required for this. This is dealt with later in this chapter. The concept of species has been introduced in chapter 2.

*Activity* ## Group discussion: Human reproduction

Ask pupils to talk to each other in small groups, then select a 'scribe' for each group and ask them to summarise the group's ideas on a piece of blank paper. You can encourage them to include drawings if they want. Do not get the groups to present to the whole class; this is an activity to give you information, not to teach the 'facts of life'. It is important that you assess the overall level of prior knowledge in the class so that you can respond sensitively to their existing knowledge, or ignorance, throughout this chapter.

## Did you know?

➡ *Pupil's Book page 153*

The average life span in Britain for men is now 82 and for women it is 6 or 7 years longer. You could ask pupils to give some reasons why it has increased and why there is a gender difference. This is a good question to set for homework or use as a web search topic using online encyclopaedias, such as Encarta.

## Human reproductive organs and fertilisation

➡ *Pupil's Book pages 153 and 154*

These sections contain essential knowledge that all pupils need to know. The teaching will take about 30 to 40 minutes, depending on what resources you use. Pupils need to learn the named parts of the diagrams; they must retrieve the information visually from the diagrams and from the text about fertilisation. There is a lot of information in the written text so a good video or other multimedia resource can be used to explain fertilisation. You may also have posters and models to help explain the internal and external sexual features of men and women. It is necessary to discuss the relative positions of the urinary system and the reproductive system because many pupils think they are one and the same thing.

## Answer

➡ *Pupil's Book page 153*

1 Each pupil needs this information in their own notebooks for revision purposes but encourage them to help each other. Give them time to do it for themselves then get them to swap lists and check each other's work. It is not intended that there is one correct list for the differences between men and women but most pupils will easily list the fact that men have deeper voices than women, women have breasts, men have penises, men have facial hair and more body hair. Some

pupils may list emotional differences that can be rather stereotyped – for example women get upset and cry more than men do, men are stronger and less emotional, and so on. How you handle this debate is up to you but set the class a time limit for any discussion (see below), otherwise it can expand to fill the whole lesson and reinforce stereotypes!

### *Activity* Group discussion: Men and women

An activity that encourages children to explore their own attitudes involves making a list of statements and asking children to work in mixed gender groups to discuss which they agree/disagree with or don't know. Statements could include:

- Men should never cry.
- Boys are always stronger than girls of the same age.
- Women and men should both care for children.
- Men should never hit women.
- Girls should never hit boys.
- Women have hairs on their legs.
- Boys are better at maths than girls.
- Girls talk more than boys.

## Answers

➡ *Pupil's Book pages 153 and 154*

**2 Man**

Testes: make sperm cells
Penis: urination and ejaculation of semen and sperm
Urethra: passage inside penis carrying urine or ejaculate
Prostate gland: makes seminal fluid
Ureter: carries urine from kidneys to bladder
Bladder: stores urine
Foreskin: protects the tip of the penis

**Woman**

Ovary: makes egg cells
Oviduct: carries egg cells to uterus; fertilisation will take place inside here
Vagina: during copulation, penis is inserted here to transmit sperm; also the birth passage for a baby
Womb/uterus: the fertilised egg grows in here into a baby
Urethra: carries urine from the bladder
Bladder: stores urine
Cervix: opening to the uterus (womb)

**3** Inserting the sperm directly inside the woman's body, through the penis, ensures a moist environment.

**Attainment targets**

Work in the previous sections should provide evidence that pupils are working towards the following attainment levels.

| Select information from sources provided | Level 4 |
|---|---|
| Use scientific names and identify major reproductive organs of body and identify the position of these organs in the human body | Level 4 |

# 2 *Sex cells*

## Learning outcomes

Pupils:

- identify and describe how sperm and egg cells are adapted to their function
- explain that sperm and egg each have half the inherited information needed
- know that a new life starts when a sperm fertilises an egg
- describe fertilisation as the fusion of cells
- sequence changes in sperm and eggs during and after ovulation
- calculate simple ratios, proportions
- read scales

This section links to chapter 7 Cells. Pupils should already know that all cells have a nucleus and that they can be different to suit different functions (Level 4). Start the lesson by asking pupils to each jot down five things they could tell you about cells. Go round the class and collate this information on the board. Pupils can be surprised about how much they already know collectively. Alternatively, arrange the information in a concept map as each pupil gives you one fact from his/her list.

*Activity* ## Information processing: Comparing male and female sex cells

➡ *Pupil's Book page 155*

Pupils may need calculators. Questions 2 to 4 develop pupils' mathematical skills and understanding of proportionality (a CASE reasoning pattern). Make sure pupils measure the egg and sperm cells that are drawn to the same scale, that is 500 times larger than life. The larger labelled sperm cell diagram is not to scale.

This is best done as a group activity. It helps if you group pupils by mathematical ability so that the more able can move on to Worksheet 8.1 (see below) and you can give more support to the less able. Do not expect to teach the whole class how to do the calculations; circulate and teach each group as appropriate.

## Answers

1 Differences include:
the sperm cell has a tail; the egg cell has a very large nucleus; the sperm cell does not have as much cytoplasm as the egg cell; the egg cell has a jelly coat; the sperm cell has a different shape; the egg cell is round.

2 Size (measured from diagram) of egg cell is 50 mm, length of sperm cell is approximately 45 mm (if you want greater accuracy get pupils to use a length of cotton to measure the curves of the tail). This scale diagram is 500 times bigger (this information is given in the text) than real life so the measurements must be divided by 500 to get the real size.

3 The answers must be calculated. 50/500 is 0.1 mm (100 μm) and 45/500 is 0.09 mm (90 μm). (Point out that the head of the sperm cell is really tiny.) This calculation is difficult so you may have to do it for most pupils so that they can attempt Q4.

**4** The ratio is a comparison of the diagram size to the real life size. Some of your more able pupils will spot that you have already given this information, the drawings are 500 times bigger than real life so the ratio is 500:1 (scaled up) but many will get it the wrong way around (1:500) so go through the concrete strategy of dividing the drawing size by the calculated real size. A real egg cell would fit inside the diameter of this drawing 500 times.

**5** We have to draw 'scaled up' to see them.

## Comparing cell sizes

➡ *Worksheet 8.1: Comparing cell sizes (K)*
Worksheet 8.1 is an extension activity for more able pupils (Level 6) to give them practice at the mathematics involved (scales, ratio and proportion calculations). It can be given as homework and is useful in developing numeracy skills.

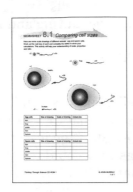

## Answers

| Egg cells | Size of drawing | Scale of drawing | Actual size |
|---|---|---|---|
| fish | 6 mm | × 2 | 3 mm |
| frog | 10 mm | × 2 | 5 mm |
| snake | 50 mm | × 2 | 25 mm |
| hen | 60 mm | × 1 | 60 mm |
| human | 1 mm | × 2 | 0.5 mm |

| Sperm cells | Size of drawing | Scale of drawing | Actual size |
|---|---|---|---|
| fish | 30 mm | × 50 | 0.6 mm |
| frog | 40 mm | × 50 | 0.8 mm |
| snake | 50 mm | × 50 | 1 mm |
| hen | 40 mm | × 50 | 0.8 mm |
| human | 20 mm | × 50 | 0.4 mm |

## Time to think

➡ *Pupil's Book page 155*
This 'reflecting back' time is required for construction and consolidation. You have given pupils a lot of information to assimilate. It makes a good homework session or alternatively you can divide the class into two quiz teams.

## Answers

- Fertilisation takes place in a woman's oviduct.
- As a sperm penetrates the egg's surface a chemical change happens to make the egg cell too tough for other sperm cells to enter.
- All other sperm cells die.
- A woman makes egg cells in her ovaries.
- A man makes sperm cells in his testes.

- Large numbers of sperm are made because so many die before they can swim up through the womb and into the oviduct to fertilise the egg cell.
- The sperm and egg cell fuse to create a zygote.

**Attainment targets**

Work in the previous sections should provide evidence that pupils are working towards the following attainment levels.

| | |
|---|---|
| Make observations and measurements | Level 4 |
| Calculate ratios, choose scales, communicate quantitative data | Level 6 |
| Describe simple cell structure, distinguish fertilisation from other processes | Level 6 |
| Explain how ovum and sperm are adapted for their function | Level 7 |

# 3 *Egg production*

## Learning outcomes

Pupils:

- recognise that rapid growth occurs at different times in the human life cycle
- describe the menstrual cycle
- make calculations to do with stages of the menstrual cycle
- recognise egg production as a cyclic activity
- know some of the reasons for infertility
- relate the concept of genetic inheritance to creation of identical and non-identical twins

## The menstrual cycle

➡ *Pupil's Book page 156*

Introduce this section with a software simulation of the cycle or make an overhead of the diagram on page 156 of the Pupil's Book and use it to give a brief talk on how to 'read' it. Girls vary enormously in what age they start their menstrual cycles so great sensitivity is required for this topic. Pupils should work in groups to answer the questions.

## Answers

4 Bleeding starts on day 1.
5 Fertilisation can take place between day 10 and day 15.
6 The lining comes away and leaves through the vagina as menstrual blood or a 'period'.
7 The lining thickens to be prepared for a fertilised egg cell. It will provide food and oxygen, and help form the placenta.

## Infertility

➡ *Pupil's Book page 157*

This section can be left out but infertility is increasing in our society and pupils may have already come across issues related to this in their own lives or in the media. 'Test tube babies' have often been in the news. The section on genetic modification in chapter 2 (Pupil's Book pages 51–52) could be used here as an opportunity to discuss the moral and ethical implications. Discussing infertility does help pupils understand the process of fertilisation. It is also useful to tell pupils that an unfertilised egg will not survive more than three days but that sperm may survive much longer. You could ask them what the fertile period is, taking this into account.

## Answers

**8** Infertility is the inability to conceive.

**9** A man's sperm production can be low.

**10** If the oviducts are blocked, surgery can unblock them.

**11** Hormone treatments can improve a woman's ovulation (egg production).

**12** The sperm fertilises the egg outside a woman's body, often in a glass container.

**13** Hysterectomy is a surgical operation to remove the womb or all of the reproductive system (womb and ovaries) so it is unlikely that a fertilised egg could implant and grow but it can happen and an ectopic pregnancy occurs (very rare).

## Growth
## Answer

➡ *Pupil's Book page 158*

**14** Zygote, embryo, foetus, baby.

## How twins are made

➡ *Pupil's Book page 158*

Some of your pupils may be twins; most pupils will have met twins so are usually fascinated to find out how they are created.

## Answer

**15** The series of drawings to show how triplets are made ensures that pupils look at the diagrams of how twins are made with understanding. This is a good group activity, using large pieces of poster paper. Usually multiple births occur when three or more eggs are produced at the same time, often as a result of using fertility drugs. Triplets formed in this way will be non-identical.

## What do you think? Science and society

➡ *Pupil's Book page 159*

You may have a more topical and up-to-date example to substitute here.

*Activity* ## Debate: Siamese twins

This is a good activity as part of a PHSE programme. It also develops debating skills and an awareness of many perspectives. The underlying issue is one that occurs time and time again through science and technology. Just because science and technology allow something to be done that could not be done before, does that mean it should be done? You could enlist the support of the Drama department and ask them to take up this issue as a role play activity.

## Answers

Answers to Q16 to Q19 will depend on pupils' views.

# 4 *Fertilisation*

## Learning outcomes

Pupils:

- note key points about reproduction in birds
- explain the advantages of internal development over external
- explain that there is a greater chance of developing eggs surviving from internal fertilisation and development

## Fertilisation in other animals

➡ *Pupil's Book page 160*

➡ *Worksheet 8.2: Survival rates (D)*

This section on other animals highlights the differences between internal (human and bird) and external fertilisation (fish and frogs).

Worksheet 8.2 on caterpillar data is a useful homework activity which consolidates earlier lessons and develops links with other concepts such as variation and adaptation (key scientific idea: interdependence).

## Answers

➡ *Pupil's Book page 160*

**20** Internal fertilisation gives the sperm cells more protection.

**21** The zygote grows attached to the yolk of an egg.

**22** Springtime is the best time of year when the weather is mild and food plentiful.

**23** Birdsong and bright plumage attract mates.

**24** If frogs mated on land the sperm cells would shrivel and die in the air. They could not swim over the female's egg cells (spawn).

**25** For frogs and fish the survival rate of fertilised eggs is low, as predators eat them. Both birds and humans can protect their young more by building protective environments (nests, homes).

**26** The tough jelly coat around fish- and frogspawn may deter some predators. Some fish do make protective 'nests' (for example the stickleback) and some frogs and fish do search out cracks in rocks to lay their eggs in.

## Answers

➡ *Worksheet 8.2: Survival rates*

**1** 5

**2**

| Cause of death | Number | Percentage of total sample |
|---|---|---|
| caterpillar disease | 260 | 53 |
| parasites of caterpillars | 152 | 31 |
| eaten by birds | 51 | 10 |
| disease of pupae | 24 | 5 |
| parasites of pupae | 8 | 2 |

*Note:* the percentage answers given here have been rounded up to whole numbers.

**3** Pupil's pie chart.

**4** 1%
Pupil's pie chart.

**5** Colour of caterpillar.

**6** All caterpillars were made from dough; all were the same size; all were placed on the upper surface of green plants; time.

**7** Number of caterpillars remaining; measured according to number of each colour remaining.

**8** Red.

**9** Green, red and brown.

**10** Yellow and white.

**11** Pupils may give one of the following answers: red is generally a warning colour, so that predators may think they are poisonous and/or toxic; predator may be red–green colour blind. Any plausible answer clearly explained should be accepted.

*Activity* ## Research: Other life cycles

You need to assemble secondary sources of information such as video clips, photographs and posters. A library loan box is useful. Ask the librarian for resources for Key Stage 2 as well as Key Stage 3. If you have enough resources this can be done as a research project, with pupils working in pairs on an animal of their choice. They can be asked to make a poster for display. If you have insufficient resources, give pupils about 30 minutes to answer the questions in writing. More able pupils should be asked to write in continuous prose using the questions as a guide.

### Equipment
- sources of information
- pens and pencils
- paper for posters

### Attainment targets
Work in the previous sections should provide evidence that pupils are working towards the following attainment levels.

| Describe the main stages of life cycles | Level 4 |
|---|---|
| Explain distribution and abundance of organisms affected by environmental factors such as predation | Level 5 |

# 5 *Development and birth in humans*

## Learning outcomes
Pupils:

- state that mammalian young are fertilised internally and develop in the uterus
- explain that measurable changes in growth result from cell division and increased size

- identify the structures in the uterus of a pregnant woman
- explain the function of amniotic fluid
- describe how nutrients get from the mother's digestive system to the foetus brain (in general terms)
- state that oxygen, water and food pass to the foetus, and waste and carbon dioxide pass from the foetus' blood to the mother's blood
- know the effects of drugs, alcohol and smoking on a baby's development
- recognise that a pregnant woman should avoid rubella

## Development and birth in humans
### Answer
➡ *Pupil's Book page 161*

**27** The level of response to this question is a good indicator for pupils at different levels. Level 4 pupils will simply state that menstrual bleeding stops when a woman becomes pregnant. Pupils capable of higher levels will indicate that the cycle stops because there is no more ovulation once a woman is pregnant, the lining of the womb does not break down, so there is no bleeding.

*Activity* ## Information processing: Human embryo development

➡ *Pupil's Book page 161*
➡ *Worksheet 8.3: Human development (S)*

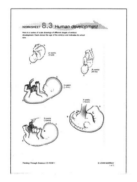

Start with Worksheet 8.3 (pupils cut out and stick pictures of embryo development). Each pupil should have this information in his or her own notebook for revision. The activity should take around 25 minutes and pupils can check each other's sequences before they are stuck down permanently. This task supports and reinforces earlier work in this chapter.

Q2–5 in the Pupil's Book develop pupils' understanding of proportionality.

## Answers
➡ *Pupil's Book pages 161 and 162*

**1** This gives pupils an opportunity to construct their own meaning from the diagrams. It is essential that pupils talk about what they see so that their observation skills are sharpened.
**2** The pictures are all approximately 4 times larger than life.
**3** The ratio is written 4 : 1 but many pupils will get this the wrong way round (1 : 4) or invent their own notation, based on the right kind of thinking (1/4, a quarter, a fourth of one whole, and so on).
**4** The pictures are all scaled up.
**5** They are drawn to scale (all the same scale – about 4 times larger than real life) so that they can be compared with each other.

Looking at the photograph on page 162:

**6** 20 weeks is about 5 months' pregnant.
**7** 4 months remain.

# Answers

➡ *Worksheet 8.3: Human development*

| Age from conception | Actual size in real life (written by each picture) | Size in picture (from A to B) | Scale |
|---|---|---|---|
| 5 weeks | 10 mm | approx. 60 mm | × 6 |
| 8 weeks | 13 mm | 65 mm (or 6.5 cm) | × 5 |
| 9 weeks | 1.8 cm | 7.2 cm | × 4 |
| 24 weeks | 37 cm | 3.7 cm | × 0.1 |
| 36 weeks | 46 cm | 4.6 cm | × 0.1 |
| 38 weeks | 52 cm | approx. 21.5 cm | × 0.4 |

*Activity* # Data processing: Human embryo growth

➡ *Worksheet 8.4: The growth of a human embryo (K)*

The rest of this lesson is for data processing activities so pupils need to work in groups of four, each group having someone who is competent at using a calculator and checking calculations. All pupils need to do Worksheet 8.4: The growth of a human embryo (plotting and reading line graphs) or something similar to practise graph-plotting skills.

## Answers

1 Line graphs as mass v. time has to be compared against length v. time.
2 Pupil's line graphs.
3 7–9 months.
4 3–6 months.
5 Mass at 1 month < 1 g; length at 7 months = 410 mm.
6 At 5 months: mass ≈ 250 g; length = 250 mm.

## The placenta

The placenta is difficult to understand for pupils so you need to use as many and varied visual aids as you can.

### Equipment
- ultrasound scans
- photographs
- software simulations

*Activity* # Group discussion: Inside the womb

Use the questions in the textbook (page 163) as the basis for discussions. Pupils need to discuss their existing ideas about how babies live inside the womb before they are given the scientific facts. This is done best in small groups. You may like to get one or two groups to tell the whole class what they think or you may get them to make some brief notes. They can look back at these and see if their ideas changed as they worked through the rest of this chapter.

## Answers

➡ *Pupil's Book page 163*

28 Children are often surprised and intrigued to find their 'belly button' is where they were joined to their mother's womb.

**29** You may need to get pupils to turn back to their work in chapter 2. The characteristics are respiration, nutrition, reproduction, sensitivity, growth, excretion, and movement.

**29** and **30** The foetus gets its food from the food the mother eats. She digests her food, and glucose is released into her blood, which gets carried to the placenta. There is no solid waste (faeces) for a baby to get rid of before it is born because it has not eaten any food. Waste is sent back into the mother's bloodstream via the placenta.

The foetus does show all characteristics of living things. It does respond to light and sound. The amniotic fluid is protective.

**31** Pupils do not need to know why the blood supplies are kept separate but this is a good opportunity for them to generate their own hypothesis and to use deductive reasoning (Level 6).

The two blood supplies do not mix for several reasons: their blood pressures are different (think of the relative sizes of hearts and bodies); the mother's bloodstream contains chemicals (for example, large protein molecules, some hormones) which are prevented from entering the babies' bloodstream by the membranes of placenta acting as a barrier; and the baby may be a different blood group from the mother.

## Harming the unborn baby

➡ *Pupil's Book page 164*

This is part of the PSHE programme. Pupils should make their own notes after being encouraged to talk to each other and at home. They could carry out some research using the library or local health centre. The school nurse or a local midwife may be prepared to come and give a short (no more than 10 minutes) talk and give out samples of health care leaflets designed for prospective parents.

## Answer

**32** A display of published posters and leaflets and the pupils' own posters could be made.

# 6 *Pregnancy times and birth*

## Learning outcomes

Pupils:

- explain the process of birth
- know that the length of aftercare is related to the level of development of young at birth
- describe how a newborn baby gets nourishment for growth
- recognise that breast milk contains antibodies to build the baby's immune system
- plot and read growth data from graphs
- sequence the stages of foetal growth and birth

*Activity* Information processing: Lifespans and pregnancy times

➡ *Pupil's Book page 165*

It is best if pupils do this section individually so you can assess their data processing skills and help pupils who struggle. It will take between 30 and 40 minutes. The table provides information that needs re-ordering if pupils are to see that there is a correlation between lifespan and gestation. A suitable graphing software package is helpful. Spreadsheet 'Lifespans.xls' on the CD-ROM can be used for this activity.

## Answers

**1** The variables are species of mammal, lifespan and gestation time.

Pupils are not expected to list all the values of the variables, as they are already written in the table. This is an important exercise to ensure they understand the difference between variables and values. The values for the variable 'mammal' are the names of each type of animal, the range of values for the variable 'lifespan' is from 1 to 85 years and the range of the variable for 'gestation time' is from 15 days to 84 weeks.

Questions 2 and 3 are exercises for transforming data from one form to another.

**2** There is a relationship: the longer the lifespan, the longer the time taken for the young mammals to develop inside the mother before they are born.

**3** Encourage groups of pupils to try out different methods, for example, pie charts, bar charts. Display pupils' work and ask the class to evaluate them. Which look most attractive? Which are easy to read? Which show the relationship most clearly? Are they all showing data correctly?

ICT link: web search for www.newton.dep.anl.gov and 'Ask the scientist' about human lifespan. You might ask:

• Has the human lifespan increased over the years? If so, why?
• What was the average lifespan of Neanderthal man or woman?
• Why do women live longer than men on average?
• Could we predict how long the average lifespan will be by the end of the twenty-first century, using past trends?

## Gestation

➡ *Worksheet 8.5: Gestation in domestic and wild cats (K)*
This worksheet involving variables, values and relationships, and scatter graphs, can be used as an extension activity or for homework. It is useful for developing graphing skills. Part A is for pupils working below Level 4 and part B is for pupils working at Level 5 or above.

## Answers

### A Gestation in domestic cats

1 Average gestation time is 1135 ÷ 18 = 63 days (rounded up to whole day).

2 One cat has exactly the same gestation time as the average.

3 A larger sample would give a more accurate average gestation.

4 Ask the vet any of these questions:
Were the cats selected randomly?
Do they all live close together?
Do they come from lots of different places?
Are they all the same age or do they represent the whole age range of fertile cats?

5 Diet, age, general health are all factors that might affect gestation time.

6 Draw a bar chart of the number of cats with particular gestation times.

7 Easier to see how many cats show the same gestation time.

8 The table shows individual cats. The bar chart does not.

### B Gestation in big cats

1 There is probably a correlation because as the gestation time increases, the mass generally increases.
Pupil's scatter graph.

2 The variables are:
Species
Gestation time
Mass

3 Range for gestation time is 66–106 days. Range for mass is 8–250 kg.

4 Scatter graphs show correlation patterns better than other types of graphs.

*Activity* ## ICT: The birth of a baby

→ *Pupil's Book page 166*
This is a description that could be read individually as homework or read through in groups. It is useful to show a film of the birth of a baby at this stage but make sure it has been made for this age range.

### Equipment
• suitable video of the birth of a baby

## Answer

33 Some pupils may not know any details about their own birth. You may want to send a letter home warning parents that their children may ask them for details. In primary school, many pupils will have brought photographs of themselves to school. You could ask them to do this again and do a 'spot the baby' naming quiz – include your own photograph or other science staff (with their permission!).

# 7 *Development*

## Learning outcomes

Pupils:

- recognise that there is wide variation in the development of children
- present height and other human development data in a graph
- read and interpret growth and development graphs and tables
- suggest reasons for differences between class and national data and explain in terms of sample size
- describe observable changes of puberty and know they are a consequence of growth and circulating hormones
- provide examples of how physical and emotional development proceed at different rates
- share information and discuss ideas
- distinguish between aspects of reproduction – fertilisation, gestation, pregnancy and birth

## Human development

➡ *Pupil's Book page 167*

It is useful to begin this section by finding out if anyone has baby brothers or sisters and asking them to tell the class what progress they have noticed in their siblings from birth to their current age. In Key Stage 2 pupils will have described the human life cycle in terms of infancy, childhood, adolescence, maturity and ageing. Use resources such as video clips showing responses of a newborn baby, and other animals, for example deer, birds, kittens, immediately after birth/hatching.

## Answer

**34** After pupils have discussed the purpose of each reflex, they could write their own notes. This could be done for homework. The swallowing and sucking reflex helps ensure the baby gets sufficient milk from the mother's breast. The 'rooting' reflex helps the baby find and grip the mother's nipple in his mouth. The grasping reflex may be from a time in our evolution when babies had to hang on to their mother's bodies as they moved about. This reflex is particularly strong in monkeys who have to hang on as their mothers swing through trees! The startle reflex and the falling ('moro') reflex also help a baby to stay securely fastened to an adult. The walking reflex helps strengthen babies' muscles in preparation for standing upright and learning to walk. It is important for young mammals of some species to be able to walk and run as early as possible – foals, calves and lambs all stand and walk within an hour of birth and quickly learn to run. These are all grazing animals that could be preyed on by carnivores.

## *Activity* Research

➡ *Pupil's Book page 168*

The research activity here could be linked to the 'Harming the unborn baby' section above. It could be given as a homework/after school activity over several weeks. Think about dividing the class into groups, each of which researches a specific aspect, for example immunisation, drugs, alcohol, smoking, good nutrition for weaning a baby, helping babies learn to speak, creative play, hygiene.

*Activity*  ## Information processing: Growth patterns
➡ *Pupil's Book page 168*
Ask pupils to look at the data in groups and talk about what they think the diagram is about. Get a response from each group then ask them to complete the questions. This is an unusual diagram to look at because it shows the relative increase in size of head, trunk and legs as well as overall growth. Human growth is not linear and the head grows relatively slowly compared to the trunk and legs.

### Answers
1  Measurements of the head size (top to bottom) in the diagram are: 1.8 cm, 1.4 cm, 1.1 cm, 0.9 cm, and 0.8 cm.

2

| Age | Head (cm) | Body (cm) | Ratio (to nearest whole number) |
|---|---|---|---|
| newborn | 1.8 | 6 | 1 : 3 |
| 2 years | 1.4 | 6 | 1 : 4 |
| 6 years | 1.1 | 6 | 1 : 6 |
| 12 years | 0.9 | 6 | 1 : 6 |
| 20 years | 0.8 | 6 | 1 : 8 |

At birth the baby's head is nearly a third of the total body length, at 2 years it is about a quarter of the body length, by 6 years it is about a sixth, by 12 years it is still about a sixth and by adulthood it is about an eighth. Remind pupils that brain growth is rapid in humans (look at the development data on page 167 of the Pupil's Book to see how much children learn to do in the first 18 months of life after birth) and this correlates with head growth.

3  This is a question for discussion and there is no right answer. Pupils are expected to make reasoned suggestions. Importance of sample size was made clear in chapters 1 and 2. Remind pupils that samples should be representative. The larger the sample, the more representative it is. Selection should also be representative, for example, different ethnic origins would be represented, maybe geographic location, economic circumstances of the parents, and so on.

## Puberty in humans
➡ *Pupil's Book page 169*
Again this is a sensitive issue because children vary enormously in their rate of development at this age. Pupils need reassuring that they are 'normal' and do not want to be different from their peers. It is useful to leave a box of easy-to-read books and pamphlets about adolescence for pupils to browse through. The English department can recommend suitable novels dealing with adolescent changes.

## Answers

**35** For women changes include: menstruating, growing breasts, skin texture changing (possibly becoming greasier and less delicate), hair growth in groin and under arms, gradual deepening of the voice, emotional and sexual feelings become stronger.

Men's voices 'break' – get lower dramatically, darker hair growth on chest, groin, under arms and on legs and arms, testicles enlarge and descend, skin may become more greasy, sexual and emotional feelings grow stronger.

**36** Menstruation is sometimes known as a 'period' or 'monthlies'. Your pupils may know other names. This may be a question you do not wish to draw attention to but let pupils read for themselves to avoid embarrassment in mixed sex classes.

## *Activity* Data collection

➡ *Worksheet 8.6: What is 'normal'? (K)*

This worksheet should be done by all pupils working in groups. You may give each group a different set of data to collect and process and then make a class display. If you used Worksheet 2.7 in chapter 2 (Being average) then your class may have already collected some or most of the data requested here. You could continue to process this and, if not already on a spreadsheet, create a spreadsheet-based activity or use the existing spreadsheet. Note that the questions asked here are different to those on Worksheet 2.7 so pupils are not being asked to do repetitive tasks. As well as developing ICT skills, this worksheet encourages the investigative skills of pattern seeking and clarifying.

### Attainment targets

Work in the previous sections should provide evidence that pupils are working towards the following attainment levels.

| Describe the main stages of the life cycles of humans | Level 5 |
|---|---|
| Identify and explain functions of reproductive organs in humans | Level 6 |
| Describe some of the causes of variation between living things | Level 6 |

# 8 *Consolidation*

## Learning outcomes

Pupils:

- draw conclusions about the number of offspring and investment in aftercare by comparing frogs and humans
- produce an account identifying key points and linking them in an appropriate sequence, using links of time and cause

## Frog development

➡ *Pupil's Book page 170*

This section again returns to comparing human development with that of another animal, an amphibian.

*Activity*

## Information processing: Birth rates

➡ *Worksheet 8.7: Birth rates (K)*

Before starting to make life cycles (Q37 in the Pupil's Book) pupils could do Worksheet 8.7 (ranking and plotting data as a bar chart) to reinforce their graphing skills.

## Answers

**1–5** Answers will depend on pupils' views. Note for Q5: biologically, some women over 45 years may have already experienced the menopause.

**6** Pupil's graph. This needs to be a bar chart, because of the different age ranges.

**7** Age on horizontal axis. Number of births on vertical axis.

**8** Between 19 and 20–25.

**9** Girls under 11 years do not usually ovulate (release eggs).

*Activity*

## Enquiry: Looking at life cycles

### Equipment

- video clips and photographs about reproduction in animals where fertilisation is external, for example in fish, frogs

### Safety

If live frogs or fish are examined ensure that up-to-date health and safety recommendations are followed (see ASE or CLEAPSS websites, for details see Appendix).

## Answers

➡ *Pupil's Book page 170*

**37** Pupils are encouraged to represent information in different ways, as a life-cycle model (Level 5). How they do this can be as creative as you and they want. Provide lots of coloured paper, crayons and photocopied pictures to cut out and stick. Printing labels using a computer adds to the appearance of the finished products.

Q38–40 are to promote group discussions in class. Each pupil can then write up his or her own answers for homework.

**38** and **39** Humans develop slowly because the parents invest time and energy in parental care, suckling, protecting and teaching the young baby. Frogs have no parental care so many young tadpoles get eaten by predators or die because they get cold.

**40** This is a matter of opinion but discouraging the young from creating babies at too young an age is strongly recommended! It is worth stating that the average age a woman has her first baby in this country has gone from about nineteen 50 years ago to the mid-twenties now. Be sensitive, as some pupils may have very young or very old parents and may feel they are being criticised.

## Time to think

➡ *Pupil's Book page 171*
This is a self-assessment section. It is best done by giving pupils no more than 10 minutes to jot down their individual responses to the questions and then 10 minutes to work with a partner or in a group of friends to compare their responses. Alternatively, use it as homework.

## Review

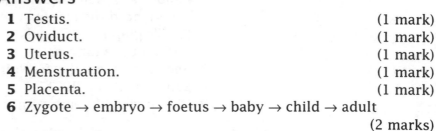

➡ *Worksheet 8.8: Test on reproduction*
This worksheet provides a 20 minute test to check on understanding of this chapter.

## Answers

**1** Testis.                                                                (1 mark)
**2** Oviduct.                                                             (1 mark)
**3** Uterus.                                                               (1 mark)
**4** Menstruation.                                                    (1 mark)
**5** Placenta.                                                           (1 mark)
**6** Zygote → embryo → foetus → baby → child → adult
                                                                                (2 marks)
**7** Divides/cell division.
    Travels to uterus/implants.                              (2 marks)
**8** Low sperm count.
    Blockage in oviducts.
    Under-developed uterus.
    No egg cells in ovaries.
    Problems with menstrual cycle.          (Any 2 for 2 marks)
**9** Help her produce eggs/ovulation.
    Produce *more* eggs each month/cycle.
    Control menstrual cycle.                    (Any 2 for 2 marks).
**10** Non-identical – 2 eggs produced.
    Both eggs fertilised.
    Identical – zygote splits.                              (3 marks)
**11** Fish.
    Amphibians.                                                   (2 marks)
**12** Better diet.
    Healthier because of medicines/better living conditions.
                                                                                (2 marks)

# 9 Solutions

→ ## Rationale

This chapter provides up to 8 hours of teaching materials. The first part of the chapter builds on the Key Stage 2 work on dissolving, filtration, evaporation and condensation. The pupils will have dissolved common substances such as sugar and salt in water and explained that, although they cannot be seen, they are still present (tested by taste). They will have tested one or two factors that help a solid dissolve more quickly and explained what the results show, for example 'the salt dissolved faster when the water was hotter'. They will have probably done some separations with sieves and filter paper and explained that mixtures can often be separated because the large grains won't go through the holes but the small ones will (for example a sieve will separate marbles from water but not sand and water, whereas a filter will separate sand from water but not water and dissolved salt). They will have described how a dissolved solid can be recovered from water and used the term evaporation.

The main aim of the chapter is to build on ideas about the particle theory introduced in chapter 4 Solids, liquids and gases. Pupils extend their knowledge of dissolving by looking at saturated solutions. They will be introduced to the idea that mass is conserved when a solid dissolves in water and begin to use the particle model to explain what happens. They will extend their knowledge of the separation of the components of a mixture by filtration, distillation and chromatography and relate this to particle theory. They begin to distinguish between a 'pure' substance and a mixture. There will also be opportunities to apply the particle model of solids, liquids and gases in a range of contexts to enable pupils to recognise that the model can be used to explain a range of phenomena.

In terms of scientific enquiry, pupils develop their skills at controlling variables, measuring mass and evaluating when comparing the solubility of sugar and water. In a study of the effect of temperature on solubility, for example: they choose equipment; measure temperature; plot a line graph; identify patterns in data about solubility and make predictions from these; identify anomalous results; evaluate reliability and accuracy.

This chapter takes the ideas developed in chapter 4 on particle theory further and provides opportunities for pupils to use the model more broadly, before moving on in Year 8 to Atoms and molecules, and Compounds and mixtures. In Year 9 progression is encouraged in various topics and the idea is developed considerably in Using chemistry.

# Overview

The textbook sections, activities and worksheets have been arranged into 1 hour blocks to aid lesson planning. Clearly several of the activities and worksheets could form part of a homework session. The planning includes reading time for individual sections but some teachers may prefer to organise this as homework preparation for the following lesson. Five types of worksheets – extension (E), support for an activity (S), practical (P), key skills (K) and developmental (D) – allow for differentiation and to fit with teachers' preferred practice. The actual timing and emphasis on different sections will depend on the current knowledge base of the pupils, the ability of the teaching group and the preferences of the teacher.

| Lesson | Worksheets |
|---|---|
| **1** Solutions | |
| **2** Dissolving | Worksheet 9.1: The dissolving story (K) |
| **3** Measuring solubility | Worksheet 9.2: Which is more soluble: salt or sugar? (P) |
| **4** Increasing the solubility | Worksheet 9.3: The effect of temperature on solubility (P) Worksheet 9.4: Accuracy and improvements (D) |
| **5** Separating salt from rock salt | Worksheet 9.5: Separating salt from rock salt (P) |
| **6** Separating water from salt water | Worksheet 9.6: Separating pure water from salt water (P) |
| **7** Chromatography | Worksheet 9.7: Separating a mixture of coloured dyes (P) |
| **8** Applying the particle theory | Worksheet 9.8: Solution definitions card chase (S) |
| Review | Worksheet 9.9: Test on solutions |

# ➡️ *Chapter plan*

| | Demonstration | Practical | ICT | Activity | Word play | Time to think |
|---|---|---|---|---|---|---|
| **Lesson 1** | Dissolving<br><br>Tom's plan | | | Evaluation: Where has the solute gone? | | What do you know? |
| **Lesson 2** | Get cleaning | | Simulation/ Video | Helpsheet: The dissolving story<br><br>ICT: Dissolving | | Dissolving |
| **Lesson 3** | | Which is more soluble? | | Information processing: Different solutions<br><br>Enquiry: Which is more soluble: salt or sugar? | Scientific language | |
| **Lesson 4** | | Solubility of benzoic acid at different temperatures | | Enquiry: To investigate the effect of temperature on the solubility of salt using method 2<br><br>Extension: Accuracy and improvements<br><br>Information processing: Solubility data | | |
| **Lesson 5** | | Separating salt from rock salt | Internet/ CD-ROM/Video | Research | Salt | Extracting salt |
| **Lesson 6** | Separation of water and paint | Separating pure water from salt water | | | | Extracting water |
| **Lesson 7** | Making a wick | Separating a mixture of coloured dyes | | | | Chromatography |
| **Lesson 8** | | | | Revision: Time to think | | Solutions and particle theory |

# ➡️ *Expectations*

**At the end of this chapter**

**in terms of scientific enquiry**

**most pupils will:** control the variables in a fair test; make measurements of temperature and mass; present experimental results as line graphs, pointing out patterns; describe observations and explain them; identify patterns in data about solubility, and make predictions from these; interpret data from chromatograms

**some pupils will not have made so much progress and will:** explain why a test is fair; make measurements of temperature and mass; produce simple line graphs of results and point out patterns in these

**some pupils will have progressed further and will:** make measurements of temperature and mass; choose their own scales in plotting a line graph; identify anomalous results and suggest a possible explanation; interpret and explain the significance of data from chromatograms

**in terms of materials and their properties**

**most pupils will:** classify some solids as soluble or insoluble and explain the meaning of the term 'saturated solution'; describe how mixtures can be separated by filtration, distillation and chromatography and begin to use the particle model to explain what happens when a solid dissolves in water, explaining why mass is conserved

**some pupils will not have made so much progress and will:** name some soluble and insoluble solids; describe how salt can be separated from rock salt, pure water can be obtained from sea water and how different colours can be separated from some inks

**some pupils will have progressed further and will:** use the particle model to explain a range of phenomena

# ➡ *Links with CASE*

In this chapter pupils will further develop their reasoning skills in the recognition of variables and in the control and manipulation of variables. These skills will be utilised when pupils plan a fair test.

The reasoning pattern of ratios and proportionality is used when pupils are asked to compare the concentrations of different solutions both qualitatively and quantitatively. This provides access to the reasoning pattern at both concrete and formal operational levels.

The particle theory is used to explain phenomena such as dissolving, evaporating, condensing and chromatography, allowing pupils to utilise thinking through formal models. It is not expected that all pupils will be able to carry this out successfully, as the cognitive demands of explaining a range of phenomena through a model is very high.

# ➡ *Pupils' misconceptions*

| Misconception | Scientific understanding |
|---|---|
| Dissolving and melting are the same process. | Melting occurs when enough attractions between the particles of a solid are broken so that they are no longer arranged in fixed positions. |
| When a solid dissolves in a liquid, it disappears. | When a solid dissolves in a liquid, the component particles separate from each other and mix in with the solvent particles. |
| When a solid dissolves in a liquid, the mass of the solution is less than the mass of the solid + liquid. | All of the solute is still present in the solution and mass is conserved. |

# → *Literacy, numeracy and other cross-curricular links*

There will be ample opportunity to develop speaking skills through discussion in this chapter. Explanations, descriptions of ideas and using models are all very useful in promoting speaking skills. Writing skills are encouraged through DARTs activities (Directed Activities Related to Text) and story writing.

Numeracy skills are developed through calculations, analysing and interpreting graphs, and ratio.

## Language for learning

By the end of this chapter pupils will be able to understand, use and spell correctly:

- words and phrases relating to dissolving and the separation of mixtures – solution, solute, solvent, insoluble, saturated solution, filtration, distillation, chromatography
- words and phrases relating to explanations using the particle model – particle, attracted, vibrating
- words and phrases relating to scientific enquiry – prediction, evaluate, interpret
- words with similar spelling but different meanings, and use them in a consistently correct way – affect, effect
- words that have different meanings in scientific and everyday contexts – solution.

They will also understand the etymology of words such as 'salary', 'chromatography'.

# 1 *Solutions*

## Learning outcomes

Pupils:

- state that the mass of a solution is the same as the mass of the solute and solvent, for example if you dissolve 10 g of salt in 50 g of water, you will get 60 g of salt solution
- describe, for example using annotated diagrams, how solute and solvent particles mix
- explain that as the particles mix no matter is lost, so the mass remains the same
- name some solids that dissolve in water and some that do not
- state that some solids dissolve more in some liquids than in others

## What do you know?

→ *Pupil's Book page 172*

This topic is concerned with the separation of mixtures by dissolving substances or changing state. The purpose of this first, short activity is to check on prior learning.

## Answers

**1** In this Cloze activity, the missing words have been given as **key words**. It is best to get some feedback on this question before tackling Q2.

A = boiling
B = filtering
C = dissolving
D = freezing
E = melting
F = condensing

**2** It is quite likely that the pupils will have done some of this work before. There is an advantage in having pupils from different feeder primaries in each group so that there is a range of experiences to share.

Two possible methods for the separation are:

- Use a kitchen sieve to let through the small sugar grains but not the glass. The problem is that there could be some small pieces of glass that could pass through the holes in the sieve.
- Dissolve the mixture in hot water, filter the sugar solution through filter paper and then evaporate.

After comparing answers, ask 'How does a filter paper work?'. A sieve only lets small grains of a substance through. A filter paper only lets the smallest particles of matter through (refer back to chapter 4). This reference back to particle theory could be extended by asking for an explanation of 'How could some of the water particles in the hot coffee end up as condensation on the window?'

## Is there a solution?

➡ *Pupil's Book page 173*

Several studies have shown that the two major misconceptions relating to dissolving are:

- **conservation of mass:** even at 15–16 years old, only half of the students believed that the mass of a solution of salt would be the same as the mass of the solute and solvent. The problem is that the salt has 'disappeared' – it cannot be seen, so it has no mass.
- **dissolving/melting:** the terms 'dissolve' and 'melt' are often used synonymously. Although this misusage decreases with age, it is still commonly heard, even from adults.

*Activity* ## Demonstration: Dissolving

The teacher could demonstrate the two types of aspirin mentioned in the Pupil's Book (page 173) by stirring them in water. Most brands of soluble aspirin do not fully dissolve. Also demonstrate a simple solubility test for the following four solids in water: sand, copper sulphate, stearic acid and salt. A simple method is to place four test tubes in a rack and half fill with water. Add a small spatula end of each substance, stopper and shake for 10 seconds. (*Note:* this is a test to see if a solute dissolves or not. Later experiments will test how much dissolves.) Compare results. Encourage the pupils to use the key words.

**Equipment**
- aspirin tablets: 'normal' and soluble
- two beakers (250 cm³) and two stirring rods
- small samples of sand, copper sulphate (CARE: harmful), stearic acid and common salt
- four stoppered test tubes

*Activity* Evaluation: Where has the solute gone?
## Answers
➡ *Pupil's Book page 174*
1 Zoe's plan was too dangerous. You should never taste anything in a science laboratory.
2 Nisha's plan was to evaporate the water, leaving behind the salt.
3 Tom's plan was to show that the mass of water and salt at the beginning of the experiment was the same as the mass of the solution at the end.
4 Pupils should use the words soluble, solute, solvent and solution.

*Activity* Demonstration: Tom's plan
Demonstrate Tom's plan to emphasise the conservation of matter (see Pupils' misconceptions, page 182). The pupils will experience weighing and dissolving later in the chapter.

**Equipment**
- beaker (100 cm³)
- measuring cylinder (50 cm³)
- balance (0.1 g)
- container of common salt
- glass rod

# 2 *Dissolving*

## Learning outcomes
Pupils:

- describe in writing and by drawing the arrangement, the proximity and motion of particles in solids and liquids
- use the particle theory to show how particles behave when solutions are formed
- state that some solids dissolve more in some liquids than in others

## Time to think
➡ *Pupil's Book page 174*
Different groups could feed back orally and with diagrams. Key points are:

- when the particles mix, no matter is lost, so the mass remains unchanged
- the 'Particles in a box' model can show a solution very clearly – it is a liquid with two different types (colours) of particles.

*Note:* solubility is sometimes introduced with the 'dissolving salt in a beaker full of water' demonstration or the 'rice into dried peas' model. Both imply that the solute particles are so small that they fit in between the spaces of the solvent particles. This is not the case and these approaches are best avoided. The reason for the negligible change in volume when dissolving ionic solutes in water is rather more complex. In a later practical exercise (see page 188), when sugar is dissolved in water, there is a noticeable *increase* in volume on forming the saturated solution.

## *Activity* Helpsheet: The dissolving story

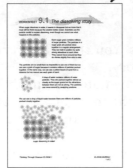

➡ *Worksheet 9.1: The dissolving story (K)*
Worksheet 9.1 offers an alternative/additional exercise to explain dissolving using the particle theory. The sheet is also designed to develop literacy skills.

## *Activity* ICT: Dissolving

If pupils are finding difficulty with these concepts, further work could involve:

- the 'marbles in a tray' model, which, if done carefully, can show the process where the particles of a solid move apart and mix through the liquid particles. By holding one group of coloured marbles in position (the solid) and gently rocking the tray to allow the second type of marble (the liquid) to dislodge the solid particles, a mixture is eventually formed.
- an ICT simulation or video clip, which can show dissolving very effectively, for example *Scientific Eye*: 'Salty water' or *Science in Action*: 'Mixtures'.

## *Activity* Demonstration: Get cleaning

➡ *Pupil's Book page 175*
It is worthwhile demonstrating this problem using the two tins of paint, with two paint brushes coated in each type of paint and two beakers each of water and white spirit. Keep the white spirit out of sight at first and pose the question 'How would you clean these brushes?'. Then show the effects of the two solvents (including the negative results), emphasising that different types of paint (solute) dissolve in different types of solvent to give a solution. Emulsion paint is insoluble in white spirit and gloss paint is insoluble in water.

You can also demonstrate that a small spatula end of stearic acid dissolves readily in a different solvent (propanone). Remind the pupils that stearic acid did not dissolve in water. Also show that salt does *not* dissolve in propanone.

### Equipment
- small tins of gloss paint and emulsion paint
- four paint brushes
- four beakers (250 cm³)
- white spirit (CARE: flammable)
- small samples of stearic acid and salt
- two stoppered test tubes
- small bottle of propanone (CARE: highly flammable)

## Answers

1  The dry-cleaning solvent left on the clothes evaporates. In an enclosed space like a car, the vapour could affect the driver.

2  **a)**  Creosote and tar.

   **b)**  Dry-cleaning fluid.

   **c)**  Solvent.

   **d)**  The solvent may damage the fabric.

### Attainment targets

Work in the previous sections should provide evidence that pupils are working towards the following attainment levels.

| | |
|---|---|
| Name some soluble and insoluble solids | Level 3 |
| Use the scientific words for physical changes, such as evaporating and condensing | Level 4 |
| Identify a range of contexts in which physical changes take place | Level 5 |
| Explain why mass is conserved in dissolving | Level 5 |
| Recognise that materials are made up of particles and begin to describe the movement and arrangement of particles | Level 5 |
| Begin to use the particle theory to picture a solution | Level 6 |

# 3 *Measuring solubility*

## Learning outcomes

Pupils:

- use proportionality to compare concentrations
- state that there is a limit to the amount of solid that dissolves in a particular volume of water
- describe differences between the amounts of different solids that dissolve in the same volume of water
- state that a saturated solution has been formed when crystals appear in the solution
- evaluate an experiment in terms of reliability

## Concentration

## Answers

➡ *Pupil's Book page 176*

3  The one on the left has less orange squash particles and more water particles than the one on the right.

4

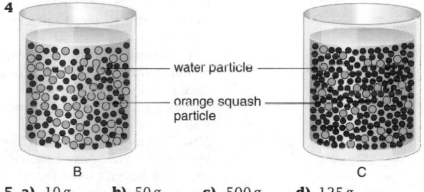

         B                    C

5  **a)**  10 g    **b)**  50 g    **c)**  500 g    **d)**  125 g

*Activity*   Information processing: Different solutions

➡ *Pupil's Book page 178*
This exercise is related to the CASE Reasoning pattern: Ratios and proportionality.

### Answers
**1 a)** Rajit's = 48 g per 100 cm³ of water.
   Anna's = 50 g per 100 cm³ of water.
**b)** Anna's is the more concentrated.
**2 a)** BigSave = 6 g per 100 cm³ of water.
   LowPrice = 5.6 g per 100 cm³ of water.
**b)** LowPrice is the more dilute.
**c)** BigSave has 3 g per 50 cm³ of water.

*Activity*   Enquiry: Which is more soluble: salt or sugar?

➡ *Pupil's Book page 179*
In an investigation, it is important that the pupils understand the question that is posed. This investigation is *not* about how *fast* the two solutes dissolve or about how to make *more* dissolve. This activity is designed to teach pupils the skills of identifying variables and evaluating a plan.

### Answers
**1 a)** The more accurate value for the outcome variable is the mass of sugar and salt.
**b)** Other important fixed variables are:

| Variable | Values |
| --- | --- |
| volume of solvent | 10 cm³ |
| temperature | room temperature |
| mixing | steady shaking for 15 seconds |

**c)** All of the variables are kept at the same value for the two experiments except the type of solute.
**2** Repeat each experiment a few times and average the results.

*Activity*   Practical: Which is more soluble?

➡ *Worksheet 9.2: Which is more soluble: salt or sugar? (P)*
This practical is derived from the above planning exercise.

As indicated in the textbook, one method is to weigh out 10 g of salt in a beaker. 10 cm³ of water is measured out into a test tube and spatula ends of the salt are added with shaking until no more dissolves. The solution is now saturated. The remaining salt in the beaker is weighed and, by subtraction, the mass of dissolved salt can be obtained. The experiment is then repeated for sugar.

To save time, each group should do either sugar or salt and combine the results as indicated on the worksheet.
*Note 1:* At 25 °C, the solubilities are, roughly, sodium chloride (salt) 3.8 g/10 cm³ of water, and sucrose (sugar) 5.6 g/10 cm³ of water.
*Note 2:* Some teachers may like to draw the pupils' attention to the relative volumes of the two saturated solutions (provided that they haven't used the 'rice and dried peas' model to demonstrate dissolving).

**Equipment**
Each group will need:

- test tube with rubber bung
- beaker ($100 \, cm^3$)
- spatula
- common salt or sugar (about $10 \, g$)
- calculator

And per class:

- at least two balances (one decimal place)

## Answers

1 A simple bar chart is appropriate since the input variable is in words and the output variable is in numbers (and there are only two results).
2 Emphasise that replication and averaging produces a more reliable result, and a good test of the reliability of the method is to examine the spread of the results.
3 Possible reasons for variation in results include: the amount of undissolved solute is likely to vary in each experiment due to the 'spatula end' method; and pupils may have not used the measuring cylinder correctly (not reading at eye level).
4 The results are not likely to be very accurate. The error in the mass of solute is due to the 'one spatula end'. An alternative, more accurate method is used later on.
5 The accuracy could be improved in this method by using much smaller 'spatula ends' or by weighing the solute and adding the same quantity each time.

## Word play
## Answers

➡ *Pupil's Book page 179*
1 Example answers:
   **a)** The sugar was dissolved in the water to form a solution.
   **b)** I have found a solution to the problem.
2 At first sight, the word solution has different everyday usage, meaning 'explanation' or 'answer'. However, in both cases, the result is that something 'disappears' – the sugar and the problem!

# 4 *Increasing the solubility*

## Learning outcomes
Pupils:

- choose sensible pieces of equipment for an experiment
- state that a saturated solution has been formed when crystals appear
- state the solubility at a particular temperature, for example 'at 70 °C, 3 g of the solid dissolved in 10 g of water'
- describe the way in which the solubility of the solute varies with temperature
- use the pattern of solubility data to predict solubility at higher and lower temperatures
- draw a line graph from solubility data

*Activity* ## Enquiry: To investigate the effect of temperature on the solubility of salt using method 2

➡ *Pupil's Book page 180*

The aim of this section is to develop the enquiry skill of selecting appropriate equipment.

### Answers

**1 a)** Although a 0–50 °C thermometer is more accurate than a 0–100 °C, it is unsuitable in this case because the crystals may form above 50 °C.

**b)** A 100 cm³ measuring cylinder would be used to make up the original solution.

**c)** A balance accurate to 0.1 g is probably the best choice. A 1 g balance would give a larger percentage error (2.5 per cent at 40 °C) and the other two balances would be far too accurate for the general method.

**d)** A 250 cm³ beaker would be used. The 100 cm³ beaker would be too small since stirring is needed to dissolve the solute.

**e)** The rubric mentions a volume of about 10 cm³, so beakers are inappropriate. A boiling tube is probably better than a test tube since it has to also contain a thermometer.

**2** The second method is more accurate because the solubility is measured when the first few crystals of salt appear. The first method uses successive spatula ends of salt giving a greater margin of error.

*Activity* ## Practical: Solubility of benzoic acid at different temperatures

➡ *Worksheet 9.3: The effect of temperature on solubility (P)*

This practical is derived from the above planning exercise except that benzoic acid is used because the 'first appearance of a few crystals' is more obvious.

*Notes:*

• Six solutions are needed of the following concentrations: 0.5, 1.0, 1.5, 2.0, 2.5 and 3.0 g/100 cm³ of water.

• 100 cm³ of the six solutions should have been previously made up and heated to about 90 °C to fully dissolve the solute.

• Samples of roughly 10 cm³ are then transferred to labelled boiling tubes in a thermostatted water bath at around 90 °C.

• The boiling tubes can be distributed to pupils when they are ready.

• Warn of the danger of the very hot solution.

• Warn about careful stirring with the thermometer – don't push the thermometer through the bottom of the boiling tube.

### Equipment

Each group will need:

• boiling tube containing one of the solutions (CARE: harmful at higher concentrations)

• eye protection

• thermometer (0–100 °C)

• rack to hold the boiling tube

• calculator

And per class:

- thermostatted waterbath(s) at around 90 °C with racks to hold boiling tubes of each of the six solutions

A rough guide to expected values:

| Concentration (g in 100 cm³ of water) | 0.5 | 1.0 | 1.5 | 2.0 | 2.5 | 3.0 |
|---|---|---|---|---|---|---|
| Saturation temperature (°C) | 33 | 50 | 63 | 70 | 77 | 82 |

A reference table for the solubility of benzoic acid:

| Temperature (°C) | 20 | 30 | 40 | 50 | 60 | 70 | 80 | 90 | 95 |
|---|---|---|---|---|---|---|---|---|---|
| Solubility (g in 100 cm³ of water) | 0.29 | 0.42 | 0.60 | 0.95 | 1.20 | 1.77 | 2.75 | 4.55 | 6.8 |

## Presenting evidence

The aim of this section of Worksheet 9.3 is to develop some enquiry skills.

## Answers

### Reliability of results

1 a) If the repeat readings obtained from the different groups are very similar, the results can be described as reliable.

   b) You can obtain a more reliable value for each temperature by taking several temperature readings at each solubility and comparing the results at each temperature.

2 If there is one result that is very different from, say, another four which are very similar, you would reject the anomalous result and decide that the other four are reliable. It is possible for the results to be reliable but inaccurate, for example if the thermometers consistently read 10 °C too low.

### Presentation of results

The table should include all of the temperature values for each concentration and the mean value.

### Plotting a graph

3 The input variable is the solubility (concentration) and the outcome variable is the temperature when the crystals first form.

4 and 5 This method produces data in which the outcome variable (temperature) is plotted on the horizontal axis. Pupils may need help with the graph, depending on their ability and experience with graphs at this stage.

### Considering evidence

6 The word relationship is used in the CASE programme to explore the link between the input and outcome variables. The graph should be a curve so the relationship is not direct proportionality.

7 Points should be read from the pupil's graph. These require interpolation and extrapolation skills.

8 The result should be about 60 °C, but take readings from pupils' graphs and discuss any deviance from 60 °C in terms of accuracy and/or reliability.

9 It should dissolve at about 80 °C.

*Activity* Extension: Accuracy and improvements

➡ *Worksheet 9.4: Accuracy and improvements (D)*

This is an optional, extension worksheet on accuracy. The discussion is more important than the 'correct' results; the order is debatable but a suggested order is:

| Order | Accuracy | Improvements |
|---|---|---|
| **1** Rajeev and Rose | Valid comments about accuracy. | 0–100 °C thermometer is a good choice. A temperature probe is probably too accurate. |
| **2** Jill and Sam | It does not matter what volume of solution is used. The concentration is still the same. Their method does limit accuracy if one student is doing both jobs. | No need to measure out the volume of the solution. Sharing the jobs would make the method more accurate. |
| **3** Tom and Alice | They have confused accuracy with reliability. There is no point in recording the temperature to three decimal places. | Using a computer to get a ten decimal place value is pointless. |
| **4** Mary and Ben | They have confused accuracy with fair testing. | Changing the boiling tube will not affect the fair test. |

*Activity* Information processing: Solubility data

Answers

➡ *Pupil's Book page 181*

**1 a)** As the temperature increases, the solubility increases.
   **b)** 46 g
   **c)** 80 °C
   **d)** 43 g
   **e)** 8 g

**2 a)** The higher the temperature, the greater the solubility.
   **b)** Approx. 24 g/100 cm$^3$ of water.
   **c)** 62 g/100 cm$^3$ of water.
   **d)** Approx. 59 °C.

**3 a)** 2.0 g/100 cm$^3$ value is anomalous.
   **b)** The point is much further from the line of best fit than the other points.
   **c)** For example, the temperature was taken too late, after much more than a few crystals were formed.
   **d)** The higher the temperature, the greater the solubility.
   **e) i)** Approx. 45 °C. **ii)** Approx. 83 °C.

**Attainment targets**

Work in the previous sections should provide evidence that pupils are working towards the following attainment levels.

| | |
|---|---|
| Explain the meaning of 'saturated' solution | Level 4 |
| Recognise that materials are made up of particles and begin to describe the movement and arrangement of the particles | Level 5 |
| Begin to use the particle theory to explain what happens when a solid dissolves in water | Level 6 |

# 5 *Separating salt from rock salt*

## Learning outcomes

Pupils:

- plan a method for obtaining a sample of salt from rock salt
- explain why the mass of the salt sample was less than the mass of rock salt
- state that salt comes from a variety of sources and list some uses

## The salt industry

➡ *Pupil's Book page 183*

Show a sample of rock salt and refer to the pictures and the text.

## Time to think
## Answers

➡ *Pupil's Book page 184*

- In hot countries, sea water is trapped in lagoons and left to evaporate using the energy of the Sun.
- In the UK, salt is obtained from brine by heating to evaporate off the water (modern methods use evaporation under vacuum in huge evaporator vessels).
- The lumps of rock salt must be crushed and the salt dissolved in hot water which is then filtered off from the insoluble 'sand'. This solution is then evaporated.

*Activity* ## Practical: Separating salt from rock salt

➡ *Worksheet 9.5: Separating salt from rock salt (P)*

It is very likely that most of the pupils will have separated salt from sand in primary school. If you wish to do the familiar practical exercise, Worksheet 9.5 provides guidelines.

The pupils may not be familiar with some of the apparatus used in secondary school, for example evaporating dish, conical flask.

- Put a selection of apparatus on display and invite the pupils to choose the appropriate ones for their plan. Include some equipment that is not necessary and some different sizes of a given piece of apparatus (for example, beaker: 100, 250, 500 cm$^3$).
- Use a felt/velcro 'word wall' with stick-on line drawings of the piece of apparatus and their corresponding names. Invite pupils to match up each diagram with a name. This is also useful when the pupils come to write up their plan.

The extension work on the worksheet requires extra steps in the plan:

- weigh the rock salt before the dissolving step
- weigh the salt after it has been extracted and dried
- obtain the mass of sand by subtraction (or weighing)
- to make a valid comparison with other groups, they should have all started with the same mass of rock salt (not likely) or use percentage or proportion.

CARE: tell the pupils that they should not evaporate to dryness because this results in 'spitting' of hot grains of salt. Suggest that it is best to use partial evaporation and leave to stand.

*Notes:*

- Place a few spatula ends of the powdered rock salt in the beaker and add about $30 \, cm^3$ of water.
- Warm on a tripod and stir carefully to dissolve the salt.
- Filter the warm solution into the conical flask.
- Transfer to the evaporating dish and partially evaporate.
- Leave to cool and crystallise.

**Equipment**

Each group will need:

- sample of 'rock salt' (a mixture of common salt and sand)
- beaker ($100 \, cm^3$)
- conical flask ($100 \, cm^3$)
- Bunsen, tripod and gauze
- filter funnel and filter paper
- evaporating dish
- eye protection

And per class:

- balance ($0.1 \, g$) if the extension work is done

**Evaluating**

For the extension work, when all of the results have been obtained, different methods could be compared in terms of how much salt is extracted or the different techniques and equipment used.

## Answers

1. The difference in mass is due to the rock (sand) that has been removed.
2. The grains of salt are too big to go through the very small holes in the filter paper. When salt is dissolved, it is split up into extremely small particles that do fit through the holes in the paper.

*Activity* ## Research

➡ *Pupil's Book page 184*

Possible sources of information include:

- video, for example *Science in Action:* 'Mixtures'
- CD-ROM, for example *Encarta*
- Internet, for example The Salt Manufacturer's Association website at www.saltinfo.com. This website is available on the CD-ROM as an intranet file that can be readily accessed through a web browser without the problems associated with surfing the web.

## Answers

1. To prevent ice forming on the roads.
2. **a)** For example: dyeing; to preserve food.
   **b)** For example: chlorine (used in swimming pools); PVC plastic.

**3 a)** It contains less sodium than table salt.
  **b)** Common salt is associated with high blood pressure.

## Word play

➡ *Pupil's Book page 184*
This information is readily found in a good dictionary.

**1** Examples of sayings about salt are:
  *Salt of the earth*
  *Worth his salt*
  *Rub salt in a wound*
  *Take with a pinch of salt*
  *To salt away*
**2** Roman soldiers were partly paid in salt which gave rise to the word salary (*salarium*).

# 6 *Separating water from salt water*

## Learning outcomes
Pupils:

* describe how a solvent can be separated from a solute by heating the solution (evaporation), followed by cooling (condensation)
* explain that separation works because the solvent changes to a gas and back to a liquid, but the solute does not

## Separating water from sea water
## Answers
➡ *Pupil's Book page 185*
**6 a)** Water vapour condenses in the condenser; pure water drips into the beaker.
  **b)** The solute (salt) does not evaporate during the heating process because it has a much higher boiling point than the solvent (water).
  **c)** 100 °C.
  **d)** A white solid would remain. This is the salt.

*Activity* ## Demonstration: Separation of water and paint
Demonstrate the separation of water from poster paint solution using the apparatus shown in the textbook for desalination, page 185. If poster paint is used instead of salt as the solute, it will show more clearly what happens to the solute and the solvent.

Start by dissolving the coloured powder (solute) in the water (solvent) to emphasise the idea that water is being separated from a solution containing a solid. Discuss how the condenser works. What will be the reading on the thermometer?

**Equipment**
* Quickfit apparatus for distillation including a Liebig condenser
* poster paint powder

*Activity* Practical: Separating pure water from salt water

➡ *Worksheet 9.6: Separating pure water from salt water (P)*
Pupils may have used distillation in primary school, for example, to separate water from ink. If you wish to do the familiar practical exercise, Worksheet 9.6 can be used.

Unlike paint, salt cannot be seen in solution. To test that the distillation has worked, we cannot use taste (for safety reasons), but there is a chemical test for salt. Demonstrate the use of a few drops of silver nitrate solution to test whether salt is present in the salt water and in the distilled water. CARE: eye protection is needed with silver nitrate.

- Show the apparatus available and compare the functions of each part with the demonstration distillation.
- Use gentle boiling to avoid salty water boiling over into the collecting test tube.
- Remove the delivery tube from the test tube when a few $cm^3$ of distilled water have been collected, before removing the heat. This avoids suck-back.
- Emphasise that the salt water should not be boiled dry.

**Equipment**
Each group will need:

- sample of salt water (approx. $30\,cm^3$)
- conical flask ($100\,cm^3$) with fitted bung and delivery tube
- beaker ($250\,cm^3$)
- test tube
- Bunsen, tripod and gauze
- clamps and stand
- eye protection

And per class:

- dropper bottles of silver nitrate solution (less than $0.2\,M$)

**Safety**
Wear eye protection when using silver nitrate solution. This solution also stains the skin.

## Answers
1 The beaker of cold water condenses the water vapour.
2 There is not enough water remaining in the flask to dissolve all of the salt.

## Time to think
## Answers
➡ *Pupil's Book page 186*
1 A lot of energy is needed to distil water on a large scale and energy is very expensive. The alternative process of reverse osmosis is often used.
2 This question presents an opportunity for the pupils to use their understanding of particle theory in some extended, creative writing.
3 This is intended to be an exercise in investigating through technology (designing something to solve a problem). Commercial products are now available which act as solar stills. They are inflated and towed behind the liferaft. The

sea water is evaporated, condensed and collected. A possible answer is shown below. Reverse osmosis hand pumps are also available.

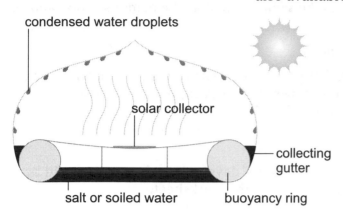

condensed water droplets

solar collector

collecting gutter

salt or soiled water

buoyancy ring

# 7 *Chromatography*

## Learning outcomes

Pupils:

- use chromatography to separate and identify different solutes
- use particle ideas to explain how chromatography works
- interpret chromatograms, explaining what the evidence shows
- describe a situation in which chromatography provides useful evidence

Chromatography involves separating a mixture of solutes.

*Activity* ## Demonstration: Making a wick

Demonstrate the filter paper/wick method:

- Place a small spot of black fountain pen ink that contains a range of colours (for example Quink ink) at the centre of a piece of filter paper.
- Cut a 'wick' into the filter paper as shown below.
- Place the filter paper on to a beaker (250 cm³) and let the water soak up the wick and spread across the paper.

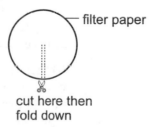

filter paper

cut here then fold down

### Equipment

- Quink ink
- teat pipette
- beaker (250 cm³)
- filter paper
- scissors

### *Activity* Practical: Separating a mixture of coloured dyes

➡ *Worksheet 9.7: Separating a mixture of coloured dyes (P)*
The practical uses the same method as the demonstration above.

**Equipment**
Each group will need:

- water-soluble felt tip pen or Smarties (use a moistened, fine paint brush to remove the colouring from a Smartie)
- beaker (250 cm$^3$)
- filter paper
- scissors

While the chromatograms are developing, the pupils could be discussing the questions on the worksheet.

## Answers

1 The same type of filter paper, solvent (water), amount of ink, and time for the chromatogram to develop.
2 The type of brown ink.
3 Measure the distance moved by each dye. Identical dyes will move the same distance.

## Analysing foods
## Answers
➡ *Pupil's Book page 187*
7 **a)** Lime sweet.
  **b)** The lime sweet contains an extra colouring, Patent blue.
  **c)** Only the lemon sweets are safe.
  **d)** Both sweets are safe.

## Forensic science
➡ *Pupil's Book page 188*
The uses described in the Pupil's Book, and the investigation on Worksheet 9.7, demonstrate the practical roles of science in everyday lives. This is often very motivating for pupils and can be linked with popular detective films, programmes and novels.

## Word play
➡ *Pupil's Book page 188*
1 **a)** In cells.
  **b)** Because scientists use a coloured dye as a stain in order to see them.
  **c)** Chromium forms many coloured compounds.
2 It records earthquakes.

**Attainment targets**
Work in the previous sections should provide evidence that pupils are working towards the following attainment levels.

| | |
|---|---|
| Describe how simple mixtures can be separated by filtration, distillation and chromatography | Level 4 |
| Use knowledge of separation techniques to suggest ways in which various mixtures can be separated | Level 5 |
| Interpret and explain the significance of data from chromatograms | Level 5 |
| Begin to use the particle theory to explain what happens in a range of separation techniques such as dissolving, filtration, distillation, chromatography | Level 6 |

# 8 *Applying the particle theory*

## Learning outcomes

Pupils:

- recognise the key words from the chapter and pair them up with their descriptions
- show by modelling how particles behave when solutions are formed or components of solutions are separated
- describe what the models show

*Activity* ## Revision: Time to think

➡ *Pupil's Book page 189*

### Card game

➡ *Worksheet 9.8: Solution definitions card chase (S)*

This is intended as a quick revision exercise relating to the large number of new words covered in this chapter. There are two alternative approaches to the card game. The pupils can make their own as indicated in the Pupil's Book, or there is a prepared set of cards on Worksheet 9.8.

The words and definitions on the worksheet should be photocopied onto card and then cut up to give 26 word/definition cards. Distribute all of the cards to the class (depending on numbers and ability, pupils with reading problems could be paired up with others, and some pupils could have more than one card).

Explain that each card has a word on the left and a definition for a different word on the right. Ask one pupil to read out a definition. The pupil with the correct word shouts out the word and then reads out the definition from the right hand side of their card. Help may be needed. Measure the time taken to complete the task. Then repeat it to see how much improvement can be made.

### Presentation

The presentations of the four topics outlined in the Pupil's Book can be made in various ways:

- poster or OHT
- PowerPoint
- 'Pupils as particles' role play (as in chapter 4, Worksheet 4.2). For this activity the group size should be roughly 10 pupils. Lab stools and/or benches will be useful in some cases (for example they could represent filter paper or a container). Pupils need to think how they can represent two or three different types of particle. Each group could be asked to prepare two of the listed changes.

Instructions for the evaluation are given in the Pupil's Book.

# Review

→ *Worksheet 9.9: Test on solutions*

This worksheet provides a 20 minute test to check on understanding of this chapter.

# Answers

**1** Liquid/mixtures.

Dissolves.

Soluble.

Insoluble. (4 marks)

**2 a)** A solution with a lot of solvent (e.g. water) but only a small amount of solute/solid dissolved. (2 marks)

**b)** The mass of solute in a set volume of solvent; a solution with a lot of solute dissolved in a small volume of solvent. (2 marks)

**3 a)** 9 g in 100 cm$^3$ of water. (1 mark)

**b)** Econoway's because it has only just over 8 g of ethanoic acid per 100 cm$^3$ of water (*or* less ethanoic acid dissolved per 100 cm$^3$). (2 marks)

**c)** $9 \times 15$.

135 g. (2 marks)

**4 a)** Yes.

**b)** No.

**c)** Yes.

**d)** No. (4 marks)

**5** Detecting small traces of explosives on people.

Detecting small traces of drugs on people.

Analysing small traces of substances on clothing.

Identifying the type of ink used, e.g. for forged signatures. (Any 2 for 2 marks)

**6** Desalinisation (also allow distillation). (1 mark)

# The Solar System

## ➡ Rationale

This chapter provides about 9 hours of teaching materials. It builds on Key Stage 2 work, particularly the material in Unit 5E The Earth, Sun and Moon.

Most children are fascinated by space and astronomy, and bring to lessons a wealth of detailed knowledge that can be utilised to take everyone's knowledge forward. Astronomy is probably the oldest of the sciences and an historical perspective, using the specific example of the Mayan culture of Central America, is provided in the Pupil's Book. Teachers may wish to choose a different historical perspective, such as that of the Ancient Greeks or the Chinese.

The chapter looks at the Earth and our Solar System, the Moon, and the Sun. It then considers the Solar System in general, finishing up with a brief look at the place of our system in the Milky Way galaxy and within the expanding Universe. Information is provided through analysis of data and the use of models.

## ➡ Overview

The textbook sections, activities and worksheets have been arranged into 1 hour blocks to aid lesson planning. Clearly several of the activities and worksheets could form part of a homework session. The planning includes reading time for individual sections but some teachers may prefer to organise this as homework preparation for the following lesson. Five types of worksheet – extension (E), support for an activity (S), practical (P), key skills (K) and developmental (D) – allow for differentiation and flexibility to accommodate teachers' preferred practice. The actual timing and emphasis on different sections will depend on the current knowledge base of the pupils, the ability of the teaching group and the preferences of the teacher.

| Lesson | Worksheet |
|---|---|
| **1** Identify pupils' needs | Worksheet 10.1: The Solar System and beyond (S) |
| **2** Historical perspective | |
| **3** Modelling the Earth, Sun and Moon | |
| **4** The Sun and Earth | Worksheet 10.2: Making a clinometer (P)<br>Worksheet 10.3: A cola can sundial (the shepherd's dial) (P) |
| **5** The Moon | Worksheet 10.4: Phases of the Moon (1) (S)<br>Worksheet 10.5: Phases of the Moon (2) (S)<br>Worksheet 10.6: Moonwatch (P) |
| **6** The Solar System (1) | |
| **7** The Solar System (2) | Worksheet 10.7: Tunguska explosion in Siberia (K) |
| **8** The Universe | Worksheet 10.8: Powers of ten (S)<br>Worksheet 10.9: The millionaire quiz (S)<br>Worksheet 10.10: Planets and stars (S)<br>Worksheet 10.11: A Ride On A Comet (E) |
| **9** Sc1 investigation: The impact of craters | |
| Review | Worksheet 10.12: Test on the Solar System |

# ➡ *Chapter plan*

| | Demonstration | Practical | ICT | Activity | Word play | Time to think | Ideas and evidence |
|---|---|---|---|---|---|---|---|
| **Lesson 1** | | | CD-ROM | Discussion: What do you know?<br><br>ICT: Movement of Earth and Sun | | What do you know? | |
| **Lesson 2** | | | CD-ROM/ Internet/video | | | | The origins of astronomy |
| **Lesson 3** | | Using models | Using a spreadsheet/ simulation | | Star | | |
| **Lesson 4** | Energy from the Sun | Making a clinometer<br><br>Making a shepherd's sundial | Using a spreadsheet Simulation Datalogging | Reasoning: Sunrise to sunset | | | |
| **Lesson 5** | Phases of the Moon<br><br>Eclipses | | CD-ROM/video<br><br>Video/simulation | Revision: Phases of the Moon | | | |
| **Lesson 6** | | | CD-ROM/ Internet | Information processing: The Solar System<br><br>Information processing: Scale models | | | |
| **Lesson 7** | | | | Reasoning: Considering evidence | | Planets | |
| **Lesson 8** | | | Video | ICT: Powers of ten<br><br>Revision: The Universe | | | |
| **Lesson 9** | | | | Enquiry: Craters | | The Solar System | |

# → *Expectations*

**At the end of this unit**

**in terms of scientific enquiry**

**most pupils will:** describe and explain a phenomenon of the solar system, for example, solar eclipse; describe ways in which evidence about the solar system has been collected; interpret patterns in data with respect to a model of the solar system, for example, the tilt of the Earth causing seasonal variation; select information from secondary sources to present a report about a planet and evaluate the strength of evidence from data

**some pupils will not have made so much progress and will:** describe a phenomenon of the solar system using some scientific terms; describe patterns in seasonal variation, for example, day length, climate; use simple secondary sources to collect information about a planet

**some pupils will have progressed further and will:** describe and explain a phenomenon of the solar system, showing that explanations have changed over time; use a model of the Earth, Moon, Sun system to explain patterns in data, for example, seasonal variations, and relate this to real observations; and use a range of secondary sources in finding information to report on aspects of the solar system

**in terms of physical processes**

**most pupils will:** relate eclipses, phases of the Moon and seasonal changes to a simple model of the Sun, Earth and Moon system; describe the relative positions of the planets and their conditions compared to Earth; state that the Sun is a star and that stars are light sources, while planets and other objects in the solar system reflect light

**some pupils will not have made so much progress and will:** describe how the Moon orbits the Earth and the Earth spins while orbiting the Sun; identify some differences between features of the Earth and other planets; recognise that the Sun and stars are light sources but the Moon reflects light

**some pupils will have progressed further and will:** explain, using models, patterns or associations in data about the Earth and other planets in the solar system, for example, relationship between distance from Sun and orbital period; use large numbers appropriate to these; make comparisons between the Sun and other stars

# → *Links with CASE*

In this chapter there are many references to the use of models to explain the motion of the planets in the Solar System. In addition pupils are encouraged to look for patterns in data about the planets.

# ➤ *Pupils' misconceptions*

| Misconception | Scientific understanding |
|---|---|
| The Earth is stationary. | The Earth moves around the Sun once a year. |
| The Earth is flat. | It is spherical.<br>We live on the surface. |
| Day and night is caused by the Sun moving round the Earth once a day. | The Earth rotates on its axis (spins) once every 24 hours. |
| The Earth is nearer the Sun in summer and further away in winter and this causes the seasons. | The Earth's axis is tilted and always points in same direction. This causes the seasonal changes. |
| The Sun and the Moon move round the Earth. | The Moon orbits the Earth.<br>The Earth (and Moon) orbit the Sun. |
| The Earth is the biggest astronomical object. The Moon and the Sun are about the same size. Stars are very small. | The stars (including our star, the Sun) are much larger than the planets including our planet Earth, which is larger than the Moon. |
| The shadow of the Earth covers the Moon. | The Moon's phases depend on the portion of the illuminated Moon which we can see from the Earth. |

# ➤ *Literacy, numeracy and other cross-curricular links*

Literacy is developed through speaking and writing in this chapter. Reading from newspaper articles, comprehension activities, extended writing and imaginative writing all have a part to play in this development. The short story 'A Ride On A Comet' by Carl Sagan and Ann Druyan was written to celebrate the return of Halley's comet. It provides the opportunity for extended reading. The article from *The Times* allows pupils to consider evidence presented factually in a newspaper article and consider writing for a specific audience.

Numeracy skills are developed in this chapter in a different manner than in other areas. Pupils will have the opportunity to use very large numbers and begin to get an understanding of their meaning. They will also make scale comparisons using large numbers.

There are strong links with the History curriculum. The Year 9 Unit 21 From Aristotle to the atom: scientific discoveries that changed the world? covers the ideas of people in ancient civilisations concerning the structure and functioning of the Universe. Aristotle's idea of a geocentric Solar System dominated thinking for over 1500 years until the work of Copernicus. There is also opportunity to consider the attitude of the Roman Catholic Church to Galileo and why he was tried for heresy, which allows pupils to consider science and society issues.

## Language for learning

By the end of this chapter pupils will be able to understand, use and spell correctly:

* words that have different meanings in scientific and everyday contexts – poles, atmosphere, crescent, wax
* words relating to the Solar System – constellation, asteroid, eclipse, orbit, planet, satellite, comet, galaxy, revolution, anticlockwise, axis, meteor, equinox, clinometer, wane, annular
* words and phrases relating to historical and more general contexts – hieroglyphics, codex, equator, Arctic circle, Mayan civilisation, hemisphere, elliptical.

# 1 *Identify pupils' needs*

## Learning outcomes

Pupils:

* represent the Sun, Earth and Moon by spheres and identify them in a model or diagram representing the system
* use the model to explain why the Sun appears to move across the sky during a day

*Activity* ## Discussion: What do you know?

➡ *Pupil's Book page 190*
➡ *Worksheet 10.1: The Solar System and beyond (S)*

The approach suggested here is to encourage pupils to construct a concept map to show their understanding at the start of the topic. Teachers may then wish to revisit this at the end of the topic so that pupils can update their concept maps in the light of their new knowledge.

Another way to encourage pupil discussion is to provide a number of statements on cards around the laboratory. Pupils can go round in pairs considering the statements, before they are discussed as a class group. A sample set of statements are provided on Worksheet 10.1 that can be cut and pasted from the document to make up cards. A separate table for the answers and comments is also provided.

## Answers

➡ *Worksheet 10.1: The Solar System and beyond*

| | | |
|---|---|---|
| 1 True. | 15 True. | 28 False. |
| 2 False. | 16 True. | 29 False. |
| 3 False. | 17 False (elliptical). | 30 False. |
| 4 True. | 18 False. | 31 True. |
| 5 True. | 19 True. | 32 False. |
| 6 False. | 20 True. | 33 False. |
| 7 True. | 21 False. | 34 False. |
| 8 False. | 22 False. | 35 False. |
| 9 False. | 23 False. | 36 False. |
| 10 True. | 24 False. | 37 False. |
| 11 True (the equinoxes). | 25 False. | 38 False. |
| 12 False. | 26 False. | 39 False. |
| 13 False. | 27 True. | 40 False. |
| 14 False (*daylight* changes). | | |

## Answers

➡ *Pupil's Book page 192*

**2 a)** 'The Earth goes round the Sun' and 'the Earth spins on its axis' are both correct statements. Evidence comes from photos from space.

**b)** The Earth spins on its axis. The Earth takes 24 hours to spin on its axis, so the position of the Sun will change.

**3 a)** The Earth turns round once a day. By turning, the Sun's position will change and will 'disappear' at night.

**b)** Because the Earth takes 24 hours to spin on its axis.

**4 a)** Pupils explain this by referring to a place on the globe as the globe rotates.

**b)** It spins anticlockwise when viewed from the North Pole, so the Sun 'rises' in the East and 'sets' in the West.

*Activity* ## ICT: Movement of Earth and Sun

If teachers have the facilities, there are a number of CD-ROMs available such as 'RedShift 3' to simulate the relative movement of the Earth and Sun in space. ('RedShift 3' is avilable from Focus Multimedia, www.focusmm.co.uk.) An alternative would be to get pupils to demonstrate the relative movements, or use an orrery.

### Equipment

• orrery

At the start of this topic teachers may wish to distribute Worksheet 10.6: Moonwatch, on which pupils are asked to draw their observations of the Moon.

### Attainment target

Work in the previous sections should provide evidence that pupils are working towards the following attainment level.

| | |
|---|---|
| Pupils demonstrate knowledge and understanding of physical phenomena such as how the apparent position of the Sun changes over the course of a day | Level 4 |

# 2 *Historical perspective*

## Learning outcome

Pupils:

• extract information from sources to create a composite picture that represents the understanding that people in ancient civilisations had of the Universe and the Earth's place in it

## Ideas and evidence: The origins of astronomy

➡ *Pupil's Book page 193*

This historical perspective is an approach that may not appeal to all teachers; in which case it may be combined with later work in lesson 6. However, this is a rich area in which pupils may be allowed to consider the wider aspects of scientific development. As well as the discoveries of the Mayans, pupils could investigate the discoveries of the Greeks, Babylonians or Arabs. They could produce a time-line on astronomical discoveries. They could use the Internet, the Encarta CD-ROM or reference books to find out about myths, legends and beliefs of others such as the Australian Aborigines, the Chinese, or Hindus. They could find out about the measurement of time, the development of the chronometer, or the astronomical telescope.

A different approach would be to introduce the material through a selection of video clips such as 'Powers of Ten' (see lesson 8 notes, page 215).

### Equipment
* relevant reference material or videos

## Answers
1 He wrote a book on astronomy.
2 Central America.
3 In the tropics at certain times of year, the Sun is directly overhead and so there is no shadow cast.
4 In leather-bound bark-paper books, using a hieroglyphic system.
5 The Spanish invaders destroyed them.
6 Halley's comet was first recorded by the Chinese in 240 BC.

# 3 Modelling the Earth, Sun and Moon

## Learning outcomes
Pupils:

* describe how differences in orbit and rotation time affect phenomena, for example day length, year length
* use models to explain how day and night occur, involving the Earth's rotation on its axis from west to east
* use the model to explain the passing of a month and of a year and to explain that a day is the time for one revolution
* describe that the axis of spin of the Earth is at an angle to the Sun (the Earth is tilted on its axis at about 24° to the orbital plane)
* observe that the Sun and stars seem to move from east to west, and use the idea of the Earth's rotation to explain this apparent movement
* distinguish between luminous and non-luminous objects and explain that the Sun is our source of light
* explain that we can see the Sun and other stars because they are light sources

Lessons 3, 4 and 5 all link together and so the time spent on each can be adjusted according to the pupils' interests, their ability and prior knowledge. In the first part teachers will need to establish that pupils understand the difference between the Sun as a source of light and the Moon as a reflector of the Sun's light.

*Activity* ## Practical: Using models
Pupils will need a physical model to demonstrate the Earth spinning on its axis from west to east and to demonstrate the orbit of the Earth around the Sun (and the Moon around the Earth). It is worth making sure that the model used is clearly

visible by all as it can be used effectively to show day and night, the variation in day length throughout the year, the seasons, the phases of the Moon and eclipses.

During this topic teachers will have several opportunities to further discuss the use of models in science. In lesson 6 the use of models is again referred to in the activity *Information processing: scale models*. A spreadsheet 'Scalemodels.xls' is provided on the CD-ROM to accompany this activity. The diagram of the marbles, balls and so on in the Pupil's Book on page 194 shows, for example, the use of a variety of objects to represent the relative sizes of the planets. Any set of objects may be used as long as they are to the same scale.

Some schools may possess an orrery, in which case this could be demonstrated. It will be an alternative way of discussing the use of models in science – in this case to represent the movements of the bodies in the Solar System. (The name orrery is in honour of the Earl of Orrery who purchased one in 1712 from John Rowley, who manufactured them in London.) Teachers may wish to discuss whether the parts are to the same scale in terms of both planetary size and their distance from the Sun.

An alternative to a mechanical orrery is a demonstration using a computer simulation. This is easily demonstrated to the whole class if the laboratory has either a large screen monitor or an LCD projector.

**Equipment**
- models of the Solar System

## The Earth, Sun and Moon
## Answers
➡ *Pupil's Book page 195*
1  The time for the Earth to spin once on its axis.
2  A day would last much longer; it would be colder during the night and warmer during the day.
3  The Sun. (Proxima Centauri is the next nearest star.)
4  To compensate for the fact that the Earth takes $365\frac{1}{4}$ days to circle the Sun.

# 4 *The Sun and Earth*

## Learning outcomes
Pupils:

- identify on a diagram or model parts of the Earth which are experiencing different seasons, due to their relative position with respect to the Sun
- explain that a year is the time for the Earth to orbit the Sun once
- explain why the height of the Sun in the sky varies predictably both during the day and during the year
- construct and use a clinometer
- explain that the seasons are due to the tilt of the Earth's axis
- explain how sundials can be used to measure time, and construct a sundial

*Activity*   ## Reasoning: Sunrise to sunset

➡ *Pupil's Book page 197*

The textbook refers to the use of a clinometer to measure the altitude of the Sun and there is an activity to plot the results from an experiment using a clinometer. These are deliberately not perfect results and there is an opportunity for teachers to discuss lines of best fit.

### Answers

1  7.00 a.m. to 7.00 p.m. 12 hours.
2  The graph is a similar shape but has a lower slope. The highest point is at midday because clocks/watches are changed for British Summer Time by setting 1 hour back.
3  Approximately 7½ hours.
4  Approximately 16°.
5  East.
6  East.
7  North.

*Activity*   ## Practical: Making a clinometer

➡ *Worksheet 10.2: Making a clinometer (P)*

Pupils can construct their own clinometer and Worksheet 10.2 gives detailed instructions. The use of a clinometer and the height of the Sun in the sky links to the explanation of seasons that is covered in the Pupil's Book. Teachers may wish to demonstrate the reason for the seasons using a globe and lamp or using an ICT simulation. This will reinforce earlier work on the Earth's orbit.

### Equipment
• card
• scissors
• straw
• protractor
• small weight on thread as a plumb line
• transparent sticky tape
• glue

## Sundials

➡ *Pupil's Book page 198*

The work on sundials is an interesting way of extending the work from Key Stage 2, Unit 5E on shadow sticks. A number of books give suggestions for constructing sundials, as do a number of sites on the Internet.

### Answers

5  **b** = About 2.30.
   **c** = About 4.15.
   **d** = About 9.30.
6  Shortest is around midday and longest is first thing in the morning and just before sunset.
7  In winter the shadows are longer.
8  Because the further west you go the later the Sun rises.
9  May, June and July.

*Activity* Practical: Making a shepherd's sundial

→ *Worksheet 10.3: A cola can sundial (the shepherd's dial) (P)*
The worksheet gives details of how to make the sundial.

**Equipment**
- copies of hour line sheet
- cola can
- glue
- Blu-tack
- card

*Activity* Demonstration: Energy from the Sun

The relative strength of the Sun's energy could be demonstrated using a lamp and temperature probe embedded in a sand tray. The light source illuminates the tray from different angles and for each position the temperature change is logged over a period of time. This needs to be carefully set up and is worth practising beforehand. The sets of readings may be superimposed on the same graph using suitable datalogging software such as 'INSIGHT'. This has links to 'Energy from the Sun' in chapter 12.

**Equipment**
- datalogging equipment
- lamp
- sand tray

**Attainment target**
Work in the previous sections should provide evidence that pupils are working towards the following attainment level.

| Use simple models to explain effects caused by the movement of the Earth | Level 5 |
| --- | --- |

# 5 *The Moon*

## Learning outcomes
Pupils:

- explain that the Moon reflects the light from the Sun
- know that the Moon orbits the Earth
- sequence the phases of the Moon over a 28-day period
- explain how the view from the Earth of the Moon causes the phases in a regular sequence
- explain that the Moon's phases are due to the portion of the illuminated Moon visible from the Earth
- sequence a series of images showing stages of an eclipse
- explain, using a model and diagrams, how eclipses of the Sun and Moon occur, in particular that eclipses of the Sun occur when the Moon passes directly between the Sun and the Earth, and eclipses of the Moon occur when the Earth is directly between the Sun and the Moon
- describe the evidence that eclipses provide about the Solar System, for example relative sizes and distances of the Moon and the Sun, and other phenomena, for example roosting of birds
- describe the experience of a solar eclipse

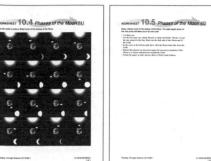

*Activity*   Revision: Phases of the Moon

➡ *Worksheet 10.4: Phases of the Moon (1) (S), Worksheet 10.5: Phases of the Moon (2) (S), Worksheet 10.6: Moonwatch (P)*
Pupils will have covered the changes in the Moon's appearance in Key Stage 2, Unit 5E. For revision pupils should have the opportunity to demonstrate their understanding of this by sequencing a set of images. Worksheets 10.4 and 10.5 are provided for this purpose. In 10.4 the shapes of the Moon are given and the pupils only have to get the sequence correct. Worksheet 10.5 is more demanding and requires the pupils to complete the shapes themselves. Alternatively teachers may wish to utilise CD-ROMs or video clips to reinforce the topic. With the advent of digital cameras it is also relatively simple to produce a sequence of photos of the Moon taken over a period of a few weeks. An alternative night-time activity would be for the pupils to look at the Moon at the same time each evening and draw the Moon's shape and position in the sky. A sample worksheet is provided for this, Worksheet 10.6.

*Activity*   Demonstration: Phases of the Moon

The reason for the phases of the Moon is often not understood and teachers will probably wish to demonstrate this experiment, which is described in the Pupil's Book (page 201).

**Equipment**
• overhead projector
• ball (the size of a tennis ball) mounted on a stick

## The Moon
### Answers

➡ *Pupil's Book page 201*
**10** You would see half the Moon illuminated.
**11** The Moon is increasing towards full Moon from half Moon.

*Activity*   Demonstration: Eclipses

The formation of eclipses can be demonstrated or pupils could watch a video or use ICT for a simulation.

**Demonstration 1**
To show the relative positions of the Earth, Moon and Sun during an eclipse.

**Equipment**
• reading lamp to represent the Sun
• ball to represent the Moon
• pupil is the Earth

**Demonstration 2**
To show the stages of an eclipse.

**Equipment**
• OHP          • card          • scissors

Cut a circular disc from the sheet of card. The hole (about 4 cm diameter) represents the Sun. The disc represents the Moon. Place the card on a projector. Shine the 'Sun' onto the screen. Push the 'Moon' across the 'Sun'. Pupils may record the successive stages of the eclipse.

## Eclipses
### Answer
➡ *Pupil's Book page 202*
**12** Where the Moon's shadow falls on the Earth's surface.
### Attainment target
Work in the previous sections should provide evidence that pupils are working towards the following attainment level.

| Use simple models to explain the phases of the Moon and eclipses | Level 5 |
|---|---|

# 6 *The Solar System (1)*

## Learning outcomes
Pupils:

- label a diagram showing the Sun, planets and asteroid belt and the natural satellites of the planets of the Solar System
- explain that the planets orbit the Sun as does the Earth, but that their orbits take different times to complete
- describe how information on the planets in our Solar System is obtained and used
- present data on comparisons between characteristics of planets in a suitable way, for example a table, chart or graph
- present evidence of relationships in data on aspects of planets
- present relevant information about a planet in the Solar System in an appropriate form, for example for a future visitor

*Activity* ## Information processing: The Solar System
➡ *Pupil's Book page 205*
Lessons 6 and 7 cover the same area but if teachers wish to use ICT then it will take two sessions for pupils to prepare and present their work. From earlier work pupils should already be clear on the relative positions of the planets in the Solar System.

This is an area that allows ICT to be used effectively. Pupils may use the Internet to research the planets' characteristics such as distance from the Sun, diameter, temperature, number of moons and orbit time. The best known Internet site is nineplanets; it has a number of mirror sites such as:

www.ex.ac.uk/Mirrors/nineplanets/
www.gly.bris.ac.uk/www/teach/virtrips/nineplanets/
nineplanets.html

Alternatively information can be extracted from a CD-ROM such as RedShift 3 (see page 206 for details) or Encarta.

Possible approaches include asking the pupils to produce a travel brochure, poster or PowerPoint presentation describing their chosen planet for prospective travellers. In all cases where pupils access the Internet they need careful guidance, possibly through a worksheet with a series of specific questions to which they must find the answers; otherwise there will be a tendency for them to copy pages of irrelevant data.

Pupils could use a spreadsheet to model the relative sizes of the planets and also their relative distances. There are also a number of good software packages available. One is New Media's *Multimedia Science School* CD-ROM 'Planet Analyser'. Pupils analyse the planetary data to look for patterns such as the temperature of the planet and its distance from the Sun. They can be encouraged to investigate other possible relationships and patterns themselves.

*Activity* ## Information processing: Scale models

➡ *Pupil's Book page 205*

As mentioned in lesson 3, the use of models in science is an important part of this topic. Pupils can produce their own scale models of the planets. This could be in the form of a 'mobile' or scale drawings along a wall in the laboratory or down a corridor; or objects of appropriate sizes such as those shown in the table below.

| Mercury | Venus | Earth | Mars | Jupiter | Saturn | Uranus | Neptune | Pluto |
|---------|-------|-------|------|---------|--------|--------|---------|-------|
| coriander seed | peppercorn | peppercorn | lentil | ping-pong ball | super-bounce ball | marble | marble | poppy seed |

Spreadsheet 'Scalemodels.xls' on the CD-ROM can be used with this activity. This enables the pupils to enter different scales, and the measurements for each model are calculated automatically.

### Answers

**1** 58 cm

**2** 1430 cm

## Comets and meteors
### Answer

➡ *Pupil's Book page 207*

**13** This question allows for a discussion with the pupils.

# 7 *The Solar System (2)*

## Learning outcomes

Pupils:

- label a diagram showing the Sun, planets and asteroid belt and the natural satellites of the planets of the Solar System
- explain that the planets orbit the Sun as does the Earth, but that their orbits take different times to complete
- describe how information on the planets in our Solar System is obtained and used
- present data on comparisons between characteristics of planets in a suitable way, for example a table, chart or graph
- present evidence of relationships in data on aspects of planets
- present relevant information about a planet in the Solar System in an appropriate form, for example for a future visitor

This allows time for further work on the Solar System including comets and meteors.

*Activity*  Reasoning: Considering evidence

➡ *Worksheet 10.7: Tunguska explosion in Siberia (K)*

This allows pupils to consider scientific ideas and evidence. The work on meteorites allows pupils to consider and evaluate the relative strengths of scientific evidence in view of recent claims about the origins of the Tunguska explosion in Siberia. The worksheet has an extract from an article in *The Times*.

## Answers

1 Volcanic eruption, meteorite.
2 19. Remote area, political situation.
3 No meteorite remains have been found; epicentre of the explosion is in the middle of the old volcano.

## Time to think

This session also allows time for pupils to present their findings to each other.

## Answers

➡ *Pupil's Book page 207*

1 Mercury.
2 Mercury, Venus, Earth, Mars, Jupiter, Saturn, Uranus, Neptune, Pluto.
3 Pluto.
4 Saturn.
5 They are not very bright, or some are only visible just after sunset or just before sunrise. Also they are at different places in the sky at different times.
6 The time for the Earth to orbit the Sun once.
7 Some stars are always visible, others are only visible at certain times of year.
8 The Sun.
9 It reflects light from the Sun.
10 It is a galaxy and consists of millions of stars.
11 Between the near and distant planets, between Mars and Jupiter.

### Attainment target

Work in the previous sections should provide evidence that pupils are working towards the following attainment level.

| | |
|---|---|
| Use simple models to explain effects caused by movement of the Earth | Level 5 |
| Describe evidence for some accepted ideas and explain how the interpretation of evidence by scientists leads to the development and acceptance of new ideas about space | Level 6 |

# 8 *The Universe*

## Learning outcomes

Pupils:

- explain that we only see the stars at night because the Sun is much nearer to us and appears brighter
- know that the Solar System forms part of a galaxy, which is part of a larger system called the Universe
- know that our Solar System is one of many in our galaxy
- state that within our Solar System only Earth is known to support any life forms.

*Activity*

## ICT: Powers of ten

➡ *Worksheet 10.8: Powers of ten (S)*

If the pupils have not seen the video 'Powers of Ten', this would be a useful place to show it to help them get a feel for the vastness of the Universe. (The video is available from Eames Office Gallery & Store, www.eamesoffice.com/powers_of_ten/powers_of_ten.html.) Worksheet 10.8 helps pupils consider the relative positions of the bodies in the Universe.

## Answers

1 To observe a simulation of the stars and planets.
2 Light year. It is the distance travelled by light in 1 year.
3 1000 m.
4 1 million metres.
5 Mercury, Venus.
6 Sometimes its path takes it inside the path of Neptune. Its path is highly elliptical rather than near-circular.
7 Milky Way.
8 In order of size: Moon, planet, star, Solar System, galaxy, universe.
  Matched with definitions: Moon, planet, galaxy, star, Solar System, universe.

## Constellations

➡ *Pupil's Book page 207*

Some teachers may wish to encourage pupils to research the constellations. Pupils could provide a sample star chart for one of the constellations using sugar paper and self-adhesive spots; or use a shoe box to make a simple constellation as described below.

### Equipment

- shoe box
- black paper for one end
- pin
- scissors
- glue

To make a shoe box constellation, pupils should cut a large square hole out of one end of the shoe box. At the other end a small circle should be cut out to use as the hole to look through. Now a constellation should be chosen and a matching pattern of holes pricked in a sheet of black paper. The square hole is covered with the black paper, making sure it is stuck on the correct way round for viewing through the shoe box. The black paper is then directed towards the window and pupils look through the round hole to view the constellation. This principle can be adapted to use a cylindrical tube or any other suitable box.

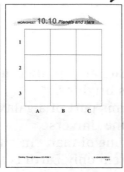

## Activity Revision: The Universe

➡ *Worksheet 10.9: The millionaire quiz (S), Worksheet 10.10: Planets and stars (S), Worksheet 10.11: A Ride On A Comet (E)*
This would be an appropriate point for pupils to consolidate their learning so far. One suggestion is 'The millionaire quiz', an activity using PowerPoint. A sample is on the CD-ROM. Pupils could be encouraged to write their own questions but Worksheet 10.9 gives some suggestions.

Another is the more traditional noughts and crosses game as shown on Worksheet 10.10. For this activity the grid, five noughts and five crosses supplied on the worksheet can be photocopied onto an OHP transparency. The noughts and crosses are cut out so that they can be laid over the grid. The class is split into two teams, and after deciding which team is to go first, ask the team which square they want and choose a corresponding question from those already prepared. If both teams get the same question wrong, give the answer and select another question from the others provided. If the question is answered correctly it can be marked off by using the noughts and crosses prepared before. The first team to produce a complete line is the winner.

Alternatively, the nine sets of questions and answers can be printed out and photocopied. The questions can then be stuck onto card, with the answers stuck on the reverse side. Split the class into groups and give each group a grid, five noughts and five crosses and a set of question/answer cards. Each group can then appoint a question reader and run the activity themselves.

This activity can be repeated with any suitable bank of questions.

Worksheet 10.11 provides the story 'A Ride On A Comet' by Carl Sagan and Ann Druyan as an opportunity for extended reading.

## Answers

➡ *Worksheet 10.9: The millionaire quiz*

| | | | |
|---|---|---|---|
| **1** B, D, C, A | **13** B | **25** B | **37** B |
| **2** D | **14** A | **26** D | **38** A |
| **3** B | **15** C | **27** B | **39** B |
| **4** D | **16** B, C, D, A | **28** B | **40** B |
| **5** A | **17** B, C, D, A | **29** A | **41** A |
| **6** D | **18** A, D, C, B | **30** B | **42** B |
| **7** C | **19** D, B, C, A | **31** C | **43** A |
| **8** B | **20** D, A, C, B | **32** C | **44** C |
| **9** D | **21** B | **33** C | **45** A |
| **10** B | **22** D | **34** A | **46** B |
| **11** A | **23** C | **35** C | **47** C |
| **12** D | **24** D | **36** A | **48** A |

# 9 Sc1 investigation: The impact of craters

## Learning outcome
Pupils:

• carry out a complete investigation

*Activity* Enquiry: Craters

➡ *Pupil's Book page 209*

This is an opportunity for an Sc1 type investigation as described in the Pupil's Book.

**Equipment**

Each group will need:

- trays of soil, sand, flour, plaster, vermiculite
- marbles or ball-bearings or small balls
- metre rule
- small transparent rulers or scales made by photocopying graph paper strips onto acetate

Pupils should experience using the equipment before devising their plan, as the choice of substrate, the height of drop, and the means of measuring crater depth will not be apparent without some initial trials.

This investigation is a practice investigation rather than one to be assessed by summative means, and is best used to develop the skills of planning, recording and evaluating.

**Assessment**

Recap, summarise, test. Teachers may then wish to refer to the concept maps pupils produced at the start of the topic so that they can update them in the light of their new knowledge.

**Attainment targets**

| Level | Planning | Obtaining and presenting evidence | Considering evidence | Evaluating |
|---|---|---|---|---|
| 3 | Respond to suggestions presented to them and put forward their own ideas about how to measure the size of craters produced | Use basic equipment to measure and make observations related to the task. Carry out a fair test with help | Explain observations and find simple patterns in results. Communicate in a scientific way | Suggest simple improvments to their work |
| 4 | Decide on an appropriate method and vary one factor while keeping the others the same. Suitable equipment is selected and predictions may be made. Realise that scientific ideas are based on evidence | Obtain a series of observations or measurements and record them clearly in a results table | Look for patterns in their results and explain their conclusions using their scientific knowledge | Suggest improvements and also give reasons for any amendments |
| 5 | Recognise the key factors in setting up the fair test and make predictions based on their scientific knowledge. If research is carried out they will refer to a range of sources | Careful measurements and observations will be made and repeated if necessary. There is a logical sequencing of results | Draw conclusions that are consistent with the data they have obtained and use/relate these to what they know and understand about how the final velocity before impact is changed by the height of release | Suggest practical ways in which their method can be improved and be critical of any differences in the repeated experiments |

## Time to think
## Answers
➡ *Pupil's Book page 209*
- 9
- 8.7 light years
- 27 days
- 365 days
- 240
- 24°
- 24 hours
- 400 times bigger
- 150 million km
- 1781
- 58 million km
- 76 years

## Review
➡ *Worksheet 10.12: Test on the Solar System*
This worksheet provides a 20 minute test to check on understanding of this chapter.

## Answers

| | | |
|---|---|---|
| **1** | Mercury, Venus. | (1 mark) |
| **2** | Pluto. | (1 mark) |
| **3** | Jupiter. | (1 mark) |
| **4** | Because it orbits the planet, Earth. | (1 mark) |
| **5** | 24 hours or 1 day. | (1 mark) |
| **6** | Clinometer. | (1 mark) |
| **7** | 12 hours. | (1 mark) |
| **8** | Sundials. | (1 mark) |
| **9** | Crescent. | (1 mark) |
| **10** | Stars that appear as a group in the sky. | (1 mark) |

**11** As the Moon orbits the Earth
the amount of the lit part of the Moon varies. (2 marks)

**12** Drawing with Sun and Earth.
Northern Hemisphere tilted away from the Sun.
Britain and Australia marked.
Australia receives more light/heat. (4 marks)

**13** (See Pupil's Book, page 202)
Drawing with Sun, Moon and Earth.
Moon between Sun and Earth.
Light rays from Sun touching Moon and passing onto Earth.
Shadow formed where Moon blocks light. (4 marks)

# 11 Simple chemical reactions

## → Rationale

This chapter provides up to 7 hours of teaching materials. It develops ideas from Key Stage 2 including Unit 5C Gases around us and Unit 6D Reversible and irreversible changes.

Pupils develop their knowledge of the chemistry of acids and they learn the chemical tests for oxygen, hydrogen and carbon dioxide. They develop their understanding of the process of combustion and link this idea to the fire triangle and fire safety. Combustion experiments are carried out with pure oxygen and simple word equations are introduced. There is further opportunity to construct and analyse graphs as well as analysing data on the combustion of elements in oxygen. Pupils complete this section by burning fuels and identifying the products of burning. Pupils learn the test for water and extend their understanding of combustion by applying their ideas to fuels such as methane (a compound of carbon and hydrogen).

In this chapter pupils further develop their process skills and are given the opportunity to carry out a full investigation. There are links with future work in Year 8, Unit 8G Rocks and weathering, and in Year 9, Unit 9E Reactions of metals and metal compounds and Unit 9G Environmental chemistry.

## → Overview

The textbook sections, activities and worksheets have been arranged into 1 hour blocks to aid lesson planning. Clearly several of the activities and worksheets could form part of a homework session. The planning includes reading time for individual sections but some teachers may prefer to organise this as homework preparation for the following lesson. Five types of worksheet – extension (E), support for an activity (S), practical (P), key skills (K) and developmental (D) – allow for differentiation and flexibility to accommodate teachers' preferred practice. The actual timing and emphasis on different sections will depend on the current knowledge base of the pupils, the ability of the teaching group and the preferences of the teacher.

| Lesson | Worksheet |
|--------|-----------|
| **1** Introduction and physical/ chemical change | Worksheet 11.1: It makes a change! (D)<br>Worksheet 11.2: Spot the chemical change (P) |
| **2** How different metals react with acid | Worksheet 11.3: Acid attack (1) (S)<br>Worksheet 11.4: Acid attack (2) (E) |
| **3** How do acids react with carbonates? | Worksheet 11.5: The fate of carbonates (P) |
| **4** Burning (1) | Worksheet 11.6: The burning question (P) |
| **5** Looking at oxygen | Worksheet 11.7: Burning elements in oxygen (D)<br>Worksheet 11.8: Measuring the percentage of oxygen in the air (E)<br>Worksheet 11.9: Pyrogallol method (D) |
| **6** Sc1 investigation: Acid rain and buildings | Worksheet 11.10: Which buildings are most at risk of attack from acid rain? (S) |
| **7** Burning (2) | Worksheet 11.11: What's in a fuel? (P) |
| Review | Worksheet 11.12: Test on simple chemical reactions |

→ *Chapter plan*

| | Demonstration | Practical | ICT | Activity | Word play | Time to think | Ideas and evidence |
|---|---|---|---|---|---|---|---|
| **Lesson 1** | | Heating chemicals | | | | What do you know? | |
| **Lesson 2** | Testing for hydrogen | Acid attack | Using a spreadsheet | Information processing: Reaction between magnesium and hydrochloric acid<br><br>Evaluation: Preparing hydrogen | | | |
| **Lesson 3** | Testing for carbon dioxide | The fate of carbonates | | | | Acid reactions | |
| **Lesson 4** | Burning<br><br>Fire triangle | The burning question | | | Flammable/ inflammable | | |
| **Lesson 5** | | Burning elements in oxygen | | Enquiry: What will happen?<br><br>Information processing: Metal and non-metal oxides<br><br>Enquiry: Acid drops investigation | | | The lakes that died |
| **Lesson 6** | | | | Investigation: Acid rain | | | |
| **Lesson 7** | Bunsen burner | What's in a fuel? | | | | Using models of atoms<br><br>Simple chemical reactions | |

# ➡ *Expectations*

**At the end of this unit**

**in terms of scientific enquiry**

**most pupils will:** obtain and present qualitative results, identifying patterns in these; work safely with acids and when burning materials; suggest how to test an idea about burning, obtaining results which can be represented as a line graph; produce rules for the safe operation of a Bunsen burner

**some pupils will not have made so much progress and will:** obtain and present qualitative results, describe some hazards of acids and of burning; work safely with acids and when burning materials; test an idea about burning and present results; us a Bunsen burner safely

**some pupils will have progressed further and will:** evaluate how well ideas about burning match the data collected

**in terms of materials and their properties**

**most pupils will:** identify that some new materials are formed during a chemical reaction and generalise that hydrogen is formed when acids react with metals, carbon dioxide when acids react with carbonates, and oxides when materials burn; describe tests for carbon dioxide and hydrogen and describe burning as a reaction with oxygen; construct simple word equations when elements burn in oxygen

**some pupils will not have made so much progress and will:** identify some products of chemical reactions and state that oxygen or air is needed for burning

**some pupils will have progressed further and will:** predict that carbon dioxide and water will be made when a hydrocarbon burns and use word equations to represent reactions in which materials burn

# ➡ *Links with CASE*

This chapter again focuses on recognition of variables and the control and manipulation of variables leading to fair testing. Pupils are asked to articulate relationships and construct graphs from which they can predict experimental results. Word equations are introduced, which force pupils to use symbolic representation. Through looking at patterns within various reactions pupils are required to make generalisations, which moves their thinking towards more formal operational mode. The use of formal modelling is also involved in some parts of this chapter and while it is not envisaged that all learners will have the capability to utilise such higher order thinking skills, most will be able to manage these tasks in a descriptive rather than explanatory mode.

# → *Pupils' misconceptions*

| Misconceptions | Scientific understanding |
|---|---|
| Many pupils consider dissolving and change of state to be chemical reactions. | Changes of state are physical changes that are reversible. |
| Pupils find difficulty in recognising when a chemical reaction occurs. | Following a chemical reaction, permanent change results in new materials being made. |
| In the everyday world the word pure implies 'untampered with', or 'natural'. Children think of rock salt as 'pure' but extracted salt as 'impure' because it has gone through a chemical process. | A pure substance comprises one single substance, rather than more than one. |
| Pupils apply the terms metal and non-metal not only to elements but often include materials such as wood and sugar. The main problem is that elements are not noticeably different from other substances. | An element is a substance that consist of only one kind of atom. It is a pure substance that cannot be split up into any other pure substance. Those pupils using a particle model will have a greater understanding of an element. |

Pupils must appreciate that matter comprises tiny particles which combine together and they must know the meaning of 'atom'. Pupils must be encouraged to overcome any reluctance to use particulate ideas in discussing elements and compounds.

Research clearly shows that pupils' understanding of the differences between elements, compounds and mixtures in particle terms is poor. It is therefore unsurprising that pupils find chemistry 'hard', as they do not understand a basic principle providing a foundation for more detailed study.

# → *Literacy, numeracy and other cross-curricular links*

Literacy skills are developed in this chapter by encouraging speaking and writing. Pupils are required to translate information from diagrams and tables into sentences, and the discussion of ideas has a major role to play in most activities. Writing for an appropriate audience is included via reports.

Numeracy skills are developed through consideration of ratio and use of percentages, as well as in graphing skills. Extension activities involve converting fractions into percentages and making calculations from raw data.

## Language for learning

By the end of the chapter pupils will be able to understand, use and spell correctly:

- names of gases and common elements and compounds – for example hydrogen, oxygen, carbon dioxide, methane, magnesium, sulphur, carbonate and oxide

- words and phrases describing chemical reactions – physical change, chemical reaction (change), reactant, product, word equation, element, compound
- words that have similar meaning – flammable/inflammable
- words that have different meanings in scientific and everyday contexts – pure, element.

# 1 *Introduction and physical/chemical change*

## Learning outcomes

Pupils:

- know how to identify a chemical change from observed criteria
- know some everyday and common laboratory chemical changes

## What do you know?

➡ *Pupil's Book page 210*

➡ *Worksheet 11.1: It makes a change! (D)*

During this chapter the idea of chemical change is pivotal to all the lessons. When considering what happens during a chemical change, children may think that:

- it just happens
- matter just disappears
- product materials are contained in the starting materials
- the product is just a modified form of the starting material.

Pupils will have studied reversible and irreversible changes at Key Stage 2 but will not be familiar with the terms physical and chemical changes. Worksheet 11.1 can be used to review their understanding of Key Stage 2 work. The exercise can be used to develop literacy. The photographs on page 211 can be used to establish the idea of reversible and irreversible changes.

## Answers

➡ *Pupil's Book page 211*

**1**

| Reversible | Irreversible |
|---|---|
| melting wax | explosion/fireworks |
| melting butter | burning candle wick |
| steam from kettle | cake baking |
| condensation of steam | rusting car |

**2** Candle: wax melting (can be reversed), candle wick and wax burning (cannot be reversed).

## Answers

➡ *Worksheet 11.1: It makes a change!*

| Reversible | Irreversible |
|---|---|
| kettle boiling | boiling (cooking) eggs |
| making coffee | toasting bread |
| diluting orange squash | bread baking |
| melting butter | Alka Seltzer for upset stomach |
| | burning gas |
| | sausages cooking |

## What is a chemical reaction?

## Answers

➡ *Pupil's Book page 212*

1 Reversible = physical; irreversible = chemical. Refer to table on previous page in answer to Q1, Pupil's Book page 211.

2 Making toast – C.
Boiling an egg – C.
A light bulb getting hot – P.
Burning charcoal in a barbecue – C.
Adding sugar to a cup of tea – P.
Making ice cubes in the freezer – P.
Setting off a firework – C.
Food going mouldy – C.
Alka Seltzer fizzing in water – C.
Brewing beer – C.
Making a cup of tea – P.
Using Rennies to cure acid indigestion – C.
Treating wasp and bee stings – C.
Diluting orange juice with water – P.
Plaster of Paris and water mixed together and going hard – C.

3 a) Salt: reversible as a little seems to dissolve. This is a physical change.
   b) Chalk: signs of a permanent change, for example bubbles, solid disappearing. This is a chemical change.

*Activity* ## Practical: Heating chemicals

➡ *Worksheet 11.2: Spot the chemical change (P)*

The main activity in this lesson is outlined on Worksheet 11.2 which suggests chemicals to be heated or mixed together. In the case of mixing lead nitrate and potassium iodide solution, recognition of the yellow stuff as a new substance is the key point. With persistent questioning, pupils admit the substance is new and 'just appeared'. The event creates cognitive conflict, as the result and the questioning challenge pupils' thinking.

The second stage involves helping pupils to extend this thinking to other reactions in the activity. Pupils need to be challenged into deciding from their evidence if the changes are temporary or permanent. Pupils find difficulty in recognising when a chemical reaction occurs. Many pupils think that dissolving and change of state are chemical reactions. Dissolving sugar or salt and recrystallising the solid from solution is commonly done at Key Stage 3 (see chapter 9). The research suggests this cannot truly be termed a 'physical change' because recrystallised solute requires an act of 'blind faith' on the part of the learner to believe this is identical to the starting material.

Pupils are provided with a checklist to help them decide on the type of change they are observing. This activity is an appropriate one for developing observation skills and for encouraging the pupils to tabulate their results in an appropriate format.

### Equipment

Each group will need:

- for heating: zinc oxide, copper sulphate (CARE – harmful), ice, wax (salol is a safer alternative), copper carbonate (CARE – harmful)
- for mixing: chalk and 0.4 M hydrochloric acid, chalk and water, magnesium (CARE – highly flammable) and 0.4 M hydrochloric acid, iron and water,

lead nitrate  and potassium iodide solutions

toxic

### Safety

Use eye protection. Control the supply of magnesium very carefully. It should always be in the possession of the teacher.

*Note:* lead nitrate solid is TOXIC. Solutions greater than 0.01 M are also TOXIC. Solutions of 0.001 M or more but less than 0.01 M: the hazard is HARMFUL. However, pupils will find it difficult to differentiate and so the toxic nature of all lead compounds needs to be made clear. Thorough washing of hands afterwards or on spillage, and cleaning bench tops is essential.

## Answers

| Chemical | During heating | After heating |
|---|---|---|
| zinc oxide | turns yellow | turns back to white |
| wax (or salol) | melts, starts to evaporate | cools down and turns back to a solid |
| copper carbonate | turns from green to black, condensation (water) drops | stays black |
| ice | melts, turns into a liquid | stays a liquid |
| copper sulphate | blue crystals turn grey/white, give off steam | stays white |

| Chemicals | Observations |
|---|---|
| chalk and water | no mixing, chalk settles at bottom |
| chalk and acid | fizzing, chalk disappears, goes cold |
| magnesium and acid | fizzes, magnesium disappears, gets hot |
| lead nitrate and potassium iodide | a very bright yellow solid settles to the bottom |
| iron and water | no obvious reaction |

1 Copper sulphate, copper carbonate.
2 Wax, ice, zinc oxide.
3 Chalk/acid, magnesium/acid, lead nitrate/potassium iodide.
4 Iron/water: no obvious result but iron does rust in water/air slowly.

**Attainment targets**

Work in the previous sections should provide evidence that pupils are working towards the following attainment levels.

| Recognise that some changes can be reversed (freezing) and some cannot be reversed | Level 3 |
| --- | --- |
| Recognise that new materials can be made through chemical reactions; predict whether changes are chemical or physical | Level 4 |

# 2 *How different metals react with acid*

## Learning outcomes

Pupils:

- generalise that when metals react with acids, hydrogen is produced
- describe and carry out the chemical test for hydrogen
- identify patterns when metals react with acids

Links to CASE 25: Explaining chemical reactions (developing formal models). One of the activities is the reaction between zinc and sulphuric acid.

*Activity* ## Information processing: Reaction between magnesium and hydrochloric acid

➡ *Pupil's Book page 213*
Teachers may wish to link back to lesson 1 and the magnesium/acid change: classified as a chemical change. Spreadsheet 'Acidsandmetals.xls' on the CD-ROM can be used for this activity.

## Answers

1 Length of magnesium.
2 Volume of hydrogen.
3 Temperature of acid, volume and concentration of acid (fixed variable).
4 Volume of hydrogen increases as length of magnesium increases. If pupils have been through CASE they should recognise the straight line relationship and be able to predict the value for 6 cm.
5 3 cm: does not fit on the line like the others.
6 **a)** 60 cm³   **b)** 15 cm³   **c)** 35 cm³
7 **a)** 5 cm   **b)** 4.5 cm   **c)** 1.5 cm
8 Accuracy of measurements: sufficient acid to completely remove the magnesium; whether the bung is placed quickly. A syringe with improved calibration or use a burette.

*Activity*   Demonstration: Testing for hydrogen

Testing for hydrogen is covered in the Pupil's Book (page 214) and how to correctly test for the gas being produced can be demonstrated using magnesium and acid. Establish that this is hydrogen and the test is the 'pop' test. Pupils can then be encouraged to test for hydrogen in their own experiments. For 'Equipment' and 'Safety' notes, please refer to the *Technician's notes* on the CD-ROM.

*Activity*   Evaluation: Preparing hydrogen

Answers

⇒ *Pupil's Book page 214*

1 Move delivery tube to point upwards: upward delivery.
2 Two reasons: density, lack of reactivity.
3 Molecules/particles of hydrogen are small enough to pass through the rubber of the balloon.

*Activity*   Practical: Acid attack

⇒ *Worksheet 11.3: Acid attack (1) (S), Worksheet 11.4: Acid attack (2) (E)*

This is a good opportunity for pupils to look for patterns in their results. Allow pupils to choose either sulphuric or hydrochloric acid. Nitric acid is an oxidising acid and does not usually produce hydrogen. This is a good opportunity for pupils to construct their own results table, although Worksheet 11.3 is available. This also contains a variables table to assist in setting up a fair test. Pupils compare the results from both acids and try to identify the pattern in order of reactivity. See if they can suggest which metal is used for hot/cold water pipes in the home and give a reason for this.

There is an extension, Worksheet 11.4 (involving predictions), which allows pupils to extend their enquiry using vinegar. It is important that pupils construct an accurate graph, as they need to read off from the graph in order to answer Q6 and Q7. This links back to the work covered in chapter 5 on acids and alkalis.

**Equipment**

Each group will need:

- test tubes
- rack
- teat pipettes
- eye protection
- access to 1 M sulphuric (irritant) and hydrochloric acid
- CLEAPPS Student Safety Sheets on acids
- small pieces of magnesium (CARE: highly flammable), zinc, aluminium, iron, copper

Extension:

- 1 M ethanoic acid

**Safety**

Control the supply of magnesium very carefully. It should always be in the possession of the teacher.

# Answers

➡ *Worksheet 11.3: Acid attack (1)*

| Variable: what will change | Type of variable | Values |
|---|---|---|
| type of metal | input | Mg, Zn, Al, Fe, Cu |
| amount of metal | fixed | lump, spatula of powder |
| concentration of acid | fixed | 1 M |
| type of acid | fixed | hydrochloric acid, sulphuric acid |
| amount of acid | fixed | 5, 50, 500 cm³ |
| how many bubbles | outcome | lots, some, few |

1 Type of metal would have most effect. Both strong acids of equal concentration (fixed variable).
2 Magnesium.
3 Copper.
4

| Position | Metal |
|---|---|
| 1st | magnesium |
| 2nd | aluminium* |
| 3rd | zinc |
| 4th | iron |
| 5th | copper |

* Aluminium probably appears less reactive than it is. If you use tin (Sn) instead the order would be: Mg, Zn, Fe, Sn, Cu.

➡ *Worksheet 11.4: Acid attack (2)*
1 Ethanoic acid.
2 pH 3/4.
3 Weak.
4 Fizz and produce hydrogen.
5 Slower.
6 As sulphuric and hydrochloric acid. Vinegar is a fixed variable and so will not affect the reaction order.

## Attainment targets

Work in the previous sections should provide evidence that pupils are working towards the following attainment levels.

| Recognise that new materials can be made through chemical reactions. Predict whether changes are chemical or physical | Level 4 |
|---|---|
| Identify and describe similarities between some chemical reactions. Use word equations to summarise simple chemical reactions | Level 6 |

# 3 *How do acids react with carbonates?*

## Learning outcomes

Pupils:

- generalise that when acids react with carbonates, carbon dioxide is produced which is evidence for a chemical change
- carry out and describe the limewater test for carbon dioxide
- state that antacids often contain carbonates which neutralise excess stomach acid
- evaluate the effectiveness of different antacids
- construct word equations involving acids and alkalis, acids and metals, and acids and carbonates

## Acids and carbonates

➡ *Pupil's Book page 215*

As an introductory activity, teachers may wish to use the photographs on page 215 as a starting point and also refer to lesson 1 and the reaction of chalk with dilute acid.

## Answers

**4** Citric, ascorbic, carbonic, ethanoic, sour milk (lactic), and so on.

**5** Corrosive, would eat away/react with the metal.

**6** Place different types of plastic into a range of different acids and look for signs of a chemical change: bubbles, colour change, disappearance of plastic, temperature change.

## Rocks at risk

## Answers

➡ *Pupil's Book page 216*

**7** Rainwater can contain dissolved chemicals which are acidic.

**8** High density, collected by downward displacement.

*Activity* ## Demonstration: Testing for carbon dioxide

**Equipment**

- chalk and dilute acid
- small flask/boiling tube with delivery tube into test tube of limewater

*Activity* ## Practical: The fate of carbonates

➡ *Worksheet 11.5: The fate of carbonates (P)*

This involves a choice of activities but with limited time the class can be divided so both activities are undertaken and each group can produce a report for whole class discussion. Worksheet 11.5 sets out the two different problems: testing rocks to identify which ones are carbonates, and testing which antacid cures contain a carbonate. A variety of carbonates can be made available. The apparatus used allows carbon dioxide to be collected and tested using limewater.

**Equipment**
Each group will need:

- eye protection
- acids (0.4 M): hydrochloric acid, nitric acid (irritant), ethanoic acid. (Sulphuric acid is not included because with calcium carbonate it will produce the insoluble salt calcium sulphate which coats the carbonate preventing any further reaction.)
- boiling tube with bung and delivery tube
- bottle of limewater
- Activity A – selection of rocks: limestone, chalk, marble, sandstone, slate, granite
- Activity B – selection of antacid cures including some with calcium or magnesium carbonate as an ingredient and a selection without a carbonate
- spatulas
- access to balance

## Answers

1 Acid and carbonate.
2 Carbon dioxide.
3 It turns milky.
4 The carbonate: because it contains carbon and oxygen.

*Activity B*
1 Neutralisation.
2 The reaction produces carbon dioxide *gas*, which can make you burp!

## Time to think
## Answers
➡ *Pupil's Book page 217*
1 Hydrogen.
2 Carbon dioxide.
3 Colour change, a milky coloured solid is formed.
4 Bubbles are produced.

## Word equations
➡ *Pupil's Book page 217*
At this stage three word equations are introduced to the pupils. Key words here are reactant and product. The goal is to establish that when chemicals take part in a chemical change, the atoms of the original substances become joined to different atoms in new combinations. This establishes the platform for lesson 5 which looks at the oxidation of a number of elements.

## Chip shop mystery
## Answers
➡ *Pupil's Book page 217*
Sodium chloride = salt, ethanoic acid = vinegar.

# 4 _Burning (1)_

## Learning outcomes
Pupils:

- explain that when a candle goes out part of the air (oxygen) is used up
- generalise that the less air is available, the sooner the flame goes out
- estimate the fraction of air used up during burning
- know that this active part of the air is called oxygen
- be aware of the fire triangle and fire safety rules

During the next three lessons it is important to be aware that many pupils have the idea that air is _one_ substance; that pupils view oxygen as necessary for burning, while they may not consider that it takes part; and that pupils may 'know' that oxygen is needed for some reactions but they may not have the key idea that it is a constituent of the air.

The questions linked with the burning candle bridge with CASE 25, which gets the pupils to construct a formal model to explain what is happening to the burning candle. The teacher may wish to use the photographs on page 218 (Pupil's Book) to initiate discussion.

## The burning question/What is needed for things to burn?
## Answers
➠ _Pupil's Book pages 218 and 219_

9 Fuels: coal, oil, gas, petrol, diesel, paraffin, other oil-related liquids, Calor gas, hydrogen, wood, paper, some plastics, fabrics, wax.

10 Chemical because new substances are produced.

11 Not once it has burnt: it is an irreversible change. (This is why a candle gets smaller.)

12 Heat and light.

13 Stored chemical energy in the wax (fuel).

14 Wax; they may offer air (perhaps even oxygen).

15 The larger the gas jar, the longer the candle burns. More able pupils may suggest a quantitative relationship. The candle in the medium sized jar burns twice as long as that in the small jar, and the candle in the large jar burns three times as long as the candle in the small jar.

_Activity_ ## Demonstration: Burning
Pupils can be asked to make predictions when different sized beakers are placed over candles.

**Equipment**
- three different sized beakers: 100, 200, 400 cm³
- tea-light candles are the most suitable for this demonstration

*Activity* ## Practical: The burning question

➡ *Worksheet 11.6: The burning question (P)*

The main activity involves the use of Worksheet 11.6 which will allow the pupils to estimate the fraction of air used up during burning. Pupils use a wooden spill that they can calibrate by marking with a biro. This will help them work out what fraction of the air has been used up. For a mixed ability group it would be sensible to have a number of spills marked up in simple divisions.

Pupils place a small piece of plasticine in the bottom of a beaker, fix in the wooden spill, which is then covered in water to the first mark. The spill is lit and quickly covered with a dry test tube so the bottom of the tube is just below the water level. Once the spill is extinguished they can estimate how far the water has risen up the tube.

Q2 may raise some debate with able pupils because the increased temperature may also affect the volume of gas inside the apparatus, plus some carbon dioxide may dissolve in the water. However, most pupils will accept the explanation in simple terms.

### Equipment
- 200 cm³ beakers
- plasticine
- wooden spills (using spills allows repeats to be quickly and cheaply carried out)
- test tubes

## Answers

**1** It is more reliable. One result may not have been accurate. It is like a check.
**2** Oxygen has been used up and the water rises up to replace it.
**4** Percentage of the air used up during burning is about 20%.
**5** Pie charts shows oxygen is 21% (approx. $\frac{1}{5}$). Pupils make a comparison with their data. Improved accuracy is achieved through using a finer scale on the spills or collecting the gas in a 10 ml measuring cylinder.

## The fire triangle

The chapter develops the notion of the fire triangle and the necessity for fuel, heat and oxygen. There is a research opportunity where pupils can find out how Davy's lamp operates. At the end of this lesson pupils should realise that it is the oxygen fraction of the air that facilitates combustion and that it makes up $\frac{1}{5}$ (20 per cent) of the air.

*Activity* ## Demonstration: Fire triangle

2 ml of oil is placed in a metal crucible and heated until it ignites. A damp cloth will extinguish the flame. If only this small amount of oil is used then a small tube of water attached to a metre rule can be added to show the dangers of extinguishing oil fires with water.

**Safety**
- Use a minimal quantity of oil such as 2 ml (it is advisable to practise this first to ensure that the correct amount of oil is used).
- Use a safety screen and eye protection.

## Fire fighting: The fire triangle
## Answers
➡ *Pupil's Book page 221*
**16**

| Fire fighting method | How it is used | How it works |
|---|---|---|
| carbon dioxide extinguisher | pointed and sprayed onto the fire forming an invisible blanket | smothers flame to remove supply of air |
| fire blanket | a non-flammable blanket is placed over the fire | smothers flame to remove supply of air |
| water | water is hosed onto the fire | removes heat, so cools the fire down, cannot ignite |
| sand | sand is thrown onto the fire | smothers flame to remove supply of air |

## Which part of the air is needed for burning?
## Answers
➡ *Pupil's Book page 222*
**17** $100 \, cm^3$
**18** $80 \, cm^3$
**19** 20%

# 5 *Looking at oxygen*

## Learning outcomes
Pupils:

- explain that burning is a chemical reaction in which materials react with oxygen to produce oxides
- name the products of some simple combustion reactions
- (more able pupils) classify oxides as acid, alkali, neutral
- explain why greater care is needed when materials burn in pure oxygen

This lesson follows on from the previous lesson and involves the burning of a number of elements in pure oxygen.

*Activity* ## Enquiry: What will happen?
## Answers
➡ *Pupil's Book page 223*
**1** Materials should burn much *better* in oxygen. Pupils may suggest brighter, quicker, more vigorously.
**2** Carbon dioxide.
**3** Limewater test: turns milky with carbon dioxide.

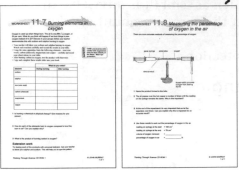

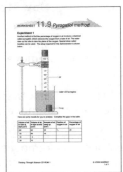

*Activity* Practical: Burning elements in oxygen

➡ *Worksheet 11.7: Burning elements in oxygen (D),*
*Worksheet 11.8: Measuring the percentage of oxygen in the air (E),*
*Worksheet 11.9: Pyrogallol method (D)*

This activity can be done as a combination of teacher demonstrations and pupil practical (Worksheet 11.7). Pupils learn the test for oxygen and look for patterns in the data. There is the opportunity for extension work (Worksheet 11.8), which uses gas syringes to measure accurately the percentage of oxygen in the air. This can easily be set up as a demonstration if required. There is also a homework sheet (Worksheet 11.9) that provides data from the pyrogallol method, from which they can calculate the percentage of oxygen. This method can also be set up as a demonstration.

➡ *Worksheet 11.7: Burning elements in oxygen*

**Equipment**

Pupils need:
- deflagrating spoons and gas jars, or combustion spoons and boiling tubes, stoppered and full of oxygen
- access to: wire wool, small pieces of charcoal, magnesium, copper, limewater

Teacher demonstration:
- deflagrating spoon, gas jars, lids, oxygen supply, sodium, sulphur

Extension:
- universal indicator solution to test oxides

**Safety**
- Use eye protection.
- Burning magnesium: look at the flame through gap between fingers that are close together.
- Burning sodium and sulphur: use a fume cupboard for these demonstrations as some of the products are toxic/corrosive.

Extension:
- Universal indicator solution to test oxides: pupils must take care since some oxides may be toxic/corrosive.

➡ *Worksheet 11.8: Measuring the percentage of oxygen in the air*

**Equipment**
- two glass syringes connected by silica tube packed with wire-formed copper and gently plugged with mineral wool to contain copper oxide in the tube

➡ *Worksheet 11.9: Pyrogallol method*

**Equipment**
- a broken burette converted into a calibrated tube with a bung at each end (flame polish any sharp ends)

Keeping the inside moist, have a small ignition tube and put in some pyrogallol and a pellet of sodium hydroxide. Put the tube into the burette, replace the bung and allow the contents to empty into the burette until the water inside goes dark brown. Place one end of the burette into a beaker of water and remove the bung under water. The water level rises to replace the oxygen that has been removed by the pyrogallol.

# Answers

➡ *Worksheet 11.7: Burning elements in oxygen*

| Element | During burning | After burning |
|---------|----------------|---------------|
| sodium | yellow flame | white/yellow solid |
| sulphur | blue flame | fumes, gas produced |
| iron (wire wool) | fierce burning, yellow sparks | brownish solid remains |
| carbon (charcoal) | red glow, yellow flame | colourless gas |
| magnesium | very bright white flame | white powder/ash |
| copper | goes black | stays black |

**1** Chemical: new substances are made, temperature increases, reactant disappears.
**2** Burning is much brighter in oxygen. Air is only $\frac{1}{5}$ oxygen.
**3** Carbon dioxide.

Extension work: This can be linked to the information processing activity on page 224 of the Pupil's Book, on the different oxides.

➡ *Worksheet 11.8: Measuring the percentage of oxygen in the air*
**1** Copper oxide.
**2** To make sure the reaction is over. All the copper has reacted.
**3** Gases expand when they are hot and take up more space.
**4** To work out the percentage of oxygen in the air:
reading on syringe at the start = $100\,cm^3$
reading on syringe at the end − $79\,cm^3$
volume of oxygen removed = $21\,cm^3$
percentage of oxygen in air = 21%

➡ *Worksheet 11.9: Pyrogallol method*
**Experiment 1**

| Volume of air in tube at start ($cm^3$) | Volume of air in tube at end ($cm^3$) | Amount of air used up ($cm^3$) | Fraction of oxygen in air | Percentage of oxygen in air |
|---|---|---|---|---|
| 100 | 80 | 20 | $\frac{1}{5}$ | 20 |
| 50 | 40 | 10 | $\frac{1}{5}$ | 20 |
| 10 | 8 | 2 | $\frac{1}{5}$ | 20 |
| 20 | 15 | 5 | $\frac{1}{4}$ | 25 |

**Experiment 2**
**1** $16\,cm^3$
**2** Oxygen.
**3** Nitrogen.
**4** $\frac{16}{80} \times 100 = 20\%$
**5** Accuracy depends on reading the scale on the tube correctly at the start and finish. The final result gives $\frac{1}{4}$ rather than $\frac{1}{5}$; this is probably due to inaccurate reading of the scale on the tube.

*Activity* # Information processing: Metal and non-metal oxides

➡ *Pupil's Book page 224*
More able pupils will be able to look for patterns in the nature of metallic and non-metallic oxides.

## Answers

1 Blue.
2 They are alkaline.
3 Red.
4 They are acidic.
5 **a)** Blue: alkali. **b)** Red: acid.
6 magnesium + oxygen → magnesium oxide
7 calcium + oxygen → calcium oxide
  sulphur + oxygen → sulphur dioxide
8 iron + oxygen → iron oxide

This section develops the use of word equations for the oxidation of some common elements. Pupils should be encouraged to draw particle diagrams to help them understand that the oxide product is a compound containing oxygen. They can be introduced to non-flammable materials that are already oxides and so cannot burn, for example water, sand.

### Attainment targets

Work in the previous sections should provide evidence that pupils are working towards the following attainment levels.

| | |
|---|---|
| Know that burning involves a reaction with oxygen | Level 5 |
| Know that combustion is an oxidation reaction involving oxygen and resulting in oxides. Recognise patterns in some chemical reactions: elements and oxygen. Use word equations to summarise simple chemical reactions | Level 6 |

*Activity* # Enquiry: Acid drops investigation

➡ *Pupil's Book page 225*
➡ *Worksheet 11.10: Which building materials are most at risk of attack from acid rain? (S)*
Pupils can construct a plan ready for lesson 6 using Worksheet 11.10 if necessary.

## Ideas and evidence: The lakes that died

➡ *Pupil's Book page 226*
This is an opportunity to consider ideas and evidence. The pupils are asked to consider who is actually responsible for the pollution in Swedish lakes.

## Answers

1 It is alkaline and will neutralise the acid in the lake.
2 The prevailing wind would blow pollution from countries like the UK, Russia and Germany over countries like Sweden.
3 The level of acid in the lakes has killed all wildlife.
4 This is an excellent debating issue that pupils can address. The pollution is not a product of pollution produced in Sweden but is 'imported'.

# 6 Sc1 investigation: Acid rain and buildings

## Learning outcomes

Pupils:

- use their knowledge of the acidic nature of oxides of carbon, nitrogen and sulphur to predict the result of acid rain on different materials such as metals, limestone, marble and chalk
- plan, carry out, draw conclusions and evaluate an investigation into acid-resistant building materials

*Activity*

## Investigation: Acid rain

➡ *Worksheet 11.10: Which buildings are most at risk of attack from acid rain? (S)*

The teacher could show the pH of the product of burning sulphur in oxygen and establish the low pH. Ask pupils to name the product. It would be useful to refer to the photograph in the Pupil's Book (page 216) showing the effects of acid rain on buildings. It would be helpful to have a brainstorming session to make a list of materials used by builders and to outline how to carry out a fair test. Worksheet 11.10 can be issued before the lesson to allow pupils time to begin the planning stage. There is a variables table to help pupils construct a fair test.

### Equipment

- use 0.5 M sulphuric acid (irritant) labelled 'acid rain'
- access to a variety of materials depending upon what the brainstorming session produces: brick, stone, limestone, marble, slate, wood, iron, aluminium, concrete, glass (this is best done with small quantities that fit into test tubes to save on resources)
- access to a balance if pupils wish to weigh materials as part of controlling variables

### Safety

- Use eye protection.

## Answers

1 Slate: roofing
   Wood: frames (roof, windows, doors)
   Brick: walls
   Aluminium: window frames
   Concrete tiles: roofing
   Glass: windows
2 Steel, plastic, foam (insulation), concrete (sand/cement), paving stones, stones, mortar.
3

| Variable: what will change | Type of variable: input, fixed, outcome | Values |
|---|---|---|
| type of material | input | brick, concrete, wood, etc. |
| amount of material | fixed | lump, spatula of powder |
| concentration of acid | fixed | 0.5 M |
| type of acid | fixed | acid rain |
| amount of acid | fixed | 10 cm³ |
| how many bubbles | outcome | lots, some, few, none |

**Assessment**

It may be useful to use this investigation as an opportunity to assess a whole investigation and to begin making the processes involved more transparent to pupils.

**Attainment targets**

| Level | Planning | Obtaining and presenting evidence | Considering evidence | Evaluating |
|---|---|---|---|---|
| 3 | Respond to suggestions presented to them and put forward their own ideas and use simple texts to research information | Use basic equipment to measure and make observations related to the task. Carry out a fair test with help | Explain observations and find simple patterns in results. Communicate in a scientific way | Suggest simple improvements to their work |
| 4 | Decide on an appropriate method and vary one factor while keeping the others the same. Suitable equipment is selected and predictions may be made. Realise that scientific ideas are based on evidence | Obtain a series of observations or measurements and record them clearly in a results table | Look for patterns in their results and explain their conclusions using their scientific knowledge of the effect of acids | Suggest improvements and also give reasons for any amendments |
| 5 | Recognise the key factors in setting up the fair test and make predictions based on their knowledge of acids and their reactions with different materials. If research is carried out they will refer to a range of sources | Careful measurements and observations will be made and repeated if necessary. There is a logical sequencing of results | Draw conclusions that are consistent with the data they have obtained and use/relate these to what they know and understand about the chemistry of acids | Suggest practical ways in which their method can be improved and be critical of any differences in the repeated experiments |
| 6 | | | Recognise patterns in some chemical reactions and use word equations to summarise simple chemical reactions | |

# 7 *Burning (2)*

## Learning outcomes

Pupils:

- name a range of fuels and explain the meaning of the word fuel
- explain that fuels containing carbon burn to produce carbon dioxide
- explain that hydrocarbon fuels such as methane produce carbon dioxide and water
- know that dry cobalt chloride paper is a simple test for water, and summarise the reaction with a word equation

The last lesson in this chapter investigates the products of burning fuels. Pupils will need to know the test for carbon dioxide and they will be introduced to a simple test for water using cobalt chloride.

## The Bunsen burner

The design of the Bunsen burner (see page 229 of the Pupil's Book) allows pupils to discuss how much air is being mixed with the gas. It is a worthwhile exercise to take a Bunsen burner to pieces to show the gas valve.

*Activity* ## Demonstration: Bunsen burner

ICT opportunity: most electronics companies will sell pyrometers to fit dataloggers. Use a basic pyrometer to compare the temperature of the three air hole positions and link this to the amount of air being mixed with methane gas. The combustion products can be demonstrated. Ethanol/methylated spirits can be used instead of a Bunsen.

**Safety**
CARE: ethanol/methylated spirits are highly flammable.
A safety screen is advisable.

## Burning fuels
## Answers

➡ *Pupil's Book page 229*

**20** Teacher to lead discussion to create a comprehensive list, based on definition in the Pupil's Book.
**21** Carbon dioxide.
**22** Acidic: causes natural rainwater to become acidic even without pollution from other acidic gases like sulphur dioxide.
**23** Hydrogen, carbon.

## The bad news about fossil fuels
## Answers

➡ *Pupil's Book page 230*

**24** Mid 1950s.
**25 a)** 10–15 ppm **b)** 15 ppm
**26** They use the carbon dioxide during photosynthesis and release oxygen into the atmosphere.
**27** Example answers:
   **a)** Turn lights off, reduce heat losses, turn thermostat down, switch appliances off when not in use.
   **b)** Encourage sustainable forests (so that as trees are felled, new ones are replanted), make it easier for individuals/companies to recycle wood and paper products, punish companies/individuals that log areas too intensively.
   **c)** Fund research into alternative energy sources, increase cost to the public of fossil fuels to pay to setup alternative sources.
   **d)** Reduce fares, improve bus/train network so that people can reach isolated places, make cars more expensive to run, introduce toll charging on congested roads/motorways, increase the number of buses/trains.

*Activity* Practical: What's in a fuel?

➡ *Worksheet 11.11: What's in a fuel? (P)*

Pupils complete the activity on Worksheet 11.11 to confirm whether carbon dioxide and/or water are produced when a number of different fuels are burnt. Pupils will be asked to link the products to the elements in the original fuel. This is a key idea. Most fuels are hydrocarbons although charcoal will be an exception. They will do well to link the carbon dioxide product to carbon being present in the original reactant. This will necessitate a good degree of question and answer interaction. The presence of water will raise the question: What is the chemical name for water? More able pupils will realise that the carbon and hydrogen present in carbon dioxide and water must have been in the fuel to begin with.

### Equipment

Each group should have:

- diagrams on page 229 of the Pupil's Book
- either combustion spoons and stoppered boiling tubes, or deflagrating spoons with gas jars and greased lids
- small pieces of spill, firelighter (metafuel), samples of simple carbohydrate foods such as bread, rice, cereals
- bottles of limewater and books of dry cobalt chloride paper (stored in desiccating jars)

### Safety

- Use eye protection.
- Avoid handling cobalt chloride paper as much as possible. Encourage pupils to use forceps and to wash their hands thoroughly at the end of the lesson.

## Answers

| Fuel | Observations | | Conclusions: the burning fuel has produced: | |
|---|---|---|---|---|
| | limewater test | cobalt chloride test | carbon dioxide? | water? |
| wood | milky | pink | yes | yes |
| metafuel | milky | pink | yes | yes |
| charcoal | milky | – | yes | no |
| bread | milky | pink | yes | yes |
| cereal | milky | pink | yes | yes |
| rice | milky | pink | yes | yes |

1 All except charcoal.
2 Charcoal.
3 All except charcoal.
4 Limewater test – negative, cobalt chloride test – positive.

## What are the products of burning gas?
## Answers
➡ *Pupil's Book page 231*

**28** The hydrogen from the **gas** has reacted with the **oxygen** from the air to produce water (**hydrogen oxide**).

The carbon from the burning gas has joined up with **oxygen** from the air to form **carbon** dioxide. This gas turns limewater **milky**.

**Attainment targets**

Work in the previous sections should provide evidence that pupils are working towards the following attainment levels.

| | |
|---|---|
| Know that burning fossil fuels releases energy and waste gases | Level 4 |
| Know that burning involves a reaction with oxygen | Level 5 |
| Know that combustion is an oxidation reaction involving oxygen and resulting in oxides. Construct word equations | Level 6 |

# Incomplete burning
➡ *Pupil's Book page 232*

The issue of incomplete burning is addressed using the Bunsen flame as an example. Teachers might wish to discuss incomplete combustion in cigarettes, which raises further concerns about the health issues involved with smoking. Carbon monoxide is one of the three main chemicals associated with cigarette smoke and this is an opportunity to explain why it is produced in such large amounts.

The issue of carbon dioxide emissions is addressed (see Pupil's Book page 230) and teachers may wish to extend this through homework and research. The data is up to date (at the time of publication) and pupils might want to consider the fact that emissions have increased more than expected during 1999–2000.

## Answers
**29** carbon + oxygen → carbon monoxide
**30** Car fumes contain carbon monoxide because the petrol does not burn completely inside the engine. Good ventilation is necessary otherwise the mechanic could suffer carbon monoxide poisoning.
**31** Very little air/oxygen is mixing with the fuel because the air hole is closed.

## Time to think
➡ *Pupil's Book page 233*

• Petrol must be a hydrocarbon fuel: complete combustion produces carbon dioxide and water, and incomplete combustion produces carbon monoxide.
• Complete combustion takes place with plenty (sufficient/enough) of oxygen, whereas incomplete combustion takes place in a limited supply of oxygen, for example in an enclosed space or where there is poor ventilation/air circulation.

- Hydrogen – 'pop' test; oxygen – relight glowing spill; carbon dioxide – turns limewater milky.
- To measure percentage of oxygen in air:
  **i)** Stick candle on to bung.
  **ii)** Light candle.
  **iii)** Place candle into inverted measuring cylinder so it is airtight.
  **iv)** When candle goes out, lower cylinder into bowl of water.
  **v)** Remove bung under water and allow water to rise up the cylinder.
  **vi)** Note the new level of the water as a fraction of the whole cylinder.
- Table of differences below.

| Physical change | Chemical change |
|---|---|
| reversible | irreversible |
| no new chemicals are produced | new chemicals are produced |
| melting | burning |
| dissolving | acids and metals/carbonates |
| boiling | cooking food |

## Review

➡ *Worksheet 11.12: Test on simple chemical reactions*
This worksheet provides a 20 minute test to check on understanding of this chapter.

## Answers

**1** 1 mark for placing each entry in the correct column.

| Chemical changes | Physical changes |
|---|---|
| burning magnesium | melting ice |
| adding marble to acid | adding sugar to water |
| a burning candle | evaporating alcohol |
| lit sparklers | |
| combustion of fuel | |

(8 marks)

**2** Reacts, hydrogen produced. (2 marks)
**3** Very light gas. (1 mark)
**4** Use a burning splint. Explodes or 'pops'. (2 marks)
**5** Tablets are calcium carbonate.
Antacid reacts with stomach acid.
Neutralisation. (3 marks)
**6 a)** Carbon dioxide. (1 mark)
  **b)** Limewater, goes cloudy/milky. (2 marks)
**7** Triangle with jagged flame inside. (1 mark)

# 12 Energy resources

## → Rationale

> 'Energy is a most abstract idea because it is a mathematical principle . . . a numerical quantity that does not change . . . it is not a description of a mechanism, or anything concrete . . .'
>
> Feynman, R., Leighton, R. and Sands, M. (1963)
> *The Feynman lectures on physics.* Volume 1.
> London: Addison–Wesley.

This chapter provides about 9 hours of teaching materials and corresponds very closely to most of the QCA's Unit 7I 'Energy resources'. The work on the Bunsen burner is not covered in this chapter as it appears in chapter 11.

Energy is an abstract concept and as such it is a topic that pupils may find difficult. The scientific ideas of energy only developed in the mid-nineteenth century. While pupils will almost certainly have come across ideas about energy, they will not have been formally taught energy at Key Stage 2. This chapter introduces energy through the idea of fuels as sources of energy. Teachers will often use models to explain some of the ideas. Work on energy transformation and conservation is largely left until later in the course. The comments made in the QCA Teachers' Guide to the Key Stage 3 Schemes of Work are worth noting here.

### Appendix 4: Teaching energy

*Pupils beginning Key Stage 3 will have ideas about energy and will have talked about it in everyday terms. Many pupils and adults associate energy with activity, and think that it can be used up. They make connections between what they eat and exercise with comments such as 'I'll need some time in the gym to work off this chocolate bar!'. This comment acknowledges several aspects of energy:*

- *the chocolate bar is a **source** of energy*
- *the human body can **store** energy*
- *human activity **transfers** this stored energy to somewhere else*
- *in some transfers the energy is **transformed** into something different, e.g. from the chemicals in the body to movement and heat*
- *activities such as gymnastics **dissipate** energy; it is effectively lost.*

*The approach in this scheme of work is to challenge and develop pupils' ideas, in contexts relevant to them. The language used is appropriate to the pupil, rather than that of formal scientific definition. This involves some simplification and care needs to be taken if pupils are not to develop misconceptions. Some detailed cautions are included in the 'Points to note' in the units. In the key units the approach in the unit is outlined at the start. These are:*

- unit 7I 'Energy resources'
- unit 7J 'Electrical circuits'
- unit 8I 'Heating and cooling'
- unit 9I 'Energy and electricity'

*In other units, for example unit 7C 'Environment and feeding relationships', there is a brief statement about teaching energy in 'Where the unit fits in'.*

### Note on the teaching of energy

*This unit [Energy resources] provides an introduction to energy through the idea of foods and fuels as energy resources. The term 'resource' is used in preference to 'source' to try to encourage the idea that energy is not just a kind of stuff, like fuel. Energy transfer is associated with change, in particular changes that can perform useful tasks, as a first step towards more formal understanding. This enables pupils to make connections between apparently disparate phenomena, as contexts are drawn from across the sciences, e.g. burning fuel, movement, eating food and plant growth. Pupils can begin to distinguish energy from stuff (the energy resource) and from linked concepts, e.g. force, power (the rate of transferring energy) and activity. A common misconception is that activity gives you energy because it makes you healthier – and so more able to do more activity.*

This chapter aims to clarify pupils' understanding of the term energy when used in a scientific context. They will understand that energy can be released from various fuels, and the difference between primary fuels and electricity. Pupils are given numerous opportunities to interpret and present information about energy consumption using graphs and charts. There is a section in which comparisons are made between renewable energy sources and fossil fuels. Pupils will understand that the Earth's fossil fuel resources are finite, and that most of the ultimate source of our energy is the Sun. The final part of the chapter links to the use of energy in industry and to energy we obtain from food.

There are opportunities for investigations. One scenario provided asks pupils to find out which solid fuel gives out the most heat when it burns.

There are many opportunities for incorporating ICT, including the use of spreadsheets for plotting bar charts and the use of the Internet to collect information on fossil fuels and on renewable energy resources.

# ➡ *Overview*

The textbook sections, activities and worksheets have been arranged into 1 hour blocks to aid lesson planning. Clearly several of the activities and worksheets could form part of a homework session. The planning includes reading time for individual sections but some teachers may prefer to organise this as homework preparation for the following lesson. Five types of worksheet – extension (E), support for an activity (S), practical (P), key skills (K) and developmental (D) – allow for differentiation and flexibility to accommodate teachers' preferred practice. The actual timing and emphasis on different sections will depend on the current knowledge base of the pupils, the ability of the teaching group and the preferences of the teacher.

| Lesson | Worksheet |
|---|---|
| 1 Fuels as sources of energy | Worksheet 12.1: Fossil fuels (S) |
| 2 Fuel consumption and measuring energy | |
| 3 Sc1 investigation: The amount of heat from burning solid fuels | |
| 4 Renewable energy | |
| 5 The Sun | Worksheet 12.2: Solar energy (P) |
| 6 Nuclear energy | |
| 7 Electricity | Worksheet 12.3: Fuel resources (K)<br>Worksheet 12.4: Using fuels in the UK (K) |
| 8 Energy in industry | |
| 9 Food | |
| Review | Worksheet 12.5: Test on energy resources |

## ➡ *Chapter plan*

| | Demonstration | Practical | ICT | Activity | Time to think |
|---|---|---|---|---|---|
| **Lesson 1** | | | Using a spreadsheet<br>Internet/CD-ROM<br>Internet/desktop publishing | Information processing: Energy sources | What do you know? |
| **Lesson 2** | | | Using a spreadsheet | Information processing: Using fuels<br>ICT: Measuring energy | |
| **Lesson 3** | | | | Enquiry: Energy from fuels | |
| **Lesson 4** | | | Internet/desktop publishing | | |
| **Lesson 5** | | How much energy from the Sun? | | | |
| **Lesson 6** | Nuclear energy | | Internet/video | | Nuclear energy |
| **Lesson 7** | Generating electricity | | Using a spreadsheet | Information processing: Different energy resources<br>DARTs: Fuel resources | |
| **Lesson 8** | | | Using a spreadsheet | ICT: Energy use | |
| **Lesson 9** | | Energy from food | Using a spreadsheet | Information processing: Energy from food | Energy resources |

**Thinking Through Science** Teacher's Book 1

# ➡ *Expectations*

**At the end of this chapter**

**in terms of scientific enquiry**

**most pupils will:** plan a fair comparison of the energy output of a range of fuels or foods; control relevant variables; reduce error by repeating readings; comment on the accuracy of results; find information from selected secondary sources about fuels and energy devices

**some pupils will not have made so much progress and will:** make a fair comparison of the energy output of a range of fuels or foods and with help produce a bar chart or line graph of results; use information from a secondary source in reporting on fuels and other energy sources

**some pupils will have progressed further and will:** compare the effectiveness of different energy-transforming appliances, for example, camping stoves, windmills; select secondary sources to provide information about the use of fuels or other energy sources

**in terms of physical processes**

**most pupils will:** state that fuels release energy when burnt and describe how renewable energy resources can be used to generate electricity and provide heating; explain why conservation of fuels is important; identify energy transfers within a range of systems including those involving living things

**some pupils will not have made so much progress and will:** name a range of fuels used domestically and in industry and some renewable energy resources; give examples of how to save fuels; identify energy transfers in some systems

**some pupils will have progressed further and will:** compare the advantages and limitations of a range of energy resources and give examples of how to use fuel economically; describe energy transfer links between the Sun, energy resources and themselves

# ➡ *Pupils' misconceptions*

| Misconception | Scientific understanding |
|---|---|
| Pupils know that homes are heated by radiators but don't know that a fuel is being used. Energy is used up. | Fuels are in limited supply and are used up. The energy is conserved but becomes 'spread out'. |
| Energy is a source of power. The word energy is used in a non-scientific, colloquial way. Energy is associated with living things and they regard inanimate objects as unable to possess energy. Energy is associated with movement such as a car or a train. | Power is the rate of conversion of energy. Energy is the capacity for doing work. We can only detect the changes that accompany energy transfer. |
| Pupils do not see a need for the idea of energy conservation. Energy gets used up. | Energy cannot be created or destroyed. Energy becomes 'spread out.' |

➡️ # Links with CASE

Many of the activities require pupils to interpret and sequence data as well as to understand the need to control variables. For example, the activity to investigate solid fuels requires pupils to consider the factors to change and those to keep the same. Pupils are also expected to group energy resources according to certain criteria.

➡️ # Literacy, numeracy and other cross-curricular links

At the start of the chapter pupils are encouraged to share ideas about energy to help them to organise their thoughts and to make sense of their own ideas. There is an emphasis on the correct use of everyday words in a scientific context.

Pupils often find difficulty expressing themselves when writing science; they are encouraged to research a variety of sources and to extract and refine the information to produce a succinct collection of relevant facts. They are given a number of passages for extended reading from which they need to extract and interpret information. They also have the opportunity to write a letter to their MP, which encourages them to express clearly their ideas and point of view about fuel consumption.

The chapter has extensive opportunities to consolidate pupils' skills in producing and interpreting information in the form of bar and pie charts and line graphs.

## Language for learning

By the end of this chapter pupils will be able to understand, use and spell correctly:

- words that have different meanings in scientific and everyday contexts – energy, decay, consumption, renewable
- words and phrases relating to energy resources – primary fuel, generate, fossil fuel, compress, non-renewable, consumption, hydroelectric, solar power, wind turbine, wave generator, tidal barrage, biomass energy, geothermal energy, heat exchanger, nuclear power, radioactive.

## ICT opportunities

One of the problems here is that there are very many websites providing information on energy, and pupils will need careful directions to find appropriate sites. Also the addresses often change and so cannot be located. They should be checked out prior to the lesson to ensure that they still exist. Apart from activities that access the Internet, there are numerous opportunities for handling and interpreting data and also an opportunity for datalogging.

## Citizenship

Issues raised include fuel use worldwide and using renewable energy resources.

# 1 *Fuels as sources of energy*

## Learning outcomes

Pupils:

- identify common fuels such as oil, gas and coal
- identify fuels as a source of energy when burnt with oxygen
- distinguish between oil, coal and gas, which are primary fuels, and electricity, which is not a primary fuel
- name several fossil fuels and explain why they are described as fossil

Pupils will have come across references to energy and they will have their own ideas, some of which will be at odds with our scientific understanding. The first lesson is concerned with finding out their ideas. It would be useful to have a display of posters to do with 'Energy' and in prior planning teachers could encourage pupils to bring in their own pictures and posters. These can serve as a focus for the introductory activity on what we mean by energy.

## What do you know?

➡ *Pupil's Book page 234*

Questions to stimulate discussion can include:

What do we mean by fuels?
What different fuels are there?
How do we use energy in our houses?
Where does the energy come from?
Where does the energy go to?

This may be a short introduction requiring no more than 10 minutes; with other groups it could be a much longer process.

## Fuel
## Answer

➡ *Pupil's Book page 235*

**1** Pupils should include electricity and gas. Other fuels may include oil and coal. Whereas elecricity will have a range of uses, the others will be more limited and will probably be just for heating and cooking. Coal, oil and gas are primary fuels.

## *Activity* Information processing: Energy sources

➡ *Pupil's Book page 235*
➡ *Worksheet 12.1: Fossil fuels (S)*

The activity to show how our use of fuels has changed is suggested as a spreadsheet activity. It could alternatively be a paper exercise but this would be more time-consuming. Differentiation may be achieved by providing spreadsheet templates at different levels of sophistication. Examples are provided on spreadsheet 'Sources.xls' on the CD-ROM. The figures in the table in the Pupil's Book (page 235) are percentages rounded to the nearest whole number. Observant pupils will note that the one column does not add up to 100% because of this.

## Answers

➡ *Pupil's Book page 235*

1 Pupil's pie chart for 1949 data. Pupil's bar charts for 1949 and 1999 data.
2 Coal.
3 Oil and gas.
4 Coal.

## Fossil fuels

➡ *Pupil's Book page 236*

The work on fossil fuels could be introduced using samples of different fuels. Teachers should discuss how we get the energy out of the fuels and where the fuels come from. This preparation will lead to the research activity, using the Internet, CD-ROMs, reference books or a range of all the resources (see below).

*Activity* ## Research

➡ *Pupil's Book page 236*

This could be run as a whole class activity or as small group work depending on the facilities. Pupils should be familiar with using a web browser and should be able to save text and images. Check with the ICT Co-ordinator to find out the pupils' familiarity with using the Internet and also with desktop publishing. There are many websites available for this area. They are listed below. Remember that the web addresses change frequently and their existence should be checked prior to the lesson.

> www.energychest.net
> www.wci-coal.com
> www.coaleducation.org
> www.esso.com
> www.fe.doe.gov/education/

### Attainment targets

Work in the previous sections should provide evidence that pupils are working towards the following attainment levels.

| Select information from sources provided for them | Level 4 |
|---|---|
| Select from a range of sources of information | Level 5 |
| Select and use sources of information effectively | Level 6 |

# 2 Fuel consumption and measuring energy

## Learning outcomes

Pupils:

- provide coherent accounts of the formation or use of fossil fuels by writing, pictures or other means, such as class wall display
- contribute to a discussion on fossil fuels

There are links to the National Curriculum (NC) Citizenship requirements here. As Citizenship is a NC requirement from September 2002, teachers may wish to check whether similar work is already being done elsewhere to avoid repetition of this section.

## Fossil fuels

## Answers

➡ *Pupil's Book page 237*

**2** Coal: 2297; oil: 2027; gas: 2047.

**3** The fuels will get used up more quickly.

**4** USA, Canada, Iceland, Norway and Sweden use most. Countries such as Sudan, Ethiopia, Somalia, Afghanistan, Bangladesh, Myanmar (Burma), Vietnam, Laos and Cambodia use the least.

## *Activity* Information processing: Using fuels

➡ *Pupil's Book page 238*

The data in the table about fossil fuel reserves should reinforce pupils' awareness of the limited supply of fossil fuels. The pupils should first be encouraged to interpret the map on page 237 and comment on any pattern they notice between the fuel consumption of different countries. This then leads on to interpreting the table. With the most able pupils teachers could further discuss the relationship between fuel consumption and GNP. The GNP of different countries of the world varies widely: £84 per person per year for the USA, £42 for the UK, £50 for Australia, £51 for Germany, £5 for Egypt, £2 for Nigeria and £1 for India.

## Measuring energy

➡ *Pupil's Book page 238*

Many different units are used when people discuss large amounts of energy. They are not all SI units. Some units pupils may meet are the kWh, the calorie, the barrel of oil, the tonne of coal and the quad.

## Answers

**5** It enables a fair comparison to be made.

**6** Example answers.

General uses: cooking and heating in homes, schools, offices and factories; raw material for chemical and pharmaceutical industries; fuels.

Specific products: from oil – chemicals, diesel, tar, plastics; from gas (+ oil) – petrol.

## *Activity* ICT: Measuring energy

➡ *Pupil's Book page 239*

The final part of this section is a further opportunity for pupils to look at the amount of energy available from different fuels and to represent the information in a suitable way. A spreadsheet may be their chosen method and a spreadsheet 'Energy.xls' is provided on the CD-ROM.

## Answer

➡ *Pupil's Book page 239*

**7** Bar chart or pie chart.

# 3 Sc1 investigation: The amount of heat from burning solid fuels

## Learning outcomes

Pupils:

- use a thermometer accurately
- present their results in a table
- produce a chart of their results
- explain the significance of their results

*Activity* ## Enquiry: Energy from fuels

➡ *Pupil's Book page 239*

This is an opportunity for pupils to perform a fuel investigation. Or, teachers may prefer to concentrate on another Sc1 Investigative skill. A selection of solid fuels is suggested. Liquids such as meths should be avoided. Teachers may wish to provide pupils with a prompt sheet in addition to the questions asked in the Pupil's Book. (Please refer to the *Technician's notes* on the CD-ROM about 'Equipment' requirements.)

**Assessment**

This is an opportunity for assessment of a whole investigation and for making the assessment processes of investigative work more transparent to pupils.

## Attainment targets

| Level | Planning | Obtaining and presenting evidence | Considering evidence | Evaluating |
|---|---|---|---|---|
| 3 | Respond to suggestions presented to them and put forward their own ideas and use simple texts to research information | Use basic equipment to measure and make observations related to the task. Carry out a fair test with help | Explain observations and find simple patterns in results. Communicate in a scientific way | Suggest simple improvments to their work |
| 4 | Decide on an appropriate method to measure the amount of energy transferred by varying one factor. Suitable equipment is selected and predictions may be made. Realise that scientific ideas are based on evidence | Obtain a series of observations or measurements and record them clearly in a results table | Look for patterns in results and explain their conclusions using their scientific knowledge | Suggest improvements and also give reasons for any amendments |
| 5 | Recognise the key factors in setting up the fair test and make predictions based on their scientific knowledge and understanding. If research is carried out they will refer to a range of sources | Careful measurements and observations will be made and repeated if necessary. There is a logical sequencing of their results | Draw conclusions that are consistent with the data they have obtained and use/relate these to what they know and understand | Suggest practical ways in which their method can be improved and be critical of any differences in the repeated experiments |

# 4 *Renewable energy*

## Learning outcomes

Pupils:

- explain that fossil fuel reserves are limited because they are non-renewable
- identify the main renewable energy resources
- explain the term 'renewable energy resource'
- describe the operation of a device driven by a renewable energy source, for example solar cell to generate electricity
- use the Internet (ICT)

This and the next two lessons all link together and different teachers will wish to provide different emphasis depending on their interests, the pupils' abilities, and the facilities available within the department. In this and lesson 6 on nuclear energy pupils are asked to use the Internet to find information about energy resources. It may be appropriate to combine this research into one activity, especially if there is limited access to Internet facilities.

## Renewable energy resources

➡ *Pupil's Book page 240*

Teachers need to ensure that pupils are aware of the difference between solar panels, in which the Sun's energy is used to heat water as it passes through a system of enclosed pipes, and photovoltaic solar cells, in which the Sun's energy is converted directly to a direct current. The latter are becoming increasingly common by the side of roads in remote areas to provide the power for telephone boxes.

## *Activity* Research

➡ *Pupil's Book page 241*

The work may be introduced through discussion of the photographs on page 240 of the Pupil's Book. The research could be run as a whole class activity or as small group work depending on the facilities. Pupils should be familiar with using a web browser and should be able to save text and images. Check with the ICT Co-ordinator to find out the pupils' familiarity with using the Internet and also with desktop publishing. There are many websites available for this area. They are listed on page 249. Remember that the web addresses change frequently and their existence should be checked prior to the lesson.

Different groups of pupils could be asked to collect information on a different renewable energy resource and they could use the information to produce a brochure or poster or even a PowerPoint presentation. If each group is looking at only one energy resource then you will need to ensure that you build in sufficient time for the groups to present their information to the rest of the class.

Alternatively, teachers may wish to perform a demonstration; or pupils could work through a circus of experiments. Possible activities would be using a solar cell to drive an electric motor; a solar garden fountain; a solar-powered calculator or radio/Walkman; a water turbine driven by the mains water; a simple windmill turned by air from a hair dryer or linear air-track blower.

While most of our ultimate source of energy is from the Sun, two exceptions are nuclear energy and geothermal energy. The textbook refers to the use of geothermal energy for community heating in the French town of Chaudes Aigues. Another example of the use of geothermal energy is to be found in Kokonoe, Japan, where three geothermal power stations have a total output of 147.5 kW.

## Answers

➡ *Pupil's Book page 242*

  **8** From heat contained within the Earth's crust.

  **9** It would 'fur up' pipes very quickly.

**10** Water from the spring passes through the coil, heating the 'mains' water in the tank, which is fed to homes.

**11** Geothermal energy is the energy contained within the Earth.

# 5 *The Sun*

## Learning outcomes

Pupils:

- make presentations, for example through oral or written descriptions, of an energy device or resource for the future
- make a written generalisation about energy resources after a discussion; for example 'wood is a useful energy resource in many parts of the world'

As mentioned earlier, the lessons on renewable energy, the Sun and nuclear energy all link together and different teachers will wish to provide different emphases depending on their interests, the pupils' abilities, and the facilities available within the department.

*Activity*

## Practical: How much energy from the Sun?

➡ *Worksheet 12.2: Solar energy (P)*

The Pupil's Book provides a range of secondary data for work on energy from the Sun. As well as the questions in the Pupil's Book (page 242), teachers may wish to allow pupils to perform an experiment to invesigate the energy collected from the Sun. Two possible activities are: heating water in shiny and black containers using the energy from the Sun; or using a temperature probe to investigate the energy produced by an umbrella solar panel.

For the first activity, pupils place equal amounts of cold water in two containers, one shiny the other black, and then monitor the temperature rise using thermometers when they are both placed in the Sun for 30 minutes. Variations to this could include using temperature probes to monitor the changes in temperature, using two trays of sand with temperature probes and a spotlight to simulate the Sun shining on one tray (this is similar to the demonstration given on page 210).

The worksheet is provided for the second activity using the umbrella solar panel.

**Equipment**
*Heating water/sand activity*
Each group will need:

- shiny container
- black container
- two thermometers
- access to a clock

*or*

- two trays of sand
- two temperature probes
- spotlight

➡ *Worksheet 12.2: Solar energy*
Each group will need:

- umbrella
- aluminium kitchen foil
- black paper
- scissors
- sticky tape
- temperature probe
- light sensor
- datalogger

## Answers

➡ *Pupil's Book page 242*

**12** There are reserves of coal to last 300 years. However, when burnt it produces large amounts of pollutants. To maintain a supply of wood, forests need to be replanted and the wood needs to be transported. Flooding the land for hydroelectric power stations can destroy habitats. Hydroelectric power does not create any air, chemical or heat pollution.

**13** The Sun provided the energy for the plants to grow. Animals ate the plants. It then took millions of years for the animals and plants to decay and compress to produce oil. The uneven heating of the Earth by the Sun causes the air to move. This produces wind.

**14** Pupils should indicate which are renewable and which are non-renewable resources, the function of the Sun, where appropriate, and a range of sensible advantages and disadvantages.

**Attainment targets**
Work in the previous sections should provide evidence that pupils are working towards the following attainment levels.

| | |
|---|---|
| Use some abstract ideas to explain the different energy resources available | Level 5 |
| Use some abstract ideas to describe and explain the advantages and disadvantages of different fuels | Level 6 |
| Apply abstract ideas to explain the comparison of different energy resources and to explain the sun as a source of energy for wind and oil | Level 7 |
| Consider energy resources from different perspectives realising the need to balance ease of use against potential pollution and economic considerations | Level 8 |

# 6 *Nuclear energy*

## Learning outcomes
Pupils:

- identify the advantages and disadvantages of using nuclear energy
- consolidate the work that they have done so far

This section provides possible links to Citizenship. (See comments in lesson 2.) In both lesson 4 Renewable energy and lesson 6 Nuclear energy pupils are asked to use the Internet to find information about energy resources. Refer to the comments earlier on using the Internet.

*Activity* ## Demonstration: Nuclear energy
As a quick introduction (if the school has the equipment), teachers could demonstrate the effect of placing a radioactive rock near a Geiger–Müller tube and counter.

An alternative approach would be to watch a suitable video on nuclear energy. At this stage pupils are not expected to have a detailed understanding of a nuclear power station. It is sufficient for them to understand that the uranium fuel becomes hot as a result of a process called fission, and this heat is used to boil water as in a fossil-fuelled power station. They should also be aware that the uranium waste products are dangerous.

# 7 *Electricity*

## Learning outcomes
Pupils:

- identify different resources for generating electricity
- explain the need to generate more electricity from renewable energy resources

Many teachers will wish to combine lesson 7 Electricity and lesson 8 Energy in industry.

## Electricity
## Answers
➡ *Pupil's Book page 243*
15 Greater demand in winter months, least demand during the early hours of the morning.
16 Surges between 08:00 and 10:00 and at about 18:00. People boil kettles and turn on lights during the evening surge.

*Activity* ## Demonstration: Generating electricity
A possible introduction to the lesson could be a quick demonstration of generating electricity using a simple dynamo. This could be the hand-driven bike dynamo or a dynamo driven from a steam engine. Pupils should understand that although this is a small-scale demonstration, the principle is essentially the same for the way electricity is generated in a power station.

**Equipment**
- 'Malvern' energy conversion kit or similar

**Thinking Through Science** Teacher's Book 1

# Generating electricity

➡ *Pupil's Book page 244*

This section shows that we can generate electricity from a variety of resources, and that different countries may differ in the type of fuel or process used.

## Answer

**17** In 1990 coal was the main fuel source. In 2000 the main fuel source was gas. Over the next 10 years gas will continue to be a major fuel source, but renewable energy resources will be used increasingly, and in 50 years gas will probably be unavailable.

*Activity* # Information processing: Different energy resources

➡ *Pupil's Book page 245*

Pupils are encouraged to reflect on the different processes used for generating electricity. There is a further opportunity to use an Excel spreadsheet to chart the energy production in France. Spreadsheet 'Resources.xls' is provided on the CD-ROM, which makes the process very simple for pupils who are less competent in using ICT. It also allows teachers to display the results on a large monitor or with an LCD projector, as a teaching point for the whole class.

## Answers

**1** Pupil's bar chart.

**2**

| 1 | H | non-renewable |
|----|---|---------------|
| 2 | G | renewable |
| 3 | I | non-renewable |
| 4 | D | renewable |
| 5 | F | non-renewable |
| 6 | J | renewable |
| 7 | C | renewable |
| 8 | E | renewable |
| 9 | A | renewable |
| 10 | B | renewable |

**3** We are using up the non-renewable energy resources and we may run out of these in the future.

*Activity* # DARTs: Fuel resources

➡ *Worksheet 12.3: Fuel resources (K), Worksheet 12.4: Using fuels in the UK (K)*

The worksheets contain text on fuel resources with suggestions for Directed Activities Relating to Text (DARTs).

# 8 *Energy in industry*

## Learning outcomes

Pupils:

- state in their own words the idea that energy is associated with changes
- link key ideas, for example in a summary, spider diagram, or concept map

This section looks at the use of fuels in industry and also at environmental issues from the perspective of an industrialist. It again gives useful links to Citizenship.

*Activity* ## ICT: Energy use

**Q18** in the Pupil's Book (page 246) is a further opportunity to use Excel to produce a pie chart. Again the CD-ROM has a spreadsheet 'Energyuse.xls' for those pupils requiring support in this area.

Note that some preparation in this lesson is needed for the next lesson on food.

# 9 *Food*

## Learning outcomes

Pupils:

- describe how they have carried out a comparison of foods, making sure the comparison was fair
- produce and present records of temperature rise to compare energy output of different foods
- evaluate reliability of their results compared with other groups, for example better control of heating, less heat 'lost'

There are possible links to Food Technology. Pupils should be clear from work at Key Stage 2 and from their earlier work in this chapter that the source of energy in food comes originally from the Sun.

## Food

→ *Pupil's Book page 246*

This section provides examples of food labels and explains how they give information about the energy that the food supplies. There is also data on daily intake of food in different countries and worldwide food consumption above and below dietary needs. Using these facts pupils can begin to understand some of the issues relating to developing and developed countries. This section also links with chapter 1 Food and digestion, which will be met in *Thinking Through Science Pupil's Book 2* at the start of Year 8.

*Activity* # Information processing: Energy from food

➡ *Pupil's Book page 248*

Teachers could introduce this activity by displaying a variety of foods. Pupils read the labels and note down the energy content per 100 g. This activity must be planned in the previous lesson so that pupils come prepared with a written list of their food intake during the previous 24 hours. For those pupils who 'forget', it is worth having a prepared diet for pupils to use. There are various programs available for analysing pupils' diets in terms of carbohydrate, protein fats, vitamin, minerals and fibre; this activity is specifically concerned with the energy values of the food items eaten. The spreadsheet 'Foodenergy.xls', provided on the CD-ROM, is adapted from the book 'Spreadsheets in Science'.

## Answers

**1–4** The answers will depend on pupils' food intake.

*Activity* # Practical: Energy from food

If teachers wish, pupils can perform the standard experiment on energy from food. They burn breakfast cereal, biscuit and so on, and measure the temperature rise of some water heated by the burning food. (Beware of burning peanuts because of possible nut allergies.) This links to Unit 8A Food and digestion.

A sophisticated version of this can be done using a food calorimeter, which could be demonstrated. Results obtained from this are usually within 10% of published values, whereas results from the burning food experiment can vary greatly from those expected. For 'Equipment' and 'Safety' notes, please refer to the *Technician's notes* on the CD-ROM.

## Time to think

The final part of the chapter allows pupils to summarise the work on energy by producing either a leaflet or a letter. Teachers may wish to allow time for pupils to plan their work in this area and also to evaluate each other's final product. This could be done using 'traffic lights' in groups and/or by pupils reading a few samples of the leaflet/letter and devising their own success criteria in groups.

### Attainment targets

Work in the previous sections should provide evidence that pupils are working towards the following attainment levels.

| | |
|---|---|
| Use some abstract ideas to explain what fossil fuels are *or* to describe what a renewable energy resource is *or* to compare the energy values of different types of food | Level 5 |
| Use some abstract ideas to describe and explain what fossil fuels are *or* to describe what a renewable energy resource is *or* to compare the energy values of different types of food | Level 6 |
| Apply abstract ideas to explain how fossil fuels are formed *or* to explain the Sun as a source of energy for wind power *or* in an analysis of the energy values of meals and/or diets | Level 7 |
| Consider energy resources from different perspectives realising the need to make informed decisions about the use of fossil fuels and renewable fuels now and in the future *or* in making decisions about choices for diet *or* advising on high or low energy food sources in situations where these are appropriate | Level 8 |
| Recognise the importance of quantitative data and make use of this when considering energy efficiency | Exceptional performance |

# Review

➡ *Worksheet 12.5: Test on energy resources*
This worksheet provides a 20 minute test to check on understanding of this chapter.

# Answers

**1** Coal.
  Oil.
  Gas.                                                    (Any 2 for 2 marks)
**2** Fossilised plants
  slowly decayed
  and compressed by overlying rocks.                      (3 marks)
**3** Once used, not replaced.                              (1 mark)
**4** Megajoules.
  Kilogram.                                               (2 marks)
**5** Hydroelectric.                                        (1 mark)
**6** Solar/photovoltaic cells.                             (1 mark)
**7** Food labels/food analysis.                            (1 mark)
**8** Geothermal energy/energy from hot springs
  heats a cold water tank
  energy is transferred.                                  (3 marks)
**9** Radioactive.
  Power.
  Reactor.
  Radioactivity may escape/terrorists may blow up
      power stations.
  Fossil.
  Acid.                                                   (6 marks)

# Spreadsheets

All the spreadsheets are protected where appropriate – no passwords are required.

| File name | Description | Chapter |
|---|---|---|
| Sweets.xls | This relates to Pupil's Book page 6. Note that there are two sheets accessed from clicking on the tabs. Sweets1 does not provide any help. Sweets2 provides a possible solution. Teachers can adapt these two provide differentiation. | Introduction |
| Partytime.xls | This relates to Pupil's Book page 34. Two tabs provide differentiated tasks. This is fairly simple. | Chapter 1 |
| Current.xls | Two versions provided on tabs. One relating to results provided in Pupil's Book page 73, the other for pupils to enter their own results and see graph being plotted. | Chapter 3 |
| Reactiontm1.xls Reactiontm2.xls Reactiontm3.xls | These all relate to Pupil's Book page 110 and to Worksheet 6.3. | Chapter 6 |
| Animalspeed.xls | This relates to Pupil's Book page 114 and provides the data as suggested for producing the bar chart. | Chapter 6 |
| MidlandMetro.xls | This is the data for Pupil's Book page 115. | Chapter 6 |
| Lift.xls | This is the data for Pupil's Book page 115. | Chapter 6 |
| Roadsafety.xls | This is the data to accompany the questions on Pupil's Book page 118. | Chapter 6 |
| Density.xls | Relates to Worksheet 6.9. Density tab 1 merely requires pupils to enter the results as indicated. Density tab 2 expects the pupils to supply the formulae for calculating the volume and density as well. | Chapter 6 |
| Stretching.xls | There are three differentiated sheets provided. Relates to Worksheet 6.10. | Chapter 6 |
| Bacteria.xls | This relates to Pupil's Book page 149. This has three simple spreadsheets. The third one allows pupils to quickly see the effect of how the bacteria multiply over time if unchecked. | Chapter 7 |
| Lifespans.xls | This relates to Pupil's Book page 165. There are four versions of this. | Chapter 8 |
| Solar.xls | This relates to Pupil's Book page 205. | Chapter 10 |
| Scalemodels.xls | Models are referred to in chapter 10 of the Pupil's book page 194 and also on page 205 | Chapter 10 |
| Acidsandmetals.xls | This relates to the activity on Pupil's Book page 213. | Chapter 11 |
| Sources.xls | This relates to the activity on Pupil's Book page 235. It may be differentiated using the three tabs: Energy1, Energy2, Energy3. Energy1 is all the completed information and graphs. In Energy2 the data is provided and the pupils will plot the graphs using chart wizard. In Energy3 pupils enter the data as well. | Chapter 12 |
| Energy.xls | 'Energy.xls' is set out in a similar way to 'Sources.xls.' It relates to Pupil's Book page 239. | Chapter 12 |
| Resources.xls | This relates to the activity on Pupil's Book page 245. The sheet has three versions to allow for a degree of differentiation. | Chapter 12 |
| Energyuse.xls | This spreadsheet uses the information on Pupil's Book page 246. Again there are three versions: the first is a completed set of graphs; the second provides the template and as pupils enter the data the graphs are displayed; the third allows pupils to use Chart Wizard to produce a suitable graph of the data. | Chapter 12 |
| Foodenergy.xls | This relates to the activity on Pupil's Book page 248. Pupils use the spreadsheet to calculate the contribution of various foods to their requirements for energy. | Chapter 12 |

# Appendix

The following organisations are recommended for obtaining up-to-date health and safety information.

Association for Science Education (ASE)
College Lane
Hatfield
Hertfordshire
AL10 9AA
Tel: 01707 283000
Fax: 01707 266532
Website: www.ase.org.uk

CLEAPSS School Science Service
Brunel University
Uxbridge
UB8 3PH
Tel: 01895 251496
Fax: 01895 814372
Website: www.cleapss.org.uk

Scottish Schools Equipment Research Centre (SSERC)
Second Floor
St Mary's Building
23 Holyrood Road
Edinburgh
EH8 8AE
Tel: 0131 558 8180
Fax: 0131 558 8191
Website: www.sserc.org.uk